THE HEINEMANN
ACCOUNTANCY AND ADMINISTRATION SERIES

General Editor
J. Batty, D. Com. (S.A.), M. Com. (Du.   A.C.M.A.,
M.Inst. A.M., M.I.P.M

N INTRODU
O BANK

orc
3.10.93.

By the same author:
Practical Bank Management (1977)

AN INTRODUCTION TO BANKING

Kenneth Toft B. Com. MSc (Econ)
F.I.B. F.B.I.M. F.R.S.A.

Head of Department of Banking and Insurance
City of London Polytechnic

Heinemann: London

William Heinemann Ltd
10 Upper Grosvenor Street, London W1X 9PA

LONDON   MELBOURNE   TORONTO
JOHANNESBURG   AUCKLAND

First published 1986

© Kenneth Toft 1986

British Library Cataloguing in Publication Data
Toft, Kenneth
  An introduction to banking.
  1. Banks and banking
  I. Title
  332.1   HG1601

ISBN 0 434 91965 9

Typeset by Deltatype, Ellesmere Port
Printed in Great Britain by
Redwood Burn Ltd,
Trowbridge, Wilts

EDITOR'S FOREWORD

The *Heinemann Accountancy and Administration Series* is intended to fill a gap in the literature that caters for accountants, company secretaries, and similar professional people who are engaged in giving a vital information service to management. Due recognition is given to the fact that there are two distinct bodies of readers: those who aspire to professional status – the students – and others who are already managing and/or serving management. Wherever possible the books are written with this distinction in mind.

The monetary system, within which banks operate, has now become a major tool in the control of a country. In recent years great reliance has been placed on political and economic control through a monetarist policy.

Within the economy individuals, companies and institutions all rely on an efficient banking system. Without adequate finance there can be no growth or even the maintenance of a stable output.

This book examines the role of banks and looks at their place in a modern community. Intended as a guide for banking students, it will be useful for degree students of banking, business studies and accountancy. Managers and those giving professional advice, such as accountants and corporate planners, will also find much of value.

J. Batty

PREFACE

The aim of this book is to introduce readers to the business of banking: to help people to understand how banks operate, to appreciate the special nature of banking services, and to recognise the importance of banks in the world's economies. My hope is that young men and women employed by banks as well as those outside the industry will find this an easy and valuable introduction to the theory and practice of banking.

A particular aim is to serve the needs of full- and part-time students enrolled on courses which either lead to a degree or which provide a preliminary qualification enabling them if they wish to proceed to the specialised examinations of the Institute of Bankers. These might include the bankers' Foundation (Conversion) course or courses leading to a BTEC award or to the proposed Banking Certificate, a qualification likely to be introduced by the Institute in 1986 and one which some bankers may wish to obtain in preference to a Banking Diploma.

Banking is an activity requiring a sound knowledge of business subjects, in particular accounting, economics, and law. It is beyond the scope of one book to examine these subjects in depth and the aim is therefore to introduce the reader to these subjects by showing how in practical terms some of their principles are relevant to banking.

Whilst the needs of overseas readers have not been overlooked, it has often been necessary to refer to institutions which operate in the U.K., to examine their structural relationships, and to look at the way in which they operate in financial markets. Banks vary widely in size and in the range of services they offer and thus there are many differences in the knowledge and skills needed by their staff. However certain basic principles and practices are common to banks everywhere, despite differences in the legal, economic, and political frameworks in which they operate.

Personal assignments are given at the end of each chapter and a short series of case studies is provided to assist with the learning process. Those who wish to test their knowledge can attempt the self-examination questions at the end of the book and those wishing to broaden and deepen their understanding of banking should consult the books listed for further reading.

K.T.

For Jessie

CONTENTS

Editor's Foreword   v
Preface   vi

Chapter 1 The Nature of Banking   1
International Banking   1
What is a Bank?   2
Credit   4
Banking for Profit   5
Bank Management   6
Financial Intermediation   10
Banking Controls   12
A Bank Is . . .   13
Personal Assignments   14

Chapter 2 The Financial Network   15
Central Government Finance   15
National Savings   16
Personal Saving   19
Building Societies   21
Company Finance   22
Investment and Unit Trusts   25
Life Assurance and Pension Funds   26
House Purchase   27
Consumer Durables   28
Bank Lending   30
Personal Assignments   31

Chapter 3 The History of Banking   32
U.K. Commerical Banking   32
Joint Stock Banking   33

The Bank of England   34
U.K. Banks Overseas   37
Bills of Exchange   38
The Discount Market   40
Merchant Banking   42
Wholesale Money Markets   44
Personal Assignments   45

Chapter 4 Accounting and the Banker   46
The Balance Sheet   46
Trading and Profit and Loss Accounts   48
The Accounts   51
Bank Balance Sheets   52
Liquidity and Profitability   57
Back to Accountancy   59
Personal Assignments   60

Chapter 5 Economics and the Banker   61
The Economic Environment   61
Supply and Demand   63
Foreign Exchange Rates   67
The Balance of Payments   68
The Eurocurrency Markets   70
Interest Rates   71
The London International Financial Futures Exchange   73
Personal Assignments   75

Chapter 6 Money   76
The Functions of Money   78
The Forms of Money   80
Notes and Coin   82
Money and Near Money   83
The Value of Money   84
Money Creation   87
Personal Assignments   90

Chapter 7 Monetary Policy   91
Economic Objectives   91
Economic Weapons   92
Monetary Theory   94
The Money Supply   95

Controlling the Money Supply   96
The Role of Monetary Policy   98
Personal Assignments   102

Chapter 8 Bank Lending   103
Lending Principles   103
Personal Borrowing   106
Company Borrowing   108
Interest Rates   112
International Lending   113
Risk Capital   116
Lending Supervision   116
Personal Assignments   119

Chapter 9 Payment Mechanisms   120
Currency   120
Cheque Clearings   121
Credit Clearing   124
The National Girobank   125
Periodic Payments   126
BACS and CHAPS   127
Plastic Cards   128
The Trustee Savings Bank   130
International Payments   131
Personal Assignments   133

Chapter 10 Banking Services   134
Executor and Trustee Services   135
Taxation Services   139
Insurance   140
Instalment Credit   141
Leasing   141
Factoring   141
Merchant Banking   143
International Services   143
Other Bank Services   146
Personal Assignments   148

Chapter 11 Marketing Bank Services   149
Marketing and the Corporate Plan   149
Marketing Strategy   150

Market Segmentation 151
Delivering Bank Services 152
Sales Promotion 154
Public Relations 155
Bank Marketing 156
Personal Assignments 158

Chapter 12 The Legal Framework 159
The Banking Act, 1979 159
The Consumer Credit Act, 1974 162
The Fair Trading Act, 1973 163
The Bank's Customers 163
Banker-Customer Relationships 165
The Liability of Banks 169
Personal Assignments 171

Chapter 13 Negotiable Instruments 172
Cheques and Bills 172
Paying Cheques 174
Endorsements 175
Crossings 176
Risk and the Paying Banker 176
Collecting Cheques 177
The Holder in Due Course 179
Cheque Cards 180
Other Negotiable Instruments 180
Bills of Exchange 181
Personal Assignments 183

Chapter 14 Security for Advances 184
Life Assurance Policies 186
Stocks and Shares 187
Merchandise 188
Land 189
Valuation 190
Debentures 191
Guarantees 192
Safe Custody 194
Personal Assignments 196

Chapter 15 Bank Staff Today and Tomorrow   197
   Bank Operations   198
   Staff Planning   198
   Staff Development   199
   Banking in the Future   200
   Banking as a Career   201
   Personal Assignments   203

Appendix   204
Self-Examination Questions   209
Case Studies   210
Further Reading   216
Index   217

CHAPTER 1

THE NATURE OF BANKING

Although banks are in many ways the same as other firms there are, as we shall see, important differences. If a manufacturing company goes out of business, the owners and creditors may lose the money owing to them by the firm. If a bank fails, however, the loss also extends to all those who have entrusted their money to it for safekeeping and the results can be catastrophic, particularly if the bank is a big one. Banks are therefore very important bodies. It is difficult to imagine a modern economy working without them.

International Banking

Banking is now an international industry. If you walk through the financial centres of London, New York, Hong Kong or Singapore you will find banks which are household names in your own town or village. In London, a major financial centre, there are no less than 450 banks from countries outside the U.K. and it is not unusual to find branches of these banks in other British cities.

A bank operating in another country may be heavily involved in serving the community in competition with the local banks. However, in addition to providing a domestic service overseas it may also be engaged in international transactions, taking funds in a variety of currencies from abroad and lending to overseas residents, perhaps to large multinational companies or to foreign governments or their agencies. Of course not all banks are heavily engaged in international operations. For example, many of the 14,000 U.S. banks are small – some with a staff of less than fifty – and concentrate their efforts on serving the needs of their local community. However, the development of banking on an international scale has made it more complicated as well as more interesting and bank staff now have more opportunities of working overseas than was the case in the past.

The growth of international banking has also helped to make it more competitive and the larger banks in particular have developed a wide range of services for their customers. It is not unusual to find a large bank offering over 200 separate services which it will add to and develop in its attempt to win business from its competitors. Many bank staff now need to know about investment, taxation, leasing, factoring and credit cards. They are likely to be involved with many different types of customer, from the large corporation to the person struggling on a small pension. They may well be called on to advise customers on a wide range of financial matters – some quite simple, others calling for a high level of expertise. In many countries competition from non-banking financial institutions has also increased as these have sought to extend their range of services.

Banks therefore face heavy competition from both inside and outside the industry and their success depends on their ability to meet this challenge. They need to be highly efficient and this in large measure depends on the quality of the workforce. The personal qualities of bank staff have to be developed by education, training, and varied work experience and to be successful a bank must ensure that satisfactory staff development takes place. It shares this responsibility with its employees, who must seize every opportunity of following education and training programmes and of consolidating and expanding their knowledge and expertise through practical experience if they are to enjoy a successful, satisfying and profitable career in banking.

What is a Bank?

It is not easy to give a precise definition of a bank. In the U.K. there are *recognised banks* and *licensed deposit-takers* but not all the recognised banks include the word 'bank' in their name and some of the licensed deposit-takers call themselves banks and provide banking services. For our purposes it is sufficient to say that an organisation is called a bank if its activities are those normally associated with banking.

It is helpful to regard a bank as a *system* established for a particular reason. Many types of system have been constructed to serve different purposes – a school, for example, is a system which provides education; a factory is one which produces goods. The name we give to a system is determined by its *output*. A system established to provide education or cars would not be called a bank because the output is not regarded as a banking activity.

The output of a system can be divided into two main classes – goods and services. It is difficult to think of a bank that provides goods; the role of a bank is to provide a service and normally this is a financial service, although in some countries there is evidence that banks are extending their activity into the provision of non-financial services, such as helping people to buy and sell houses.

Banks are not the only bodies which provide a financial service – building societies, firms of accountants and moneylenders also do so although the variety of services they offer is more limited than in most banks. Figure 1 illustrates the main categories of the services produced by a banking system, the bank's output. These are of three main types:

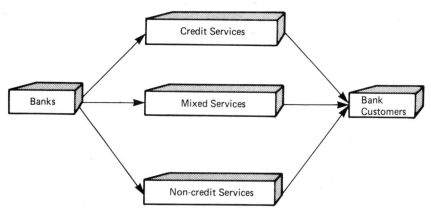

Figure 1. Banking Services

1. Those involving the provision of credit.
2. Those not involving the provision of credit.
3. Mixed services which may or may not involve the provision of credit.

When a bank lends a customer money it is providing a credit service; when it gives investment advice or sells a customer another country's bank notes it is quite clearly providing a non-credit service.

Some services however may or may not involve the granting of credit. For example, banks issue customers with cheque books to enable them to pay their bills. When these cheques are presented to a customer's bank they are debited to his account which may be in credit or, if the bank is lending him money, may be overdrawn, that is to say in debit. It follows that the cheque service offered by the bank will lead to the provision of credit when cheques are paid for a customer who is overdrawn. If his account remains in credit there is no question of lending the customer money and so no credit needs to be provided.

Credit

A bank may be regarded as a body that buys and sells credit. Clearly the granting of credit is a dominant aspect of the services it provides. The provision of credit enables a person or organisation to do something immediately which would otherwise be impossible. It implies the provision of money now in return for a promise to repay later, in commercial transactions the lender receiving a reward for the service given.

The word 'credit' is connected with the word 'trust', credit being granted to those you feel you can trust. When a customer deposits money with a bank it is because he trusts the bank to look after the money properly. The bank in effect is using its good name to encourage people to place deposits with it: should doubts arise about its stability customers will demand their money back and there is likely to be a run on the bank. In a similar way, a banker's lending to a customer is based on trust, on his belief that the customer will honour his debts and repay the loan in due course. Because banks sell services rather than goods, their output is intangible. When we consider a bank's credit services we find again the intangibility of its operations: nothing could be less tangible than trust.

The provision of credit need not necessarily involve money. A farmer might borrow seed to sow on his land on the understanding that seed would be returned when he harvested his crop. In a modern community it is far more convenient to use money for the transaction, the farmer borrowing money in order to purchase his seed, repaying the money, plus interest, when he has harvested and sold his crop. Sometimes a credit transaction may not involve the payment of interest. A shopkeeper may not have to pay for his purchases immediately. He may be given credit for a month or two on the understanding that if he pays cash he will be allowed to deduct a discount from his payment. Again, a father might lend his son or daughter money to buy a car on the understanding that it is to be repaid monthly over two or three years but without interest being charged.

As well as possessing a dimension of time, the provision of credit can also have a geographic dimension, for example when people with money to spare in one part of the country lend it to people in another part who put it to good use to the benefit of the country as a whole. A similar process occurs in the international credit markets. A rich country may lend to a poorer country to help it develop its economy, a bank may take funds from people in one country and make them available to those in another country for projects they need to finance.

The essential feature of credit is that something is made possible that otherwise could not have been carried out. For example, in the nineteenth century the development of the railways was made possible by the provision of credit while more recently the development of North Sea oil supplies would have been impossible without the provision of massive amounts of credit. From a banker's viewpoint, the satisfaction lies in the knowledge that his activities have enabled something to happen that might otherwise have been impossible. This is his important and creative role in society, a role often tinged with a touch of romance.

Banking for Profit

Whilst most of the institutions examined in this book are profit-making institutions, it is important to appreciate that not all banks are in the business of earning profits. Many countries have *central banks* or similar institutions whose main purpose is to provide a number of essential services rather than to generate profits. These services will be examined when we consider the role of the Bank of England, the U.K.'s central bank.

In some countries *development banks* have been established with the aim of procuring economic growth and raising the living standard of the people. The primary aim of such banks is not profit. The same applies in centrally planned economies such as those of the Eastern bloc countries where communist systems operate or in countries that have undergone a socialist revolution. Here the economy operates under the guidance of an economic plan and the usual role of the banking system is to provide finance to assist with the implementation of the plan.

Even in those countries with a capitalist economy, that is one based on the pursuit of profit, it is not unusual to find banks being called upon to undertake activities or organise their affairs to meet the needs of the state. They may be required to open unprofitable branches in order to help the government's aim of spreading the banking habit. They may be required to limit their lending to certain sectors of the population, such as property developers, and to increase their lending to other sectors, such as farmers and exporters. Sometimes special schemes are introduced to encourage banks to undertake business that they feel is either too risky or likely to be unprofitable. For instance guarantee schemes may be set up whereby the banks are asked to make special efforts to lend to those wishing to establish a new business (particularly one of an innovative nature) while the government guarantees that all or part of the money lent will be repaid at the appropriate time. In some countries banks are nationalised. Whilst such a change of ownership need not necessarily alter the aims of a bank or the way it operates, clearly when controlled by the government it is likely that it may have to be run to meet state objectives rather than to earn profits.

Banks in countries like the U.K. and U.S. are usually owned by members of the public and their aim is to earn profits. A bank has been defined as a system for producing financial services; however in these cases it is also a system for earning profits. These two views of a bank are not in conflict – there is no point in providing a service if nobody wants to buy it. The bank's clear objective must therefore be to provide and develop services which it can sell at a price which will yield a profit. The main aim of a business enterprise is to remain in business – bank shareholders would not be very happy to hear their chairman talk of the excellent service the bank had given to the community but then to hear that it had failed to earn any profits and that therefore no dividends were to be paid. The success of a bank operating in a profit-orientated environment is measured by the level of its profits. If it seeks new funds to strengthen and expand its business, people will look at its profit record. If this is poor the additional funds may be difficult and costly to raise.

The attitude of a bank to profits will be largely determined by top management, since they are responsible for the style of the bank's operations. Too great an emphasis on short-term gain may lead to customer alienation with the result that in the long run profitability suffers. There are also ethical problems to be faced as when advice is being given to a customer when one possible course of action is likely to be to the bank's advantage. In this situation it is not always easy for a banker to offer disinterested advice and even when he does this is not always recognised by outside observers.

Bank Management

The level of bank profits is not determined simply by the amount of services sold or by the price obtained for them. Like other systems a bank needs *inputs* which must be organised effectively to produce the services it provides, its output. Input consists of people and things. People are needed to staff the bank, to carry out the multitude of tasks that have to be performed. The staff need buildings to work in and equipment to work with. Heating or air-conditioning as well as adequate lighting is needed and a wide range of stationery has to be provided. All these things cost money; wages and salaries have to be paid, premises purchased or rented and payments made to suppliers for everything from paper clips to computers.

Profit is the difference between these costs and the money the bank obtains for its services. After meeting the demands of tax-collectors, this profit is used to reward shareholders for their investment in the bank and to plough money back into the business to ensure its stability and growth. The management of a bank must not only ensure that it is offering the services that are needed but must also see that the right input is made to the system to achieve its aims. It must ensure that the bank has sufficient experienced and trained staff to deliver the planned output to its existing and potential customers. It must too be sure that these staff have the necessary accommodation and equipment ready for their use when and where it is needed.

The input of the bank has therefore to be organised and arranged to produce the required output and a bank as a system contains a large number of other systems to bring this about. Thus there is a system for giving a customer a loan. Lending officers know the maximum amount of money they can lend and what to do if the figure required is above that limit. There are also systems for dealing with surplus cash received by a branch, for filing letters, and many more.

Bank management has the responsibility of planning, organising, directing, coordinating, and controlling the system for which it is responsible. This system, consisting of inputs and outputs, is shown schematically in Figure 2. Bank management must consider its objectives – what range of services is to be offered to the public. It must ensure that the various inputs into the system are of the type and quantity needed to provide these services; it must make sure that the bank's operations are planned and implemented as efficiently as possible. To ensure maximum profitability it needs to focus its

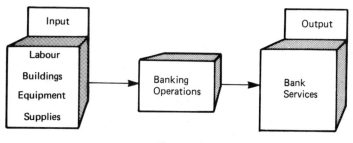

Figure 2

attention on all parts of the system – its input, its output, and the way it operates.

The Corporate Plan

These three aspects of the system are all likely to receive attention in the *corporate plan*, a planning document which sets out the objectives of the bank and how they are to be achieved. Decisions have to be made on a large range of policy matters and appropriate *strategies* and *tactics* agreed for translating policy into action.

In order to operate effectively, bank management needs *information* from both within and outside the bank. It needs to know what income is generated by each of the services it operates; it needs to be aware of the costs of the various inputs it requires. Up-to-date knowledge of the effectiveness of the bank's methods of operating is also required and these may need to be changed because of changing circumstances – for example, it may be decided to cease to offer a particular service because it is unprofitable and this in turn may mean that staff have to be redeployed or offered early retirement. If staff are to undertake different work it may be necessary to institute special training schemes to help with the transition. If staff costs are rising sharply the bank may need to seek cheaper ways of doing its work, possibly by increased automation. If property costs are increasing it may be decided to move some of the bank's departments to parts of the country where accommodation is cheaper and this in turn is likely to lead to changes in recruitment policy.

But a bank also needs to receive and constantly assess information from outside the business. Changes in society are likely to lead to changes in the range and type of services the bank offers. If the proportion of old people in a country is rising special services might be developed for this part of the community. The changing role of women in society may lead a bank to consider ways in which it can adjust its services to meet new requirements. If the importance of ethnic minorities is increasing services may be adapted to meet their special needs. Economic change must also be considered. A bank is likely to plan its immediate future differently if the countries in which it operates are facing depression rather than boom conditions. Forecasts of future changes in prices and in interest and exchange rates will likewise lead to important changes in a bank's plans. Obviously too changes in the law and the way it operates will have to be taken into account. A law compelling banks to include employees on its board of directors would clearly lead to important changes; alterations in the ways banks are supervised by the authorities may also affect its operations. A bank must also be aware of what its competitors – not only other banks but also non-bank financial institutions – are doing. Knowledge that another bank is about to develop a new service may encourage management to do likewise. These aspects of bank corporate planning are illustrated in Figure 3.

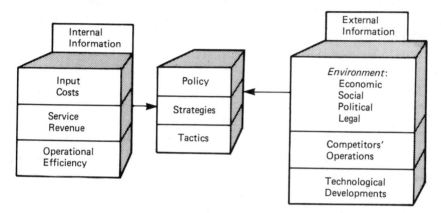

Figure 3. Corporate planning

The importance placed on knowing and understanding what is going on in the environment in which the bank operates is reflected in the rapid growth of *information technology*. The advances in computers and the introduction and development of the micro-chip have had and will have important effects on the ways in which banks operate and it is vital that a bank ensures that it keeps abreast of modern developments.

There is little point in having a plan if it is not carried out. Bank management therefore needs to monitor the system if it is to control it. For this it needs *feedback*. If a new service is to be introduced it must keep an eye on the progress being made, checking that any necessary training courses are underway, and so on. If a target has been set for an increase in the share of bank deposits it will want to know whether individual branches are likely to meet their targets, and if not, why not. Only by monitoring the system to see whether the bank's policy is being successfully implemented can management know if things are going wrong. Only if it knows that things are going wrong can it take remedial action to put things right.

If the bank's plans are known to only a few top managers or are carefully locked in a corporate planning department's filing cabinet, there is little point in having them. People throughout the bank need to know where they fit in, what contribution to the system they are expected to make, how they are to set about meeting the objectives expected of them. They do not need to know everything that is planned but they certainly need to know about the things that affect them. A target for increasing deposit share – to continue with the example cited above – would have to be broken down so that individual branches and regions of the bank would know their particular targets and what contribution they would be expected to make to the achievement of the overall goal. When it considers the progress being made, top management must be able to review the progress of individual managers to see who is not doing well, why this is, and what can be done about it. Those responsible for training need to know how much money they can spend and what changing needs the training programmes are expected to meet in order that new courses can be introduced and existing ones modified. If there are to be changes in the way certain routine operations are carried out, the staff concerned need to be warned so that the changes can be introduced with the minimum disruption to the bank's business.

Financial Intermediation

A *financial intermediary* is a body which provides a channel through which funds flow between lenders and borrowers. Banks themselves are financial intermediaries, but a variety of other bodies also exist which are classed as *non-bank financial intermediaries*. When we consider the role of banks as financial intermediaries we are obviously concerned with their credit services since a borrower from a bank is receiving credit. Clearly, by taking money from some people and lending it to others, financial intermediaries play a vital part in a country's economy and affect all our lives. Banks of various kinds are usually the most important financial intermediaries in a country but other institutions often play an important part – the U.K. building societies are a good example.

The need for financial intermediation arises because some people have an excess of income over expenditure – that is they have a financial surplus – whilst others have a deficit, in this case an excess of expenditure over income. Building societies for example receive money from the former group of people (from savers) and lend it to the latter (to those borrowing money to purchase a house). In business some firms need to borrow whilst others have a surplus of funds which they can lend. Banks are important as financial intermediaries because they lend for many purposes to a wide range of customers and accept funds from a great many sources.

The services of financial intermediaries are not always used. One firm can borrow directly from another to meet excess expenditure; people borrow from one another for various purposes; national savings certificates are purchased by the public to help finance government expenditure. In none of these cases is there a need for an intermediary.

The Economy and the Banks

A country's economy can be divided into two main sectors: the public and the private. In the U.K. the *public sector* is made up of central government, the local authorities, and the public corporations, that is the nationalised industries. The *private sector* consists of individuals in the *personal sector*, the *financial sector* made up of banks and other financial institutions, and the *corporate sector* consisting of commercial and industrial companies. To complete the picture it is necessary to include an *overseas sector* since transactions with other countries lead to a surplus or deficit.

The figures estimated by the Bank of England in Table 1 show each sector's surplus or deficit during 1984. Whilst total sector deficits must equal total surpluses this is not the case within sectors. Thus some people have a surplus and other a deficit although the personal sector on balance is in surplus. Banks and other financial intermediaries therefore form part of a financial network which, as the next chapter will show, enables funds to flow to those requiring them.

Table 1 *Surplus and Deficit U.K. Economic Sectors (1984)*

Deficit sectors	£ millions	Surplus sectors	£ millions
Public sector	−12,998	Industrial and commercial	
Banks and other		companies	+ 9,554
financial institutions	− 439	Personal sector	+10,213
Overseas	− 51		
Unidentified	− 6,279		
	−19,767		+19,767

Source: *Bank of England Quarterly Bulletin*

The Risk Factor

The financial intermediaries help in other ways, however, one of which is *risk transformation*. Those who put their surplus funds in a bank or other reputable and well-established intermediary face less risk than in lending direct to an individual perhaps not well-known to them. A bank receives a large number of deposits from many sources and lends to a large number of borrowers; risks are therefore spread widely. Bankers specialise in risk assessment, ensuring that where appropriate an advance is properly secured and making sure it is repaid at the proper time, at the maturity date.

Need for Liquidity

Maturity transformation, another by-product of financial intermediation, is of value both to borrowers and lenders. Generally speaking lenders dislike tying up their money for long periods, they are interested in *liquidity*, the ability to have their money repaid speedily and without loss. Borrowers, on the other hand, normally seek funds for a period longer than is usually available from individual lenders. Banks and other intermediaries, because they are dealing with large numbers of depositors and borrowers and have both experience and expertise, are able to reconcile the differing requirements of borrowers and lenders.

Re-Organisation of Funds

Financial intermediaries receive and lend both small and large sums of money. A bank may use a large deposit to make a number of smaller advances – a *disaggregation* of funds – or funds may be *aggregated*, a number of deposits being used to make an advance.

The process of borrowing and lending is assisted and encouraged by the standardisation of arrangements brought about by intermediaries. A good example is the current or chequeing accounts of banks. The way these operate and the terms on which they are made available to bank customers is well known to the general public and they may be regarded as standard bank products.

Banking Controls

It should be clear that banks play a vital part in the well-being of a community. Their importance to the economic life of a state will become increasingly apparent as we study the services they give and the ways in which they operate. It is because of their importance that controls are imposed upon them in a number of ways. The nature of these controls is amongst the factors banks need to take into account in their corporate planning activities since they effect the environment in which they operate.

We have seen that in some countries *economic controls* are imposed which cause banks to adjust their activities. In the U.K. for many years after the Second World War the banks from time to time were required to restrict their lending to certain sectors of the economy and to direct it towards other sectors regarded by the authorities as of greater importance.

The imposition of *prudential controls* designed to ensure the safety of banks is now common practice in most countries and has assumed greater importance in recent years as international banking operations have developed. As we saw at the beginning of the chapter the failure of a bank can be a major disaster and the job of a bank regulator is to prevent this from happening.

Banks too are usually subject to *monetary controls*, controls which form part of a country's economic policy. A recognised role of government is to secure the economic well-being of its people and its monetary policy is part of the armoury of weapons it has at its disposal for achieving this objective. Later we shall look more closely at the ways in which such policy operates but its main effect is usually to influence the amount of money lent by banks.

Like any other business banks need to conduct their affairs in accordance with the laws of the countries in which they operate. These set out the ways in which a business can be established and, among many other matters, what information it needs to disclose. Sometimes the law affecting banks differs from that covering other firms, but unlike other forms of control it is unlikely to be subject to frequent change. However current changes in the law as well as future developments have to be considered by a bank when it is planning its affairs.

A Bank Is . . .

Banks can be regarded as systems for providing a special type of service connected directly or indirectly with finance. Their activities have to be planned and directed to meet their objectives. Often they are in business for profit which means they have to maximise the difference between their receipts and outgoings. They are financial intermediaries in competition with other banks and non-bank financial intermediaries and they play important roles in the economy of a country. Because of their importance they are subject to a variety of controls, some of which change from time to time to meet the requirements of different regulating authorities.

PERSONAL ASSIGNMENTS

1 Consider the current level of profits of one bank in your country and investigate how these have changed in recent years.

2 Explain the ways in which a bank seeks to earn a profit. To what extent is it important that a bank's activities result in a favourable profit record?

3 Explain how a bank loan or overdraft has enabled someone you know to do something that would otherwise have been difficult or impossible.

4 What information does a bank need to have when carrying out its corporate planning?

5 What is a financial intermediary? Outline the functions of financial intermediaries and explain why they are important.

6 Why do you feel that it is important that controls should be exercised over the ways in which banks conduct their business?

CHAPTER 2

THE FINANCIAL NETWORK

We have seen that some sectors of the economy have deficits whilst others enjoy a surplus, the position depending on whether expenditure is more or less than income. Within these sectors however both surpluses and deficits are likely to be found. Thus although the personal sector as a whole may be in surplus, it is clear that some people will be in deficit, for example needing to borrow money to buy a house, whilst others will be in surplus, saving money perhaps for retirement. Obviously many people are doing both – borrowing money for one purpose whilst at the same time saving for another.

In a developed economy like that of the U.K. a complex network of channels exists which enables funds to flow from surplus to deficit areas. These channels are provided by a wide variety of institutions and markets. A good example of this is the market for housing finance. Funds in the market are provided by building societies, banks, and others for people wishing to buy a house, the funds available coming from deposits with buildings societies and banks.

The purpose of this chapter is to examine the U.K.'s financial network and to see more clearly the part played by banks within this structure.

Central Government Finance

Central government is the most important part of the public sector and is usually in deficit. During the financial year 1984–5 the U.K's central government expenditure was in excess of its revenue from taxation and other sources with the result that it had a borrowing requirement of over £10 billion. The main source of funds to meet this borrowing was from the private sector and the chief means of raising these funds was by increasing the government's marketable or non-marketable debt.

Non-marketable debt consists mainly of money raised through the national savings movement. Thus if a person buys a national savings certificate he is lending money to the government; government debt is thereby increased and the holder of the certificate now has an asset representing the new debt. But this is non-marketable since it cannot be sold in a market to another person, although the debt itself can be repaid at any time by surrendering the certificate.

Marketable debt consists largely of government stocks or bonds, which as we shall see can be bought and sold in a market using the facilities of The Stock Exchange. A government bond is simply a document showing how much has been lent to the government, when it will be repaid, and what interest is payable on the loan. Thus if I hold £100 of Treasury twelve per cent 1993 stock this means that I shall receive £12 interest each year until 1993 when the stock matures and I will be repaid the sum of £100. The cost of this £100 of stock will vary daily according to market conditions. For example if the price fell to £60, I would receive £12 a year on an investment of £60, in others words a *yield* of twenty per cent per annum ($^{12}/_{60} \times 100$). If the price of the £100 bond rose to £120 then the yield would be only ten per cent per annum ($^{12}/_{120} \times 100$).

National Savings

Purchasing government bonds is one way in which members of the public can invest their savings, their surplus income. Another way is to invest in national savings, the main form, as we have seen, of non-marketable government debt.

The Department for National Savings offers a range of products designed to attract the savings of members of the public and to make these available to the government. Two types of *national savings certificate* are sold, a fixed-interest certificate and an index-linked certificate. A maximum sum of money can be invested in each issue of certificates, which can be purchased from most post offices and banks. Repayment is obtained simply by sending certificates with an appropriate form to the savings certificate office. Strictly speaking certificates pay no interest, their value increasing instead by stated increments over a fixed period, usually of five years. The value of these increments becomes greater the longer the certificates are held, thus encouraging people to hold them for their full life. No income or capital gains tax is payable on the increased value of certificates and it is possible to obtain a tax-free annual income from the investment by selling some of the certificates each year, thereby taking advantage of their annual growth in value. The current issue is usually withdrawn when the general level of interest rates changes and is replaced by a new issue more in line with current conditions. Certificates can be held after the end of their normal life, their value increasing under a *common extension term* system at a rate in line with the general level of interest rates.

Index-linked certificates are designed for investors whose main concern is to protect their savings from the effects of inflation. The value of these certificates grows in line with changes in price levels measured by means of the Retail Prices Index (RPI) each month (*see* The Value of Money, Chapter 6).

In October 1983 a new security was introduced, *deposit bonds*, designed for savers with a lump sum to invest. The maximum holding allowed is greater than for a single issue of savings certificate and interest is subject to tax. The rate of interest, higher than that on savings certificates, varies according to the country's general level of interest rates and is calculated on a daily basis. Interest is added to the capital value of the bond on the anniversary of the purchase date and is capitalised, interest in the second year for example being calculated on the value of the bond at the end of the first year as determined by the initial investment plus the first year's interest. Purchases can be made through post offices or by coupons in newspaper advertising. Repayment is possible at any time on giving three months' notice.

Although an income can be obtained from fixed-interest national savings certificates by selling part of a holding to take advantage of its accrued value, it is more convenient to hold *income bonds*. These provide a regular monthly income which can be paid into a bond holder's account or sent to him direct. There is a maximum and minimum limit to the amount of bonds that may be held and the income received is based on the general level of the country's interest rates. Bond interest is calculated on a monthly basis and notice is given of changes in the rate of interest paid. This is subject to income tax but this is not deducted at source. At least three months' notice is required for repayment of bonds.

The importance of national savings certificates, deposit bonds, and income bonds in relation to other national savings products is shown in Table 2 which shows that the *National Savings Bank* offers two types of account which can be used by savers. Both can be opened and deposits made at the majority of post offices. The *ordinary account* offers a two-tier system of interest rates whereby people maintaining a prescribed minimum balance receive a higher return than those with smaller balances. The first part of the interest received is free of income and capital gains tax and interest is automatically credited to the account at the end of December each year. *The investment account* is designed for those who wish to obtain a competitive rate of interest on money which is not needed on demand. The maximum balance allowed on an investment account is higher than on an ordinary account but one month's notice of withdrawal is needed. Withdrawal of money from an ordinary account can be made on demand at a post office for limited amounts and by application to the National Savings Bank for larger amounts. Special arrangements for regular users can be made to enable them to draw larger sums from their ordinary accounts at a named post office. Regular payments may be made free of charge from an ordinary account by means of standing orders for club subscriptions, life assurance premiums, and similar payments. Ordinary account holders may also use paybills to avoid handling cash in paying bills normally payable at a post office such as those for electricity and rates.

Table 2 *National Savings Amounts outstanding (June 1985)*

		£ millions
National savings certificates:		
(Principal amounts)	Fixed interest	9,082
	Index-linked	3,072
Deposit bonds		279
Income bonds		3,033
Save As You Earn and Yearly Plan*		537
Premium bonds		1,775
National Savings Bank:	Ordinary accounts	1,737
	Investment accounts	5,303
Other (including accrued interest etc.)		5,732
	TOTAL	30,550

Source: *Financial Statistics*
Note: The Save As You Earn scheme was withdrawn in 1984.

Two products of the Department of National Savings were designed to attract funds from those wishing to save on a regular basis. A *yearly plan* is available which enables a saver to make monthly payments and to receive interest at a fixed guaranteed rate for five years from the date of the first payment. Interest is free of U.K. income and capital gains tax and can continue to be received after the end of the five-year period at the common extension term rate applicable to other savings certificates. Minimum and maximum limits are set for the monthly payments which can be made only by standing-order payments from a bank account. Subject to certain conditions, these standing-order payments can be continued after the first year by making a new twelve-month agreement. The fixed and guaranteed rate of interest for the new agreement will be determined by the general level of interest rates applicable at that time.

An index-linked *Save As You Earn* contract *(SAYE)* was another means of saving on a regular monthly basis, but in this case the monthly payments were expected to be made over a five-year period. The main advantage of the scheme was the protection it gave against the effects of inflation, the value of the investment being linked to the Retail Prices Index (RPI) in the same way as index-linked national savings certificates. No further payments were made after the end of the fifth year but, if held for another two years, a tax-free bonus would have been earned equal to two of the monthly contributions. In recent years supplementary payments were made to improve the scheme's attraction at a time when interest rates were high and the rate of inflation lower than in previous years. The scheme was withdrawn in 1984.

These schemes are designed to attract different types of saver – those with a lump sum to invest and those wishing to save on a regular basis; those needing an income and those wishing to preserve the real value of their savings. *Premium bonds* are designed to appeal to yet another class of saver – those who like to gamble. They provide the means for taking part in a regular draw for tax-free cash prizes. A prize fund equivalent to the interest obtainable on the total value of bonds issued is used to distribute prizes at weekly and monthly draws. These are made by means of *ERNIE* (Electronic Random Number Indicator Equipment) which produces the winning bond numbers. A maximum amount is specified on the value of bonds that can be held. Bonds can be bought from post offices and banks and have to be held for a minimum period before they are eligible for prizes in a draw.

Personal Saving

We have seen how savings by individuals are lent to the government either by the purchase of government stocks (popularly known as 'gilt-edged') or by using one of the National Savings schemes. These two methods come together through a *National Savings Stock Register*. This enables a wide and representative range of government securities to be

Table 3 *Personal Sector's Holdings of Financial Assets (end of 1984)*

	£ billions
Notes, coin and deposits	69.0
Building societies	90.3
National Savings	28.2
Government securities and loans	19.7
Company securities	81.4
Overseas securities	10.2
Unit trusts	8.5
Life assurance and pension funds	227.3
Trade and other debtors	26.0
Other	8.2
	568.8

Source: *Financial Statistics*

purchased at fees which are attractive for small- and medium-sized investments.

However, there are many other ways in which savings can be used. Holdings of financial assets by the personal sector at the end of 1984 are shown in Table 3. People's deposits with banks and other financial institutions are clearly important financial assets, their attraction often depending on the ease with which they can be used to buy goods and services. A current account at a bank is a very liquid asset because cash can be drawn on demand and the account used for paying bills by cheque. A seven-day deposit account is almost as liquid. Although technically seven days notice should be given before cash can be drawn, in practice funds may be obtained on demand, but usually with a penalty of seven days loss of interest on the money drawn. Money can be deposited with banks for longer periods normally at higher interest rates than for shorter periods. Cheques can usually be drawn only against balances on current accounts, which normally pay no interest. Commission charges are levied on holders of these accounts, often based on the number of transactions and the level of the balance maintained. In recent years banks have sought to attract deposits in a number of ways. Sometimes accounts with limited chequeing facilities but which also pay interest are available. Other accounts are designed to attract savings from particular sectors of the community such as children.

Building Societies

Table 3 shows that personal sector deposits with banks are smaller than those with other financial institutions and why competition from building societies in particular has been of concern to the major banks.

The first building societies were founded towards the end of the eighteenth century, each comprising between twenty and thirty members who banded together to build themselves houses. When all had been housed, the society terminated. By the middle of the nineteenth century the societies were becoming permanent institutions which supplemented their funds by borrowing from those not needing homes. By this time they had ceased to build houses but instead lent money not only to finance the building of new homes but also to those wishing to buy an existing property.

Since the Second World War there has been a massive expansion in the size of societies. Their numbers have diminished substantially since the beginning of the century but their branch network has grown so that they have become major savings institutions with their share of short-term liquid assets in the personal sector rising from ten per cent in 1950 to forty-five per cent by 1980.

Building societies derive their powers from special legislation and are supervised by the Registrar of Friendly Societies. They are effectively owned by their customers rather than by shareholders. Borrowers have to become members of a society before they can borrow and most funds are obtained through share investments. However a shareholder in a building society is in a very different position to one in a company. He obtains his shareholding without cost and the value of his investment goes neither up nor down. His position is very similar to that of a depositor with a bank.

Building societies may lend only on first mortgage (where there is no prior loan from another lender secured on the property) and they can raise funds only for this purpose. Most of a building society's funds are obtained by accepting money on share accounts. These pay a slightly higher rate of interest than on the much smaller sums taken on deposit account since deposit holders would be repaid before those with share accounts in the unlikely event of a society ceasing business.

In recent years building societies have become more competitive and now offer a range of accounts designed to attract savers. Apart from traditional share and deposit accounts it is now possible to open accounts paying higher rates of interest but which do not permit funds to be withdrawn on demand. On some accounts it is possible to draw

Table 4 *Building Society Assets and Liabilities (end of 1984)*

Liabilities		Assets	
	£ millions		£ millions
Shares	88,078	Mortgages	81,879
Deposits and loans	8,426	Cash and	
Tax and liabilities	1,894	investments	19,614
Deferred taxation	173	Other assets	1,195
General reserves	4,117		
	102,688		102,688

Source: *Building Society Fact Book, 1985*

cheques and funds are also taken in the wholesale markets largely by the issue of certificates of deposit (*see* page 42).

Company Finance

We have seen how the government finances its borrowing requirements by means of marketable and non-marketable debt. Table 3 shows how much of this debt is held by the personal sector which also holds company securities, the means whereby companies raise money to meet their financial requirements.

During the nineteenth century it became increasingly clear that firms engaged in industry and commerce required greater financial resources to support their rapid growth than could be provided by a single person or a group of persons operating on their own or in partnership with others. At the same time, growing wealth meant that people needed improved channels through which savings could be put to profitable use. The pressures from those wishing to have access to greater financial resources and from those with increased funds to invest led to the development of the *joint stock company*, an organisation recognised by law as a legal entity comprising a large number of members but with its own identity separate from that of its members. As years went by the concept of *limited liability* was developed to ensure that those becoming members of a company could be protected from large-scale losses. Their liability could be restricted to the sums invested in a company and this protection made it possible for firms to raise more easily and on more favourable terms the large amounts of capital needed.

Many firms today are in the hands of sole-traders. Others are run by two or more partners. But large enterprises are usually joint stock companies with limited liability. These are formed under the Companies Acts by an application to the Registrar of Companies. The most important documents to be submitted with the application are the *memorandum and articles of association*. The memorandum deals with the external affairs of a company whilst the articles govern its internal operations. Thus the memorandum gives the name of the company and whether the registered office is in England or Scotland, details of its capital structure and whether the liability of members is limited or unlimited, as well as setting out the objects of the company and thus the limits to its powers. The articles deal with such matters as the issue and transfer of shares, proceedings at general meetings, the voting powers of members, the accounts, and the powers and duties of directors – that is those selected by the members to conduct the company's affairs. A company if it wishes can adopt, in full or in part, a model set of articles contained in the Companies Acts. When the memorandum and articles have been registered a *certificate of incorporation* is issued – in effect the company's 'birth certificate'. The company now has a legal status, whereas before the issue of the certificate the company had no legal power to do anything.

Companies are of two main types: private and public. A private company depends on private sources for its funds whilst a public company is able to appeal to the public at large by inviting them to subscribe for its shares. It is not unusual to find a successful private company which wishes to expand changing its status by 'going public'. The shares it is then able to offer to the public are of two main types, ordinary and preference shares. *Preference shares* pay a fixed rate of interest which must be paid out of profits before any dividends are paid to holders of *ordinary shares*. If the preference shares are cumulative any payments not made to holders in earlier years must be paid before the ordinary shareholders can receive payment.

The *nominal* or *authorised capital* is the figure mentioned in the company's memorandum and that part taken up by shareholders is known as the *issued capital*. Sometimes shares are issued in partly-paid form and the amount subscribed is referred to as the *paid-up* capital. Thus the capital structure of a company could be as follows:

Nominal capital:	£1,000,000
Issued capital:	£500,000 (in ordinary shares of £1 each, £0.50 paid)
Paid-up capital:	£250,000

In this example each owner of an ordinary share is liable to pay the company £0.50 when required. As there are 500,000 shares in issue the unpaid capital is £250,000.

The services of an *issuing house* are used when a public company seeks to raise money through an issue of shares. A number of firms undertake this work including merchant banks. They must ensure that the issue of shares is in accordance with the requirements of the Companies Acts and, if the shares are to be dealt with on The Stock Exchange, that the rules of the Exchange are complied with. With the exception of some preference shares which are redeemable by a company at some future date, purchasers of shares know that the money they invest will not be repaid by the company. Clearly this could be very inconvenient for a shareholder in need of funds or who would prefer to see his money invested elsewhere. As a result a secondary market has developed through which a shareholder can realise his investment by selling his shares to someone else.

Today The Stock Exchange provides this secondary market where shares can be bought and sold at a price determined by the strength of supply and demand within the market (*see* Supply and Demand, Chapter 5). These transactions have no direct effect on the finances of the company concerned since they simply involve an exchange of shares already issued by the company, whose share register is amended to record the name of the new owner. Important changes which will affect the working of The Stock Exchange in the late 1980s are already taking place, but traditionally members of The Stock Exchange have been of two types – *brokers* and *jobbers*. Brokers are agents of the public and carry out their instructions for which they receive a commission. A person wanting to buy shares must arrange for a broker to do this for him, either by a direct approach to the broker or by asking a bank to approach a broker on his behalf. Brokers execute a client's orders by dealing with jobbers who are allowed to deal with brokers only, not with the general public. Jobbers usually specialise in particular types of share and are remunerated by the differences in the buying and selling prices of the shares they deal in. It is the broker's responsibility to obtain the best price for his client and he will approach a number of jobbers to determine the most attractive price for the shares he is buying or selling.

However, the issue of shares is not the only way in which a company can raise money. Loan stocks and debentures can be issued in which case similar dealings as those for shares are possible on The Stock Exchange. However holders of these securities are not shareholders.

They are not part-owners of the company but since they have lent money to the company they are its creditors and interest on their loans must be paid even when no profits have been earned. It is for this reason that a company must be careful not to raise too much money in this way: a bad year making it impossible to pay the interest due on this borrowing could lead to disaster.

Investment and Unit Trusts

Dealings in government securities also take place on The Stock Exchange, the provision of this secondary market making it easier for the government to raise funds. It follows that the holdings of government and company securities shown in Table 3 could have been obtained either by purchase through The Stock Exchange or by a successful application for a new issue of securities. However, a large part of the public's investment in securities arises not in this direct way but indirectly through a variety of institutions such as *investment trusts*. These are companies whose shares can be bought and sold on The Stock Exchange but who are in business not as manufacturers or traders but as holders of investments in other organisations. Their shareholders receive dividends in the same way as other shareholders, but these are paid out of income received on security holdings rather than as a result of commercial operations. To the investor, investment trusts offer a number of advantages. The investment trust is able to invest in a wider range of securities than would normally be possible with the funds available to a single investor. It is therefore possible to spread risk, poor performance of one investment being offset by a better performance elsewhere. Management of the investments is in the hands of professionals who look after the buying and selling of investments, collect the income, and pay dividends to the shareholder who is thus relieved of a good deal of burdensome paper work.

A *unit trust* has many of the advantages of an investment trust but is not a company and the investor holds units, not shares. The proceeds from the sale of units are invested by the unit trust managers over a range of companies and these investments are held by trustees, usually an insurance company or a bank (*see* Executor and Trustee Services, Chapter 10). Unlike an investment trust whose share values are determined by supply and demand, the value of a unit trust investment is determined by the value of the underlying securities which have been purchased. The managers use these values to work out the price of a unit and to quote a buying or *bid price* and a selling or *offer price*.

Whereas an investment trust can only expand if it raises more capital, a unit trust is more flexible. If more units are held by the public, the managers increase the amount invested in underlying securities. If the number of units issued falls then some of the underlying securities are sold. The managers buy and sell units according to the public's demand and part of their remuneration comes from the difference between bid and offer prices. Usually there is an initial charge when units are purchased and an annual charge based on the total value of the trust fund.

Unit trusts are authorised by the Department of Trade which sets rules for their operation. Before authorisation the Department examines the trust deed creating the trust to ensure that it meets its requirements. This regulates the methods by which bid and offer prices are to be calculated and the managers remunerated.

A large variety of unit trusts now operate in the U.K. Some are designed to yield a high income while others have capital growth as their objective. Some concentrate their resources in particular industries, for example energy, high technology, or finance, while others concentrate their investments in particular geographic areas such as the U.S. or the Far East. Some trusts are cumulative, automatically reinvesting the income due to a unit holder, while others are linked to life assurance schemes. It is often possible to buy units through a saving scheme, whereby regular payments are made each month the number of units purchased depending on their price at the time.

Life Assurance and Pension Funds

Table 3 shows how important life assurance and pension funds are as a means of chanelling personal savings to those who need to borrow. A major motive for saving is obviously to provide an income in later life for oneself and one's dependants. One method is to take out a policy of life assurance. A *whole-life policy* provides a lump sum payment on the death of the life assured. An *endowment policy* provides a lump sum either when the person concerned reaches an agreed age or on his death, whichever is sooner. The premium payable to obtain cover under both types of policy is determined by a number of factors: the age and sex of the person taking out the policy, and in the case of an endowment policy the number of payments to be made before the policy matures.

The premiums collected from policy holders form a fund which is invested and which provides the means for making payments when policies mature. As with investment and unit trusts, therefore, savings are collected which helps to provide finance for both companies and the government. Holders of both whole-life and endowment policies by paying higher premiums can participate in the profits made as a result of fund operations. Holders of *with profits* policies accumulate bonuses which are added to the value of the policy when it matures. Given sound investment management of the fund it is possible that in the later years of a policy's life the bonuses declared can be greater than the premiums paid.

This channelling of savings to where they are needed is also implemented through pension schemes. Payments made by employers and employees under a scheme operated by a company or by an insurance company on its behalf form a fund out of which the pensions are paid, these payments being met in part by those currently contributing to the scheme and in part from investments held by the fund.

House Purchase

As well as being placed in financial assets through the channels we have examined, large sums are also invested in physical assets such as houses. The figures in Table 5 show the size of these investments at the end of 1984. It is quite clear from these figures and from those given in Table 3 that the most important assets people own are the homes they live in. The purchase of a house or flat is likely to be the largest item of expenditure a person makes. Most have to make the purchase with borrowed money and because of its size the loan is normally repaid only over a long period.

Building societies are by far the most important providers of housing

Table 5 *Personal Sector's Holdings of Physical Assets (end of 1984)*

	£ billions
Dwellings	425.4
Other land and buildings	57.3
Consumer durables	89.1
Other	25.4
	597.2

Source: *Financial Statistics*

loans, despite the fact that in recent years the major banks have entered the market in competition with the societies. At the end of 1983 about seventy-five per cent of housing loans was provided by building societies and roughly sixteen per cent by banks. The remaining nine per cent came from local authorities, insurance companies, pension funds, and other sources.

Building societies do not earn profits in the traditional sense: no dividends are paid as in the case of companies and their reserves of cash and investments are modest. Since loans to their borrowers are for long periods whilst most of the money placed with them can be withdrawn quickly, the interest they pay must be at rates which enable them to compete in the market, notably with banks and the national savings movement. Thus although the societies seek to avoid frequent changes, movements in the general level of the country's interest rates are reflected in the cost of borrowing from the societies.

Consumer Durables

As Table 5 shows, the other main class of physical assets held by people consists of consumer durables, that is goods which in time will wear out or be consumed but which last longer than consumer goods such as food and clothing. A washing machine is a good example of a consumer durable.

Finance for purchases of consumer durables comes largely from banks or *finance houses*. Personal loans (*see* Personal Borrowing, Chapter 8) are generally regarded as particularly appropriate for financing the purchase of cars and consumer durables or for making home improvements. Traditionally finance houses have been associated with the provision of consumer credit, particularly of instalment credit in the form of hire purchase finance.

A *hire purchase* contract is an agreement to hire with an option to purchase when the last instalment is paid. Ownership of the goods remains with the finance house until this option is exercised. A *conditional sale* is similar to hire purchase except that the customer is legally bound to purchase the goods by completing the payments at which point he becomes the owner of the goods. A *credit sale* agreement gives the purchaser an immediate title to the goods for which he pays by instalments.

Very often consumer finance is arranged at the point of sale. Sometimes too finance is provided for the seller. Thus a car manufacturer when sending a car to a motor dealer may invoice the finance house who pays for the car and charges the dealer interest for the *stocking facility*. When the dealer sells the car he pays the finance house who then provides instalment finance to the purchaser if he needs it. Finance therefore is provided from the time of manufacture until the purchaser finishes the payment of instalments to the finance house.

Finance houses provide not only finance to consumers for motor vehicles and household goods and furnishings but also for home improvements such as the installation of double glazing or central-heating systems. Finance is also available for holidays and leisure activities. Some finance houses have now entered the house mortgage market, providing loans in a similar way to banks. Finance is available to the consumer through the finance houses' own branch systems as well as at the point of sale.

Table 6 *Bank Lending to U.K. Residents. Amounts outstanding (August 1985)*

	£ millions
Manufacturing industry	26,815
Agriculture, forestry and fishing	5,859
Oil and natural gas extraction	3,033
Other energy industries and water	2,398
Construction	4,945
Retail motor trades	2,160
Other retail distribution	6,055
Wholesale distribution	9,645
Hotels and catering	3,238
Transport and communications	3,740
Building societies	1,958
Investment and unit trusts	3,595
Insurance companies and pension funds	2,405
Leasing companies	6,630
Other financial	20,057
Central and local government services	2,231
Property companies	6,592
Business and other services	14,243
Persons: house purchase	19,551
other	19,245
	164,395

Source: *Bank of England Quarterly Bulletin*

A large part of the finance houses' facilities is in the form of credit to commercial and industrial firms. A company can use these facilities for purchasing cars and commercial vehicles as well as for plant and machinery, computers, and office equipment. Some houses are prepared to finance the purchase of retail businesses such as newsagents or sub-post offices. A very important part of their activities in recent years has been the provision of leasing facilities, the finance house purchasing and itself owning equipment but allowing it to be used in return for a rental payment (*see* Leasing, Chapter 10).

Bank Lending

Obviously a good deal of finance for the purchase of assets is self-generated. Thus a large part of company finance is derived from profits which instead of being distributed to owners is ploughed back into the business to allow it to expand and to improve its operations. Many people likewise prefer to save their money to buy for example a dishwasher or refrigerator rather than to pay for it later through a bank or finance house.

As the figures in Table 6 show, lending by banks is made to all sections of the community. This diversity requires a high standard of expertise in bank lending skills.

PERSONAL ASSIGNMENTS

1 Examine in detail the conditions under which the current issue of national savings certificates is offered to the public.

2 How does the current issue of index-linked national savings certificates differ from those giving a fixed return? Compare the advantages of holding each type of issue.

3 What are the advantages and disadvantages of holding deposit bonds and income bonds at the present time?

4 What benefits does a saver receive by placing funds in a national savings yearly plan? How do these benefits compare with those obtained from an investment in premium bonds?

5 Examine the ways in which a major bank seeks to attract deposits from the general public.

6 Examine the ways in which a major building society seeks to attract deposits from the general public.

CHAPTER 3

THE HISTORY OF BANKING

'History is bunk', said Henry Ford. Although he may have been correct in some respects there is no doubt that to understand clearly the functions of banks in the twentieth century it is useful to know something of their past.

History finished yesterday but is being made today. This is certainly true of banking. Every day reports are received from somewhere in the world of important events affecting banking; every day a bank somewhere is taking decisions that will affect its future history.

U.K. Commercial Banking

Banking has a long history. When the Bank of England was founded towards the end of the seventeenth century the Banco di Rialto in Venice had already been established for over 100 years and the Bank of St George at Genoa was even older. However there seems little doubt that in 1750 in England and Wales there were very few people outside London conducting a business confined to banking.

In London banking as we know it today had its roots in the activities of the *goldsmiths* who for many years had supplied traders with foreign currency and whose business has been described as a 'hotch-potch of pawnbroking, gold and silver smithery, money changing and true banking'. (W. J. Thorne: *Banking* (Oxford University Press, second edn, 1962.)) Above all they became recognised as providing a secure home for people's valuables and money, an important service for those without their own safe-custody facilities. Gradually the goldsmiths developed a range of services which can be recognised as forerunners of the banking services provided today. They received money for safekeeping, lent a portion of it to those requiring finance and issued receipts for the money that was deposited. These receipts developed into *bank notes* whilst the written instructions given to them by depositors to pay money to other people developed into *cheques*.

Expanding trade at home and overseas in the latter half of the seventeenth century led to major developments in the financial system both in London and in the country. In the early stages of this expansion, merchants of various kinds developed a subsidiary banking business in very much the same way as the London goldsmiths. These merchants were men trusted by the community to look after its money, men who were honest and whose IOUs were accepted in return for the gold left with them for safekeeping. Gradually these country bankers came to realise that part of the money deposited with them could be lent profitably with the result that they gave up their original activities to concentrate on the business of banking.

Joint Stock Banking

But prudence as well as honesty is needed for sound banking and the early bankers had to learn from experience what proportion of the money deposited with them they could safely lend. Sound judgement was needed, judgement of the safety of lending to a prospective borrower, judgement of how to use funds not so lent.

It became increasingly evident in the nineteenth century that prudence and honesty as well as sound judgement were not sufficient. New inventions stimulated industrial growth and there was a rapid expansion in the U.K.'s population. The small private banks were inadequate and during a crisis in 1825 over seventy stopped payment. Until this point the Bank of England had been the only bank in England and Wales permitted to have more than six partners. Things in Scotland were different and banks there had developed mainly as joint stock enterprises with many owners (*see* p. 22). They had weathered the crisis well and the lesson of their experience led to legislation in 1826 and 1833 which despite opposition from private banks and the Bank of England allowed *joint stock banks* to operate throughout the U.K.

It now became possible to have banks with more than six owners which could draw on the savings of large numbers of people rather than on the wealth of a few. Banks could be bigger if not better. Joint stock banks ran into difficulties in the same way as private banks when prudence, honesty and sound judgement were lacking. But despite legal difficulties and strong opposition from private bankers and the Bank of England, joint stock banking flourished. By the end of 1833 there were nearly 50 joint stock banks in England and around 10,000 people had an ownership stake in them. By 1836 the number had grown to over 100 and some of them had started to open branches.

In 1844 England and Wales had over 100 joint stock banks and more than 330 private banks. But the importance of the private banker was in decline and by 1884 they numbered little more than 200 although, like the joint stock banks, they had responded to the growth in the banking habit by developing a branch network. At the same time amalgamation of banks to form increasingly large units was in progress, a movement which has continued until recent times and which has resulted in the formation of four large banking groups in England and Wales with an extensive branch network.

Although some of the largest world banks are to be found in the U.S., legislation there has to a large extent prevented the amalgamation of banks into large units with the result that the system is essentially one of unit banks rather than one of branch banks as found in the U.K. and other countries. In the last thirty years competition between banks has increased and the large banking groups have extended their range of services in a variety of directions. The extent of these services is now very great and will be considered in Chapter 10.

The Bank of England

The Bank of England, established in 1694 by men in the City of London led by the Scot William Paterson, had a monopoly of joint stock banking for many years, a monopoly which greatly contributed to the weakness of the early banking system. Founded largely as a means of securing a loan to enable war to be conducted against France, the founders could not have foreseen that in time the Bank would develop functions which came to be recognised as typical of *central banking*.

From its inception the Bank competed vigorously with the other banks. Its note issue drove notes of other London banks out of circulation and legislation in 1844 gradually had the effect of giving the Bank its current monopoly of the note issue in England and Wales. It quickly became banker to the government and although it competed with the private banks, these found it convenient to keep balances with it. The Bank of England thus became a bankers' bank as well as the government's bank.

During the eighteenth century the Bank increasingly dominated the banking scene, but it was only in the latter years of the nineteenth century that it came to accept responsibility for monetary control and for the safety of the banking system. Its present role as an arm of government responsible for implementing monetary policy will be examined in Chapter 7 whilst its functions as a bank controller operating under the 1979 Banking Act will be scrutinised in Chapter 12.

The nationalisation of the Bank of England by the *Bank of England Act* of 1946 had little immediate effect on the way it operated. Its relationship with the Treasury was already close and it had assumed a number of responsibilities from its position as banker to the government. Thus it had responsibility for exchange control until the regulations were removed in 1979. It has the responsibility of raising funds for the government through the issue of Treasury bills and bonds, maintains registers of holders of these bonds, and ensures that interest payments are made to these holders at the proper time.

Despite its close links with the Treasury, the Bank of England still looks after the accounts of a small number of private customers as well as those of overseas central banks and international organisations. It deals in a number of markets, notably in the discount market and when appropriate in the foreign exchange market. It provides a channel of communication between the financial institutions and the government, collects a range of statistics, and provides an independent view of the state of the economy. More generally it collects information on current conditions in trade and industry throughout the country, and generally and increasingly exercises a beneficent influence over a range of markets such as The Stock Exchange.

In 1844 the *Bank Charter Act* provided that no new bank could issue notes, that existing issues could not be increased, and that any banks that amalgamated would lose their existing right of issue. It was the continuing process of amalgamation that led in 1921 to the Bank obtaining its present note issue monopoly in England and Wales when Fox, Fowler and Co. was absorbed by Lloyds Bank. The Act also established a means for controlling the Bank's note issue and required that it should publish a weekly return showing figures for its note issue separate from those relating to its other activities. Banks in Scotland and Northern Ireland were subject to separate legislation which allows them to issue their own notes provided that all but a very small amount are backed fully by Bank of England notes.

The return shown in Table 7 reflects some of the main functions of the Bank. The sole liability of the Issue Department is the value of the notes it has printed which are either in circulation with the public or held as a reserve by the Banking Department. No longer is there any gold backing for the note issue, assets in the Issue Department consisting of government debt – an original loan of 1694 and

Table 7 *Bank of England Weekly Return. Wednesday 20 November 1985*

£ millions			
ISSUE DEPARTMENT			
Notes issued:		Government debt	11
In circulation	12,041	Other government	
In Banking Department	9	securities	1,339
		Other securities	10,700
	12,050		12,050
BANKING DEPARTMENT			
Capital	15	Government securities	612
Public deposits	1,414	Advances and	
Special deposits	830	other accounts	911
Bankers' deposits	nil	Premises, equipment	
Reserves and other		and other securities	2,173
accounts	1,447	Notes	9
		Coin	1
	3,706		3,706

Source: *Bank of England*

subsequent increases – and government and other securities. These other securities include bills acquired by the Bank in the course of its market operations. An increase in the note issue is likely to be matched by increased lending to the government and thus to a rise in the Bank's holdings of government securities. In other words a rise in the note issue is a source of finance for the government.

The banking function can be seen from the liabilities of the Banking Department. Its role as banker to the government is shown by the item called public deposits, comprising the exchequer and other official accounts. Special deposits may be called for from the banks as part of monetary policy but on the day of this return were non-existent. They are shown separately from bankers' deposits, the sums held by the Bank in its role as a bankers' bank. The figure for reserves and other accounts includes balances held for overseas central banks, local authorities and the Bank's private customers. Among the Banking Department's assets the figure for advances includes any lending carried out in its support operations in the money market.

U.K. Banks Overseas

The direct interest of British banks in overseas business dates from 1918. Some of the large joint stock banks opened branches on the continent of Europe and chains of branches were established in Latin America, in the West Indies, and in Africa. This was by no means the first involvement of the British in overseas banking – the Midland Bank had in 1905 opened a special department for the business of foreign exchange – but international banking business at the beginning of the twentieth century was largely dominated by private firms and the branches of overseas banks.

Banks existing today in many of the Commonwealth countries as well as in other countries formerly under British control started in London. In the early part of the nineteenth century banking in the colonies of the British Empire was carried out by specialised banks known as *overseas banks*. The Bank of Montreal and the Bank of New South Wales of Sydney were both formed in 1817 and many more were founded in the second half of the century. The most important were the Hongkong and Shanghai Banking Corporation (1864) and the Standard Bank of South Africa (1862). Most *colonial banks* were founded by Royal Charter, the terms of which were carefully considered by the Treasury and the Board of Trade. Indeed, the terms on which such banks could be formed was much stricter than for banks in the U.K. itself and this influenced the legislation introduced in 1844 to control joint stock banks. As countries have gained independence they have often sought to take control of banks whose ownership was in foreign hands. This process of *indigenisation* has been prompted by the belief that political freedom must be accompanied by economic freedom and that this is only to be obtained when the banking system takes account of the economy's objectives of growth and development.

Despite this, the period since 1945 has seen a remarkable growth of international banking. The growth of multinational enterprises, improved travel conditions and better channels of communication has combined with the growth of international capital markets and increased competition between banks to make banking an international industry. The world's major banks have established extensive operations throughout the world, sometimes by acquiring the business of banks in other countries, often by extending their branch network overseas, and sometimes by establishing formal links with banks in other countries in order to develop profitable joint operations.

Bills of Exchange

The international banks of today and many before them have used *bills of exchange* as a means of making payments and providing finance. These instruments are simply written instructions to someone to pay a sum of money to somebody else at a particular time. The person giving the instruction, the *drawer*, draws the bill on the *drawee*, the person instructed to make payment to a third party called the *payee*. If the bill is payable on demand, the payee simply presents it to the drawee who pays the amount stated in the bill.

£1,000   London
                                                                            31 October 19....

Three months after date pay to Thomas James or order one thousand pounds.   (*payee*)

To Roy Owen (*drawee*)   Margaret Steele
   Blackpool   (*drawer*)

Figure 4.   A Bill of Exchange

But a bill need not be drawn payable on demand: it may be payable at some future time, as in the example shown in Figure 4. Since nobody is liable on a bill until he or she has signed it and since the payee is likely to want the drawee to acknowledge liability, the payee will present it to the drawee when he obtains the bill in order that the drawee may *accept* that he will pay when the bill matures, that is at its due date. If this is the case, the drawee writes 'accepted' on the face of the bill and adds his signature. The drawee is now known as the *acceptor* and the accepted bill is called an *acceptance*.

It is clear that the payee of a bill payable at a future date may be anxious to obtain funds immediately. In this case, instead of holding the bill to maturity and receiving its face value, he may sell the bill at a *discount*, that is for a figure less than the face value. The *discounter* holds the bill to maturity and receives more than he paid for it, thus providing him with a return on the money that he has advanced to the payee. We can therefore see that a bill of exchange has three primary functions:

1. It may be used as a means of payment.
2. It can be used as a means of borrowing money.

3. It provides a channel for investing money.

The bill of exchange has a long history which can be traced back to the fall of the Roman Empire. Something very like a bill of exchange was used in Italy as early as the eighth century and an instrument very similar to the modern bill was used by the Lombards in the thirteenth and fourteenth centuries.

Major reasons for the development of the bill as an important commercial instrument were that it facilitated trade over long distances and removed the risk of carrying cash. The law was concerned to develop a code of conduct to perfect its usefulness and was based initially on the practices of merchants. Not until the seventeenth century were these practices treated as part of the law of the land, applicable to all whether merchant or not. Pressure for codification of the law led in 1882 to the passing of the *Bills of Exchange Act*. This Act and subsequent legislation are of vital importance to bankers (*see* Chapter 13). The law regarding cheques is covered by the Act, the cheque being defined as a 'Bill of Exchange drawn on a banker, payable on demand'.

In modern times the bill of exchange has varied in importance at different stages in its history. For example until the opening of banks in Manchester and Liverpool in the 1770s bills were used like bank notes passing from hand to hand with numerous endorsements. As we shall see an *endorsement* is simply the signature of the payee or subsequent holders on the bill or cheque, the *endorser* assuming certain responsibilities regarding payment.

Before the amalgamation of banks to form a nation-wide system of branch banking, bills were used to avoid the danger and inconvenience of carrying cash. It was possible for example for a merchant to purchase from his country bank a bill of exchange drawn on a London banker. This he could use for settling a debt or to obtain cash when he arrived in London.

But the discounting of bills was an early and important banking function and was certainly a well-established part of the goldsmiths' business by the 1660s. Inland bills were an important source of finance for domestic trade and industry during the industrial revolution and the fact that they rose in value between the time of discount and their maturity date made them a useful investment, particularly as each endorsement added to their security. They were extensively used until the loan and overdraft services of banks were developed in the 1870s.

Largely because of the way in which monetary policy has been conducted in recent years (*see* The Role of Monetary Policy, Chapter 7) the bill of exchange has shown a remarkable increase in importance as is illustrated in Table 8.

Table 8 *U.K. Bank Acceptances*

	£ millions
End of 1980	5,558
1981	8,708
1982	13,459
1983	14,909
1984	19,053
August 1985	20,152

Source: *Bank of England Quarterly Bulletin*

The Discount Market

Before the development of a branch banking system the bill of exchange performed the invaluable function of facilitating the flow of funds from areas of the country with money to invest to other areas, often in the developing industrial regions, where there was a demand for credit. Towards the end of the eighteenth century bill brokers became increasingly important, touring the country and enabling bills to be discounted for those in need of funds making them available to those with money to invest. From about 1820 these brokers found that they could borrow money and thus obtain finance with which they themselves could discount bills, holding them as an investment. Banks came to realise that here was a way of employing funds that would provide a second line of *liquidity* and yield a return.

The liquidity of an asset refers to the speed with which it can be turned into cash without loss. Cash is the most liquid of assets but yields no return: it may even cost money to store it safely. Funds for the bill brokers – now called *discount houses* – can be lent overnight and because they can be called back at a moment's notice can be regarded as near cash. As idle cash produces no profit, banks are prepared to lend money to discount houses at a rate of interest slightly below the rate that can be obtained on bills thus making it possible for the discount houses to earn a running profit.

In 1829 the Bank of England agreed to establish accounts which came to be called discount accounts and these give discount houses the right, under certain conditions, to take bills to the Bank to get them discounted. Because of this the banker knows that if he is calling his loan the discount house has a *lender of last resort* standing by to provide it with cash if funds are unobtainable elsewhere.

From this has developed the system operating in the U.K. today: a market in which the discount houses stand between the banks and the Bank of England, a market which provides funds for commerce and industry through the discount of bills, and a market which is useful to banks as an important source of liquidity.

But business for the discount houses has varied in its profitability over the years, often as a result of changes in the use being made of bills of exchange. Bills as a source of domestic finance declined in importance towards the end of the nineteenth century but international trade was expanding and as London was an important source of finance the bill on London became important. However, the recession in world trade after the First World War and particularly in the 1930s led to a decline in the number of bills requiring discount and the discount houses faced a lean time. By using their borrowed funds for lending to the government by holding short-dated government bonds, however, the market was able to survive a period of lean bill dealing.

Table 9 *Discount Houses. Sterling Assets and Liabilities (August 1985)*

	£ millions
Liabilities	
Borrowed sterling funds	7,176
	7,176
Sterling assets	
Cash at Bank of England	6
Treasury bills	134
Other bills	3,666
Certificates of deposit: banks	2,049
building societies	457
Other lending	453
Investments in government and other stocks	615
Other sterling assets	96
	7,476

Source: *Bank of England Quarterly Bulletin*

Table 9 shows the present-day position of discount houses as far as their sterling business is concerned. Funds in other currencies are taken by the discount houses and invested in non-sterling assets, but the amounts involved are small. Most of the market's sterling funds are borrowed from the banks only about £1,300 million in August 1985 being borrowed from other U.K. sources.

Treasury bills are issued weekly and are a source of finance for the government. They were introduced in 1877 and because borrowing is for a short period – U.K. Treasury bills have a life of ninety-one days – they are usually a relatively cheap way for the government to borrow money. However in recent years there has been a decline in their importance.

Sterling *certificates of deposit* were first issued in the U.K. in 1968. They are issued to depositors by banks in round figures for amounts of between £50,000 and £500,000. A certificate of deposit (CD) certifies the receipt of money for a fixed period usually at a fixed rate of interest. Their advantage over other fixed-period deposits is that they can be sold before their maturity date. The discount houses participate in the market for CDs and holdings of these certificates are amongst their assets.

Merchant Banking

The term 'merchant bank' is an imprecise one, frequently used but difficult to define. It derives from the fact that many of the original merchant banks started as merchant traders but, rather like the goldsmiths, came to develop a financial service.

Although a number of U.K. firms call themselves merchant banks, a small group are members of the Accepting Houses Committee and this provides a clue to their early activities. Their development started in the eighteenth century – Barings, the oldest London merchant bank, can trace its history back to 1717 – and gathered pace with the growth of international trade in the nineteenth century. Merchants engaged in the business of importing and exporting came to enjoy a world-wide reputation and because of their international connections were well placed to judge the credit standing of other business men. As a result they were able to accept bills of exchange on behalf of other people in return for a commission under an agreement known as an *acceptance credit*. Because of their high business standing their acceptance of a bill was a guarantee that it would be paid at maturity, so a trader could obtain funds easily by discounting the bill at a fine rate, that is at a rate of discount lower than for other acceptances. It also meant that the Bank of England was happy to take bills accepted by a member of the Accepting Houses Committee when it was providing assistance to the discount houses.

The importance of London as a source of international finance in the nineteenth century and the reputation of the accepting houses led them to become bankers to overseas governments and to help them raise funds for the development of their country, for the building of railway networks, and for other projects such as that illustrated by the 1804 prospectus issued by Barings for the raising of a loan in London to enable the U.S. to purchase Louisiana from France (Figure 5).

London 3 April 1804
AMERICAN LOUISIANA STOCK
is irredemable for fifteen Years, and then reimbursable in the four following Years, by four equal payments.

The Stock bears Interest, at Six per Cent. per Annum, from the first Day of January, 1804; and it is agreed that the Interest shall be payable in London, half-yearly, as it becomes due, and without any protraction of time, namely, on the first Days of July and of January of each Year.

The first Dividend of Three per Cent. will be paid in July next, by Sir Francis Baring and Comp^y. of London.

The Interest is payable at the Par of Exchange of four Shillings and sixpence Sterling per Dollar, free of Commission and Charges, the risk of Bills being for account of the United States.

The Proprietor of this Stock has the option of exchanging his Certificate for one bearing Interest quarterly, payable in America.

The List of the Proprietors will be sent from Washington every half-year; and those Persons, in whose names the Stock stands on the first of January, are entitled to receive the six months' Dividend, due the first of July following; and in like manner those Persons, in whose names the Stock stands on the first of July, are entitled to receive the six months' Dividend due the first of January following.

Figure 5

Because of their expertise, knowledge, and connections, the merchant banks came to play an important part in the financial affairs of U.K. companies by assisting them to raise funds and providing financial advice. As advisers to companies they are sometimes involved with attempts by one firm to take control of another. Many of them are now engaged in investment and unit trust management. They provide investment advice and often take charge of the investments of private clients.

In recent years it has become difficult to draw a clear distinction between merchant and other forms of banking. The large U.K. commercial banks have developed a merchant banking business and often overseas banks in London have a merchant banking arm. In many cases many of the services provided are similar and the markets in which they operate are the same. However as a general rule it may be said that merchant banking is primarily a *wholesale banking* business – that is, one which (unlike *retail banking*) is concerned with taking deposits and making loans for large amounts, and whose clients are likely to be large firms and governments rather than private customers and small enterprises.

Wholesale Money Markets

Since the 1950s a number of sterling markets have developed in London parallel to the traditional discount market. The earliest was the *local-authority market* which enables local authorities to borrow for short periods. There are also markets in *yearling bonds* issued by local authorities and also in *local-authority bills*.

The most important of the new markets is the *inter-bank market*, a market enabling one bank to borrow from another but in which non-bank lenders can participate. Unlike the discount market, lending is usually on an unsecured basis, that is to say no security is normally required from the borrower. Borrowers and lenders are brought together by *money brokers* who receive a commission for their services, deals being struck over the telephone. The market has grown in importance and has enabled banks to acquire funds when needed in addition to the deposits made with them in traditional ways. Interest rates in the market are now of great importance to banks and the *London Inter-Bank Offered Rate* (LIBOR), is frequently used as a basis for lending to large borrowers. Closely linked to the inter-bank market is the *inter-company market* which enables firms to lend to one another or to take funds from banks through this channel.

Although the growth of the parallel markets has provided individual banks with a source of liquidity, if the banking system as a whole is short of cash the ultimate source of funds is through the discount market operating with the Bank of England as the lender of last resort.

PERSONAL ASSIGNMENTS

1 Write a brief history of one bank in your country.

2 What are the main functions of a central bank? In what way is the work of a central bank of value to the country in which it is established?

3 Examine the growth and development of merchant banking in a country of your choice.

4 Describe the methods used for paying for goods and services in your country.

5 Explain how the work of the U.K. discount market differs from that of the inter-bank market.

6 Examine the procedures used for the issue of Treasury bills in the U.K.

7 Prepare a statement showing the current sources and use of funds of the London discount houses.

CHAPTER 4

ACCOUNTING AND
THE BANKER

One of the most important skills a banker needs is the ability to read a set of accounts. This is because an accounting system, by the use of figures, reflects as clearly as possible what is happening in a business or similar enterprise. A banker, as with others in business, needs not only to know how his own affairs are progressing but also to be able to assess how those of his customers are getting on.

The Balance Sheet

Methodical accounting systems operate on well-established principles. For example the affairs of an enterprise are usually regarded as separate from those of the people who establish or own it. Thus a local badminton club will enjoy an income separate from that of its members: if it owns equipment that can be regarded as the club's property and not that of individual members.

A fundamental principle is that of *double entry*, which derives from the notion that every transaction has a twofold aspect. Thus if I buy a pair of shoes costing £20, I gain a pair of shoes but lose £20 in cash. The other party to the transaction, in this case the shopkeeper who sells me the shoes, gains £20 but loses a pair of shoes.

These principles can be illustrated quite simply if we imagine using £1,000 of our savings to establish a small business. We are concerned only with recording the affairs of the business and we wish to keep these separate from our own affairs. We can do this by producing the balance sheet shown in Table 10, which is rather like taking a photograph of the business at the time it was born. This balance sheet shows that at the start of business on 1 January the new firm owed £1,000 to its owners – a *liability* – but owned cash of the same amount – an *asset*.

Table 10 *Balance Sheet as at 1 January 19..*

Liabilities	£	Assets	£
Owners' capital	1,000	Cash	1,000

Assume that in the first few weeks of January the firm started operating, using part of its cash to purchase a stock of goods to sell. The picture of the business in the middle of the month might be that shown in Table 11.

Table 11 *Balance Sheet as at 15 January 19..*

Liabilities	£	Assets	£
Owners' capital	1,000	Cash	700
		Stock	300
	1,000		1,000

Now let us suppose that by the end of the month one-third of the stock had been sold for £125. The value of the stock would have fallen by £100, cash would have risen by £125 – the amount received for the goods sold – and a profit of £25 would have been made. This is kept in the business but as it belongs to the owners it is part of the firm's liabilities. The balance sheet for the end of January would be as shown in Table 12.

Table 12 *Balance Sheet as at 31 January 19..*

Liabilities	£	Assets	£
Owners' capital	1,000	Cash	825
Profit	25	Stock	200
	1,025		1,025

So far we have considered the results of only one month's trading in which all transactions have taken place in cash. If we now assume that trading has continued throughout the year and that some of the goods bought by the firm and some of those sold to its customers have not been for cash but have been purchased on a credit basis, we might end the year with the balance sheet shown in Table 13. This now shows figures for the amounts owing to the firm by its *debtors* as well as for the amounts the firm owes to its *creditors*.

Table 13 *Balance Sheet as at 31 December 19..*

Liabilities	£	Assets	£
Capital	1,000	Cash	1,000
Profit	200	Stock	250
Creditors	200	Debtors	150
	1,400		1,400

Because the year's profit has been retained by the business, the owners' stake in the firm is increased from £1,000 to £1,200, a figure equal to the total of the firm's assets less its liabilities to creditors. This *net worth* of the firm is shown in Table 14. Had the firm's owners decided to withdraw half of the profits from the business in cash, the figures for both profits and cash would have been reduced by £100 and the net worth would have fallen to £1,100.

Table 14 *Net Worth as at 31 December 19..*

		£
	Cash	1,000
	Stock	250
	Debtors	150
		1,400
less	Creditors	200
		1,200

Trading and Profit and Loss Accounts

Since each balance sheet of an enterprise only gives us a view of its affairs at a specific point in time we do not know what has happened during the period between two or more balance sheets. Thus we know the level of stocks at the beginning and end of the period concerned but we do not know the value of goods purchased or sold during that period. We have a series of 'snapshots' but we lack a 'moving picture'.

This deficiency is made good by means of trading and profit and loss accounts similar to those illustrated in Tables 15 and 16. The *trading account* is designed to show the *direct* costs of trading – that is the costs which vary with the amount of goods purchased and sold. In the example it is assumed that there are no direct costs, for example the cost of delivering goods to customers, and thus the *gross profit* is determined by the difference between the cost of goods sold and what they have been sold for. In some cases wages are treated as direct costs, the classification adopted depending on the nature of the product and operation.

Table 15 *Trading Account for the year ending 31 December 19..*

		£		£
	Stock at 1.1.19..	Nil	Sales	5,500
add	Purchases	2,500		
		2,500		
less	Stock at 31.12.19..	250		
	Cost of stock sold	2,250		
	Gross profit carried down to profit and loss account	3,250		
		5,500		5,500

Clearly there are many other costs to be taken into account before the *net profit* can be calculated to show how the business has performed during the accounting period. Premises have to be provided, insured, and heated, and staff have to be employed to run the business (unless counted as a direct cost). These *indirect costs* are incurred as long as the firm continues to conduct its business and are unaffected by the level of trade that it undertakes.

Indirect costs are taken into account and the net profit (or loss) arrived at by means of a *profit and loss account* similar to that shown in

Table 16. Gross profit is transferred to this account from the trading account and then used to find the net profit by taking account of the indirect costs for the period. In this example it is assumed that the year's profits are to be retained in the business. When this is not the case, an *appropriation account* is used to show how the net profit is to be divided amongst the firm's owners and what proportion is to be left in the business.

Table 16 *Profit and Loss Account for the year ending 31 December 19..*

	£		£
Wages	1,750	Gross profit brought	
Rent and rates	1,000	down from trading	
Heating and lighting	250	account	3,250
Insurance	50		
Net profit	200		
	3,250		3,250

The trading and profit and loss accounts together with the balance sheet are the final accounts for an accounting period. Whilst they provide us with an extremely useful picture of what has happened during that period they do not tell us everything. For example we know from the balance sheet that the firms debtors owe it £150 but we are unable to tell whether this money is owed by one person or by many. Clearly if only one person is involved there is more danger of loss by non-payment than if a number of people owed the money. Likewise it is probably more likely that one creditor will press the firm to pay the £200 it owes than if, for example, the firm owes ten people an average of only £20 each.

It is also important to realise that although a business may be profitable it can run into difficulties because it is short of money. For example, if a high proportion of sales are on a credit basis rather than for cash the firm could run out of money since in effect it has lent money to customers to finance the purchase of its goods. Thus in the balance sheet shown in Table 13 a figure for debtors of £1,150 would be matched by a fall in cash to zero. The total assets and liabilities of the firm, its net worth, and profits would remain unaltered. However without cash it is in trouble and is likely to be visiting its bank for financial assistance. The use of a *cash flow statement*, a summary of the sources and use of cash, is an invaluable aid to businesses and to bankers and will be considered in greater detail in Chapter 8.

The Accounts

The figures used for drawing up the final accounts of a firm are derived from records of the numerous daily transactions conducted during the accounting period. Under a double-entry system of book-keeping each transaction is recorded twice according to its two-fold aspect. Thus the initial transaction shown in Table 10 would be recorded in a *cash account* and a *capital account*. The owners of the firm are in the same position as creditors in so far as the firm owes them £1,000, and the capital account therefore shows a *credit* for this amount. The corresponding part of this initial transaction is the receipt of cash and £1,000 must therefore appear as a *debit* on the cash account. Every credit must have a corresponding debit in recognition of the two opposite aspects of a transaction.

The purchase of stock shown in Table 11 reduces the amount of cash and the sum of £300 would appear in the cash account as a credit – a situation which might at first sight seem a little odd until it is remembered that when cash was received this appeared as a debit on the cash account. This now has a balance of £700, the difference between the initial receipt from the owners of £1,000 less £300 spent on stock. The *balance* of an account is simply the difference between the credit and debit items in the account. In this case we have a debit balance since the debits to the account exceed the credits.

It is useful to remember that all a firm's assets are represented by debit balances and all its liabilities by credit balances. However not all accounts represent assets or liabilities. Those that do are called *real accounts* whilst others are called *nominal accounts*. Examples of the latter are the accounts for wages, rent and rates, and heating and lighting. Payment for items like these, unlike that for the purchase of stock, does not increase the assets of the business. The money has been spent to help with the conduct of the business but not to increase its assets. For that reason, when the final accounts are prepared, the balances on nominal accounts are transferred to the trading and profit and loss accounts whilst the balances on real accounts remain and are recorded either as assets or liabilities in the balance sheet.

A great advantage of double-entry accounting systems is that a check is possible on the accuracy of the way in which transactions have been recorded. Since every debit must have a corresponding credit the total of all credits must be the same as the total of all debits. Since a balance on an account is the difference between the credits and debits it follows that the total of all credit balances must be the same as the total of all debit balances.

This means that before the final accounts are prepared a check on the accuracy of the records can be made by means of a *trial balance*. This is simply a list of all debit and credit balances in the firm's accounts, any difference in the totals indicating that a mistake has been made in recording the firm's transactions. The trial balance that would be made before drawing up the final accounts used in this chapter is shown in Table 17.

Table 17 *Trial Balance as at 31 December 19..*

	Debit balances £	Credit balances £
Real accounts		
Capital		1,000
Creditors		200
Cash	1,000	
Debtors	150	
Nominal accounts		
Purchases	2,500	
Sales		5,500
Wages	1,750	
Rent and rates	1,000	
Heating and lighting	250	
Insurance	50	
	6,700	6,700

Bank Balance Sheets

The annual published accounts of a large manufacturing and trading group of companies are likely to be complex and to include additional information in notes to the accounts, often as a result of legal requirements. A group's *consolidated accounts* will provide a set of figures showing the results for the group as a whole, that is for the *parent company* together with those for the *subsidiary companies* which it owns. A possible consolidated balance sheet is shown in Table 18. The value of the company for its owners according to the balance sheet is £887 million, a figure made up of the original capital invested in the company by its owners, reserves which have been retained from past operations to strengthen the company, and the profit and loss account showing the accumulated profits which have not been distributed among the owners.

Table 18 *Consolidated Balance Sheet as at 31 December 19..*

Liabilities	£ millions	Assets	£ millions
Capital	181	Fixed assets	971
Reserves	251	Current assets	1,043
Profit and loss account	455		
	887		
Loans	332		
Current liabilities	795		
	2,014		2,014

Fixed assets include figures for land and buildings, plant and machinery, and fixtures and fittings – assets which normally cannot be sold without harming the earning power of the business. The *current assets* are those which are not of a permanent nature but are subject to continuous change as the firm conducts its business. They include stocks of raw materials, of finished goods and those in the course of manufacture, as well as money owed by debtors, and cash. The liabilities of the firm consist of loans to the firm of a long-term nature whilst *current liabilities* include figures for the amounts owing to creditors and any short-term borrowing – perhaps by means of a bank overdraft.

The typical balance sheet of a large British banking group shown in Table 19 when compared with the balance sheet of a manufacturing and trading group of companies (Table 18) can be seen to have the following features:

1. The importance of the funds put in the bank by its customers. Deposits and customers' current account balances account for nearly eighty-eight per cent of the balance sheet total.

2. The size of the figure for published reserves. The reserve figure is more than six times the size of the owners' capital.

3. The order in which assets are listed. Unlike the balance sheet in

Table 19 *Bank Balance Sheet as at 31 December 19..*

Liabilities	£ millions	Assets	£ millions
Capital	341	Cash etc.	8,352
Reserves	2,170	Investments	2,108
Profit and loss account	253	Advances etc.	43,693
	────	Property and	
	2,764	equipment	1,292
Loans	625	Other assets	3,601
Deposits and customers'			
current accounts	51,910		
Other liabilities	3,747		
	────		────
	59,046		59,046

Table 18, current assets appear first amongst the bank's assets.

These features are all connected. Since a very high proportion of a bank's funds are obtained from customers it is necessary to ensure that the bank is always in a position – and seen to be in a position – to meet all possible demands for the withdrawal of these funds. A substantial published figure for reserves is an indication to the public of the bank's strength, that it has conducted its affairs prudently and retained substantial sums in the business from past earnings.

The need to be able to meet withdrawals of funds also explains why assets in a bank's balance sheet are presented in a different order to the presentation in the balance sheets of other companies. A bank's need for liquidity is so important that its assets are placed in descending order of liquidity. Thus in the balance sheet in Table 19 the item 'cash etc.' includes the most liquid of the bank's assets – cash, money lent for very short periods, and its holdings of bills.

To show more clearly how banks arrange their assets and liabilities, Tables 20 and 21 show the sterling part of the combined balance sheets of the London clearing banks Barclays, Coutts & Co., Lloyds, Midland, National Westminster and Williams & Glyn's – the six large banks whose chairmen formally comprise the Committee of London Clearing Bankers (page 122).

As can be seen in Table 20, firms and individuals in the private sector of the economy provide a very large proportion of the deposits, although those received from other banks in the monetary sector are important as to a lesser extent are those received from overseas

Table 20 *London Clearing Banks. Sterling Deposits (August 1985)*

		£ millions	Percentage Share
U.K. monetary sector		20,133	19
U.K. private sector		64,553	62
U.K. public sector		1,708	2
Overseas		11,537	11
Certificates of deposits		6,155	6
	Total	104,086	100
of which sight deposits		39,515	

Source: *Banking Information Service*

residents. About forty per cent of total deposits are *sight deposits*, that is deposits payable to customers on demand, and these include credit balances on *current accounts*, that is those upon which cheques may be drawn.

Certificates of deposit (CDs) in sterling certify that a deposit has been made and are repayable to bearer when presented to the issuer at the maturity date. They are issued in large amounts and because of the existence of an active secondary market they can be sold prior to maturity at prevailing market rates. They enable those wishing to deposit large sums of money with a bank to earn interest whilst at the same time making it possible to obtain money at any time by selling them in the CD market.

CDs are a component of the banks' *wholesale deposits*, that is deposits for large amounts, which include also deposits received through the inter-bank market and large sums left with the banks through their branch network. *Retail deposits* largely comprise money in current accounts or in *seven-day deposit accounts*. As the name suggests these interest-bearing accounts nominally require seven days notice before they can be withdrawn but in practice this requirement is usually waived. Deposits of the London clearing banks are predominantly received for short periods, figures published in 1977 showing that eighty-three per cent of all sterling deposits were repayable in less than a month.

The importance of ensuring that it is always possible to repay these deposits when required can be seen more clearly by studying the detailed structure of London clearing banks' sterling assets. As Table 21 shows, notes and coin, the most liquid assets it is possible to hold, appear as the first item in the banks' balance sheet. This is the money held in vaults and cashiers' tills to meet customer needs.

Table 21 *London Clearing Banks. Sterling Assets (August 1985)*

	£ millions
Cash and balances with the Bank of England	1,560
Market loans	27,448
Bills	2,459
Investments	5,484
Advances	72,698

Source: *Banking Information Service*

Balances with the Bank of England are partly withdrawable on demand and partly frozen for the reason explained in The Role of Monetory Policy, Chapter 10.

Market loans include money lent largely to discount houses, funds placed with other banks through the inter-bank market, certificates of deposit, money made available to local authorities through the local-authority market, and sterling lent in the international markets. Lending to discount houses and other U.K. banks accounts for a very high proportion of total market loans. Lending in the inter-bank market is nearly three times the amount lent in the discount market.

Bills are of various types. They include *Treasury bills* which are offered by tender every Friday by the Bank of England on behalf of the Treasury in order to raise funds to meet government expenditure. The bills mature ninety-one days after issue and are for varying amounts between £5,000 and £1,000,000. Each tender must be for at least £50,000. Bills are allotted to those who offer the highest prices and are dated on any working day of the week following the tender as selected by the tenderer. The total amount of Treasury bills issued by tender is nowadays much smaller than in the past and the main holdings of bills are *commercial bills* discounted by the banks.

Investments are made up of funds placed in British government securities and other investments including the banks' holdings of shares in associated companies.

Advances, the largest category amongst the banks' assets, represent lending by loan or overdraft to customers at home and overseas.

As well as receiving deposits in sterling, large sums are also taken in other currencies and used by the banks for lending to customers at home and overseas, including other banks, and for placing in certificates of deposit in currencies other than sterling.

There are important differences in the balance sheet structures of the different banking groups within the U.K., the proportion of funds placed in the categories of assets available depending upon the type of banking business undertaken, the source of deposits, and the proportion of deposits taken in sterling or in other currencies. Table 22 shows the relative importance of the various groups of banks as measured by the size of their deposits, both in sterling and in other currencies.

Table 22 *Deposits with banks in the U.K. (August 1985)*

	£ millions	
	Sterling	Other currencies
Retail banks*	105,654	41,183
Accepting houses	11,323	11,713
Other British banks	31,536	33,017
Overseas banks:		
American	12,992	83,810
Japanese	10,599	151,721
Other	28,937	140,592
Consortium banks	1,840	13,385
	202,881	475,421

Source: *Bank of England Quarterly Bulletin*
* Retail banks include those with extensive branch networks or who directly participate in the U.K. clearing system.

Liquidity and Profitability

We saw above how important it is that a bank should ensure that it has sufficient liquidity to meet all possible demands likely to be made on it. The liquidity of an asset is relative rather than absolute. Thus we can say that one asset is more liquid than another even if it is not possible to quote a figure to indicate their liquidity.

The most liquid asset that a bank or a person can hold is cash. The cash in your handbag or pocket provides immediate spending power.

Money in a bank that can be withdrawn on demand also possesses maximum liquidity; other assets do not possess liquidity to the same extent. For example, although national savings certificates or government stock are safe investments, it takes time to turn them into cash and this may not be possible without incurring loss. National savings certificates increase in value at regular intervals and encashment now may mean that the holder loses the next incremental increase, due perhaps only a few days later. In a similar way the prices of government securities may fall with the result that the sale of a government security may entail a loss additional to the costs incurred through selling.

The *liquidity of an asset* is thus determined by two factors;
1. The speed with which it can be turned into cash.
2. The risk of loss that might be incurred when it is disposed of.

In general the return obtained on an asset varies with its liquidity. Cash is wholly liquid but it yields no return, it may even cost money to look after it safely. A bank which kept all its customers' deposits as cash would be highly liquid but would have no income to meet its expenses and no profits to pay its owners. At the opposite extreme, it would make good profits if all the depositors' money were lent to other customers, but it would be highly illiquid and thus in danger of going out of business.

A bank therefore has two main aims: to make a profit while at the same time maintaining sufficient liquidity to ensure that it does not fail. The vital task of reconciling liquidity with profitability is performed by ensuring that the structure of its assets meets these twin requirements. In addition it will ensure that there is no mismatch between its assets and liabilities. Thus when a bank is granting a medium-term loan for a large amount it will make sure that it has adequate deposits left with it for the period concerned.

In order to ensure their safety and to maintain the confidence of their depositors banks need to demonstrate not only that they are sufficiently liquid but also that they will remain *solvent*. The value of their investments may unexpectedly fall or a sudden increase in bad debts may occur which had not been allowed for when providing reserves to cover expected lending losses. Solvency implies that the value of assets exceeds that of liabilities by an appropriate margin. This differs from liquidity: a bank can be solvent but still run into difficulties because it is unable to meet the demands of its depositors.

Back to Accountancy

In this chapter we have looked at *financial accounting* and seen how useful it can be in studying the affairs of a bank. A study of the published accounts provides a good deal more information than can be gleaned by a look at the balance sheet and it is well worth spending a little time glancing at the figures published with a bank's annual report.

A banker is frequently required to study and judge the accounts of borrowing firms and for this he needs a sound grasp of financial accounting. But he needs also to be able to use the techniques of *cost and management accounting* in the conduct of his own business. He needs to know what it costs him to provide a particular service to his customers and whether this is profitable. He needs to know which of his branches are doing well and to compare their progress with those that are performing badly. He needs to know how the bank's business overseas is progressing and to be able to measure the profitability of the bank's subsidiaries. Only through the provision of accounting information can he plan and control the bank's progress, ensuring, for example, that through *budgetary control*, expenditure by managers is kept within agreed limits, the level of a manager's budget having been determined by the bank's corporate plan.

PERSONAL ASSIGNMENTS

1 Compare the recently published balance sheet of a bank with that of a manufacturing company.

2 Compare the recently published balance sheet of a bank with that of a building society.

3 In what ways can a bank ensure that its liquidity is sufficient to enable it to continue operations safely?

4 Show by means of a specimen balance sheet how a bank seeks to reconcile profitability and liquidity.

5 Examine the ways in which a bank takes funds from its customers.

6 Write a short report detailing the changes that have taken place in the published accounts of a bank of your choice during the course of a recent year.

7 Prepare schedules to show the holdings of different banking groups in the U.K. of the following assets:
1. Treasury bills.
2. Commercial bills.
3. Sterling certificates of deposit.

8 In what ways does the structure of the balance sheets of American banks operating in the U.K. differ from that of the London clearing banks?

CHAPTER 5

ECONOMICS AND THE BANKER

Banks are economic units operating in a national and world economy and it is for this reason that they need to be aware of economic change when planning their operations. They need to understand the economic forces affecting not only their own business but also the affairs of those to whom they are offering their services. Bankers need to understand *macroeconomics* – the factors affecting the supply of money, interest rates, investment and unemployment, and so on – as well as *microeconomics*, that part of economics which focuses on individual units in the economy, the firm, the consumer, and the industry.

The Economic Environment

One of the reasons that makes economics difficult is that it deals with human behaviour, which is not always easy to predict. For example, if prices in the shops start to rise people may buy more goods because they fear that these may become more expensive later on. Because of this their level of savings may fall. But after a time people's attitudes may change as they come to realise that because of rising prices the *real value* of their savings has fallen and they are now worth less in terms of what they will buy. They may start to buy less and to save more in order to restore the value of their savings. Again, despite rising prices, people may become convinced that the rate of increase is about to slow down and this may change their spending and saving habits. Predicting changes in people's behaviour is very difficult and this is one of the reasons why economic management presents formidable problems.

Another difficulty is the complicated nature of the economic system, which is more like the human body than a piece of machinery. When we press a car accelerator we can predict with a fair degree of accuracy what will happen to its speed and petrol consumption. On the other hand if a person smokes cigarettes it is impossible to say precisely how this will affect his health. We may know from statistical studies that in general cigarette smokers may be more likely than others to die of cancer but that tells us little about the life-expectancy of an individual. A widespread anti-smoking campaign may be followed by a fall in cancer deaths and it may be thought that the two things are connected. But they may not be. We can never have the same certainty about human affairs as we have with mechanical contrivances.

The economist is more like a doctor than an engineer. Measures to restrain rising prices may have undesirable side effects such as increased unemployment; steps to increase the level of exports may lead to inflation. The control of economic ills is difficult and there are no easy solutions. Like the doctor, the economist has much to learn. He is dealing with a relatively new subject. Adam Smith, generally regarded as the father of economics, published his *Wealth of Nations* as recently as 1776; Pythagoras, the Greek philosopher, was at work about 500 years before Christ. It must be said, however, that some subjects have made greater progress in less time.

It was Adam Smith who wrote of the 'unseen hand' of the market mechanism – the conditions under which the self-interest of individuals operates for the public good, the pursuit of profit resulting in the maximisation of consumer satisfaction. The free-market economy is the hallmark of capitalism and is in contrast to the centralised *command economies* found in Eastern Europe under communist rule as well as in other parts of the world. In these economies the consumer does not determine the mix of goods and services to be produced. This is the role of the state planning mechanism which determines production levels, the level of resources to be allocated to investment and consumption, and so on. State objectives are translated into detailed plans for each sector of the economy and targets are set for productive units. The consumer can purchase only those goods and services produced in accordance with the national plan.

In a *capitalist economy* individuals have the right to own property and to accumulate wealth. The pursuit of profit is generally regarded as the economy's catalyst and largely determines the allocation of resources and the pattern of production. However it is not unusual to find *mixed economies* like that of the U.K., where attempts are made to remove the defects of the capitalist system and where some major enterprises are state-owned rather than in the ownership of individuals. Clearly the way in which a bank operates is conditioned by the type of economy in which it conducts its business. In particular, this will affect its objectives and its attitude towards the gain of profit.

As well as understanding different types of economy the banker also needs to appreciate the concept of the real economy, to realise for example that the standard of living of a country's people is determined by the supply of goods and services which on average each person can consume. A person's *nominal income* rises with a salary increase but if this is matched by price increases *real income* will remain unchanged since the goods and services that can be consumed remain unaltered.

It is easy to be misled by changes in the level of money incomes. People can suffer from '*money illusion*': because take-home pay has risen they may feel they are better off and forget that what matters is what their money will buy. Again, a firm may be pleased that its profits are rising and not realise that in real terms they may in fact be falling. Likewise it is important to distinguish between *nominal rates of interest* and *real rates*. Thus on a bank loan offered at fifteen per cent when prices are rising at ten per cent the real rate of interest is only five per cent.

Supply and Demand

It is of vital importance for the banker to understand how prices are determined. Property prices, the prices a customer can obtain for the goods he manufactures, and the price the banker himself can charge for the services he offers are all important to him. He must be interested in the price of shares quoted on The Stock Exchange, in the price of currencies as measured by exchange rates, and in the price of credit – the rate of interest he can charge borrowing customers and has himself to pay for money deposited with or lent to him.

The starting point for such an understanding is the realisation that prices are determined by the interaction of supply and demand and that both supply and demand factors need to be considered. A piece of paper is cut by the blades of a pair of scissors working together. Both blades are important. Likewise both supply and demand are important.

It is useful to accept initially that people are prepared to buy more of a product at lower prices than at higher prices and that more will be supplied at higher prices than at lower ones. Table 23 shows this more clearly.

It is clear from these notional figures that only at a price of £2 will the supply be equal to demand. This is known as the *equilibrium price* and is shown in Figure 6 where the demand and supply schedule figures are

Table 23 *Demand and Supply Schedules*

Price of commodity or service £	Demand schedule (units demanded)	Supply schedule (units supplied)
1	40	10
2	30	30
3	20	50
4	10	70

plotted on a graph to give us corresponding *demand and supply curves*. The point where the supply and demand curves meet determines the equilibrium price. If the price rises above this level (say to £3 in our example) there will be an excess of supply over demand and this will tend to push the price back to the equilibrium level. Likewise at lower prices (for example at £1) demand will exceed supply, thus forcing the price back to the equilibrium level.

In practice, it is unlikely that much will be known about the supply and demand schedules for a product. Nor can it be assumed that prices will be fixed at the equilibrium level. It is more likely that the price will

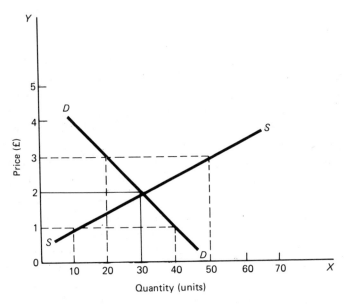

Figure 6. Demand and supply curves

fluctuate as supply and demand change, but will tend to move towards the equilibrium position.

The main use of supply and demand is to enable us to analyse price changes. Thus if we consider demand, it is evident from the demand schedule and curve that the number of units demanded will vary in accordance with the price. But many other things need to be taken into account. If people's incomes rise they may be willing to buy more of a commodity or service at a given price. The price of other goods and services may change or people's tastes may alter, factors which may in turn alter the demand schedule. Table 24 illustrates this, showing a new demand schedule beside the original one.

Table 24 *Demand Schedules*

Price of commodity or service £	Original demand schedule (units demanded)	New demand schedule (units demanded)
1	40	70
2	30	60
3	20	50
4	10	40

If we show both the schedules as demand curves together with the unchanged curve for supply we can see clearly (Figure 7) what effect there has been on the price of the commodity or service. Now the equilibrium price has risen from £2 to £3, the price at which supply and the new demand are equal. We can also see that the rise in price has been caused by new demand conditions, demand having risen from DD to D'D'. Because of this increased demand, supply has been expanded but this is due to rising prices not to any change in the supply conditions. Changes in the supply condition can of course take place, a manufacturer for example being able to supply more goods for a given price if his costs of production fall, perhaps as a result of new production methods or by using different raw materials.

When deciding what charges to levy for a banking service, a banker too will take account of the public demand. Take a simplified example. Imagine that the banker is able to sell 1,000 $50 travellers cheques per day at £2 each. His daily commission income will be £2,000. Now suppose that he lowers the price by ten per cent to £1.80. He will expect to sell more, but the important question is: how many more? This will

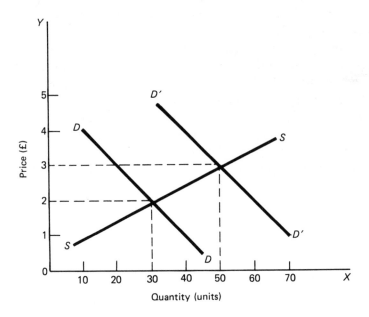

Figure 7. A change in demand

depend on the *price elasticity of demand*. If his sales rise to only 1,050, his income at the new price will be £1,890 – lower than before because the ten per cent price reduction has been matched by increased sales of only five per cent. However if sales go up by twenty per cent to 1,200 his income will be £2,160. In the first case demand was *inelastic* and in the second case *elastic*, price elasticity being measured by the percentage change in demand resulting from a percentage change in price.

But as was pointed out above, supply as well as demand factors must always be considered. Thus although it may be possible for the banker to increase his income by lowering the price he charges for travellers cheques, his costs may rise since he has to produce and sell more of them. He may be able to do this at little or no extra cost or even at a reduced *unit cost*. Very often the cost of producing something falls as the total number produced increases, a good example being home computers whose price has fallen sharply as they have become more popular and it has become possible to produce them in greater quantities at a lower unit cost.

The banker trying to decide what to charge for travellers cheques will not know with certainty how his sales will be affected. However he will be aware of the factors that determine demand elasticity. One of these is the availability of substitutes. He will know that travellers cheques issued by other banks are a close substitute for his own and that travellers also have a choice of carrying currency with them instead of travellers cheques when they go abroad. This will serve to make demand elastic but is likely to be offset by the fact that since only a very small part of travelling costs results from the purchase of travellers cheques people are not likely to be very concerned at changes in their price. Ingrained habits and convenience are also likely to be factors making demand inelastic and the banker in practice will have to judge from previous experience how these competing factors will affect the demand for his product.

Foreign Exchange Rates

The pattern of exchange rates and their likely future pattern are of great interest to bankers. An exchange rate is simply the price of one currency in terms of another. Thus if the exchange rate for the U.S. dollar in London is $1.50 = £1 the sterling cost of American goods priced at $3,000 will be £2,000. If the rate moves to $1.75 = £1, the value of sterling has increased and that of the dollar has fallen. Before the change a pound could have been purchased for $1.50; at the new exchange rate it costs $1.75. Likewise the cost of a dollar has fallen from about £0.67 to approximately £0.57.

Exchange rates between currencies exist because in general people only wish to hold their own currency. Thus an exporter who has received foreign currency for the goods he has supplied may be expected to sell it for his own currency which he can use to buy further supplies and to pay his workforce. In some countries exchange rates are fixed by the authorities but in the major countries of the West they are determined by the interaction of supply and demand in the *foreign exchange market*, in which transactions are carried out by telephone.

In the foreign exchange market currencies can be bought or sold for immediate delivery at a *spot rate* or for delivery in the future at a *forward rate*. The forward market is useful to traders since it enables them to *hedge* or protect themselves against future movements in exchange rates. Thus a British importer may be required to pay for goods in dollars in three months' time and he may wish to guard against any adverse change in the exchange rate in the meantime. He could buy the dollars at the spot rate and leave them on deposit with his banker until he needs them or buy them from his banker now at the three-month forward rate for delivery in three months time. If he chooses the first method he will lose interest on the sterling he has sold but gain interest on his dollar balance. The difference between the two rates of interest can be compared with the cost of buying the dollars forward and will determine which method he chooses. However as banks and other dealers in the foreign exchange market are seeking profitable deals, differences in the rates of interest that may be earned on balances will determine the supply and demand for currencies in the forward market. The forward rate between two currencies is therefore determined by the spot rate and the interest differences.

Interest rates in two countries will also play a part in determining the spot rate between their currencies. Thus if interest rates rise in the U.S., investors in London may decide to move funds from the U.K. to take advantage of the higher rates in the U.S. They will seek to sell sterling for dollars, demand for dollars will rise at the same time as the supply of sterling rises and the dollar will tend to increase in value whilst sterling will fall. Another influence on the supply and demand for currencies is the level of trade between countries. For example if U.K. exports to the U.S. increase whilst U.S. exports remain static, there will be an increase in the supply of dollars as British exporters sell them for sterling. This will tend to increase the value of sterling in relation to the dollar.

Among other things affecting rates of exchange are confidence factors, funds being moved from a country when, for example, there is a fear of war or internal political problems. Sometimes the operations of a government can affect exchange rates. Thus if sterling is weak and it seems desirable that this should be corrected the U.K. authorities might enter the market and purchase sterling using some of its reserves of other currencies. This will have the effect of reducing the supply of sterling and of making it more valuable.

The Balance of Payments

A country's current income and expenditure arising from transactions with other countries are recorded in a *current account*. This is divided into visible and invisible items. *Visible trade* is made up of imports and exports of goods – things like raw materials, foodstuffs, and manufactured articles. The difference in value between visible imports and exports is called the *balance of trade*.

The difference between invisible imports and exports is called the *invisible balance* and comprises such things as services; interest, profits, and dividends; and transfers. In the case of the U.K. the favourable invisible balance has been of great value since it has helped to offset a deficit on visible trade which was a marked feature of British overseas trade until it became possible to export oil from the North Sea.

Table 25 *U.K. Balance of Payments. Current Account (1984)*

		£ millions
Exports		70,409
Imports		74,510
Visible trade balance		− 4,101
Invisible balance		
Services*	+3,985	
Interest, profits		
and dividends	+3,304	
Transfers	−2,253	
		+ 5,036
Balance of payments on current		
account		+ 935
*Services**		
General government	− 923	
Sea transport	−1,151	
Civil aviation	+ 469	
Travel	− 448	
Financial and		
other services	+6,038	
	+3,985	

Source: Central Statistical Office
* Net earnings by banking institutions in 1984 = £2,339 million.

Balance of payments figures for the U.K. are shown in Table 25 from which the importance of invisible earnings can be seen. The income arising from the provision of services is very important, a major contribution to this being provided by the international business of the banking industry. In addition to the financial services provided by banking, insurance, and other sectors of the economy, an important source of income is from travel, tourists visiting the U.K. generating income that helps to cover the costs incurred by British travel overseas.

Interest, profit and dividends arise from past investment overseas. Profits earned by an American-owned company and remitted to the U.S. are regarded as an invisible import whilst dividends or interest payments received by British residents on their overseas investments represents an invisible export.

Figures recorded as transfers include many things. If someone in the U.K. receives a pension from overseas this results in a transfer of funds into the country. When the British government provides aid to a developing country that is an outward payment. U.K. payments to the European Economic Commission are very large and this is the main cause of the large deficit on transfers.

Like a private individual, a country which spends more than it earns can only do so by borrowing or using past savings. Likewise if it earns more than it spends its savings will rise or it will be able to repay some of the money it has borrowed in the past. By measuring these changes it is possible to calculate a figure equal to the balance of payments on current account. This can be seen in Table 26, a balancing item having been included since in practice it is not possible to identify all trade and monetary transactions.

Table 26 *U.K. Balance of Payments. Investment and Official Financing (1984)*

	£ millions
Balance of payments on current account	+ 935
Investment and other capital flows	−3,291
Official financing	+1,316
Balancing item	+1,040
	− 935

Source: Central Statistical Office

The Eurocurrency Markets

The growth of the *eurocurrency markets* can be traced back to the 1950s with the emergence of a *eurodollar market* in London. The market provides a source of foreign currencies additional to that of the foreign exchange market. As we have seen, the latter market enables dollars to be *purchased*; the eurodollar market allows dollars to be *borrowed*. For a variety of reasons, overseas holders of dollars may prefer not to sell them for their own currency but rather to deposit them in London as a dollar balance. The development of the market during the 1970s was stimulated by the sharp rise in oil prices and the consequent increase in overseas earnings by oil-producing countries. One consequence of this growth was the large number of overseas banks who came to London in order to participate in the market. Another consequence was the help it provided in recycling the earnings of the oil-producing countries by providing a means whereby banks could lend to international borrowers in need of finance.

The term 'eurodollar' is now something of a misnomer since balances denominated in other major currencies can now be traded in the same way and not only in London. Balances traded in the markets are for large amounts and can be made available overnight or for periods of up to five years. Balances are frequently onlent and the size of the market is therefore not easy to quantify. For example a French bank may purchase dollars from one of its customers who has received them in exchange for goods exported to the U.S. The French bank may decide that it wishes to retain the dollars and deposits them with a bank in London. The London bank in turn may lend them to an Italian bank, one of whose customers needs dollars to pay for imports from the U.S. The London bank is able to profit from this process of intermediation by the difference in the rate of interest it charges the Italian bank and the rate it pays the French bank. It can if it wishes sell the dollars for sterling but it needs to bear in mind that dollars will have to be paid to the French bank when the loan matures. When this time comes it may find that the cost of purchasing dollars has risen or that the interest it has to pay for borrowing dollars in the eurocurrency market has changed. The bank therefore has to keep a careful watch on its *currency exposure.*

Interest Rates

The cost of a loan is the rate of interest the borrower has to pay to the lender. As a general rule this cost depends on the risk taken by the lender and the length of time for which the loan has been made. A fixed-period loan to a company or to an individual is likely to be at a higher interest rate than a similar loan to the government because of the greater risk of non-payment. A loan for three months can normally be obtained at a lower rate than one for three years because of the difference in liquidity, in the amount of time that has to elapse before the loan matures.

Short- and long-term rates are closely related. If short-term rates fall people will prefer to borrow for short periods whilst lenders will prefer to lend for longer periods. The supply of funds for long-term lending will increase at the same time as demand falls and this will tend to bring down long-term rates as a reaction to the short-term fall. This relationship can be illustrated by a *yield curve* as shown in Figure 8. The yield or rate of return on money lent is plotted in relation to the term or maturity of the loan. This is the only difference taken into account, the type of borrower and the method of lending being the same irrespective

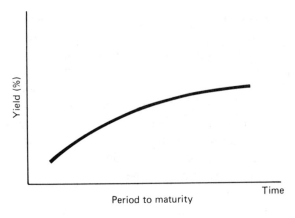

Figure 8.   A yield curve

of the period involved. It will be seen that the yield increases the longer the period that has to run to maturity.

An important factor that can affect interest rates is people's *expectations* as to future changes. For example if it is expected that rates will fall, borrowers will seek funds on a short-term basis whilst lenders will try to lend for longer periods. The effect of this can be to push longer-term rates down below those for shorter periods so that the yield curve will slope downwards, that is in the opposite way to that expected.

In the section on the Economic Environment, a distinction was drawn between nominal and real rates of interest, the difference being accounted for by the level of inflation. In a period of rising prices borrowers tend to gain and lenders to lose since the real value of the money lent, that is its purchasing power, falls at the same time as the interest payment also declines in real terms. To the extent that people realise this, nominal interest rates tend to rise as lenders seek to protect themselves from the effects of inflation. Likewise borrowers are prepared to pay more for funds, realising that in real terms the cost is low. Those who have borrowed to buy a house at such a time tend to gain substantially since the value of their property rises with other prices whilst the cost of borrowing in real terms is low or even at a negative rate of interest.

Because of the problems and uncertainties arising from inflation *index-linking* has been introduced, and this is often the way by which the U.K. government borrows money. The value of the loan is usually linked to movements in the Retail Prices Index and the nominal interest paid is low. The usual arrangement ensures that the lender's capital and interest payments are protected against inflation. In other cases loans are made at rates of interest which vary with market rates, and to the extent that these are affected by inflationary conditions some measure of protection is given to lenders. Borrowers are also protected. A borrower who takes funds at a high nominal rate of interest when the rate of inflation is high may realise that the real rate of interest is low. However if the rate of inflation falls he may regret his decision since in real terms his cost of borrowing has risen.

Close links exist between the financial markets so that changes in rates of interest are reflected in both the national and international economies. We have seen how differences between countries affect spot rates of exchange as well as rates in the forward market. High rates of interest in a country may help to maintain a high exchange rate for that country's currency but this can have adverse effects on its balance of payments by encouraging imports and making it difficult to export. Changing interest rates in the inter-bank market affect the interest rates charged by banks to their borrowers as well as the rates paid to depositors. These changes affect building society interest rates and the cost of borrowing for house purchase. If rates of interest rise the person borrowing to buy a house has less to spend on other things and this dampens the level of retail sales. High interest rates increase the costs of industry and may inhibit long-term investment projects. The level of interest rates is thus clearly of great importance both to banks and to the economy in general.

The London International Financial Futures Exchange

In September 1982 another new market was opened in London, the London International Financial Futures Exchange (*LIFFE*). Unlike the foreign exchange market, a market in which transactions are carried out over the telephone, LIFFE has a physical location, in the reconstructed building of the Royal Exchange in the heart of the City of London. Here over 370 members deal in *financial futures* and *options*, that is agreements to buy or sell a standard quantity of a given financial instrument or foreign currency at an agreed future date or, in the case of an option, the right but not the obligation to do so in the future.

These contracts enable people to protect themselves against future changes in interest rates, foreign exchange rates, or share prices. Trading companies are exposed to considerable risks and the market provides a means whereby they can hedge against them. As far as foreign exchange rates are concerned it offers an alternative to the forward exchange market where, as we have seen, it is possible to buy or sell a currency for delivery at a future date. LIFFE offers a similar facility. Thus a U.K. firm needing U.S. dollars in three months time to pay for its imports can purchase a contract whose value fluctuates daily based on the movement of the dollar-sterling exchange rate in the market. When the time comes for the importer to pay for his goods he can purchase the dollars he needs in the foreign exchange market at the same time selling his dollar contract with LIFFE. If for example the cost of dollars has risen, this rise should be offset by an increase in the value of his LIFFE contract, the purchase of the contract having provided a hedge against the adverse exchange rate movement.

In a similar way the new market can provide protection against future changes in interest rates. By buying or selling a contract the interest rate can be 'locked in'. If a contract is bought and interest rates fall, the price of the contract will rise and the trader makes a profit that offsets the loss he has incurred as the result of lower interest rates.

Futures contracts, standardised transferable agreements in which two parties undertake to purchase or deliver a specified amount of a given financial security at a future date and at a price established at the time of trade, are similar to those that have existed in the commodity markets for many years. It was realised that money can be treated as a commodity and in Chicago in 1972 the world's first centralised market for transferring financial risk was established. In London in 1981 a futures market in gas oil was opened and this was followed by a market for future trading in gold. By October 1985 LIFFE had developed ten different future contracts as well as two types of options.

PERSONAL ASSIGNMENTS

1 The prices of shares on a Stock Exchange are determined by the interaction of supply and demand. Select one share quoted on The Stock Exchange and consider what factors have affected supply and demand during recent months and what effects these have had on the share's price.

2 How has the value of your country's currency changed in relation to the U.S. dollar in recent years? What factors have caused this change?

3 Consider the main economic factors currently affecting the profitability of one of your country's main areas of production.

4 Examine the factors leading to changes in the base rate of the London banks during a recent year.

5 How has the level of your country's exports changed during the last two years? Account for the change.

6 Prepare a schedule showing the annual rate of interest that can currently be obtained by an investment in London in:
   1. Ninety-one-day Treasury bills.
   2. Three-month sterling bank deposit.
   3. Three-month eurodollar deposit.
   4. Three-month commercial bill of exchange.

CHAPTER 6

MONEY

Robinson Crusoe, shipwrecked and alone on an island, had no need of money. When he first landed, his main concern was to seek food, clothes, and shelter. A large store of money would have been completely useless as there was nobody on the island who could provide him with the things he most urgently needed. Money only exists because there is a need to *exchange* goods and services. Robinson Crusoe had landed on an uninhabited island and so exchange was impossible.

If a person is able to satisfy all his requirements by his own efforts without needing outside help, the question of exchange does not arise. There must be few people in today's world who can do this, who can supply by their own efforts all the things they need for their own survival and comfort. Most of us spend our time producing a limited range of goods or services and thus there has to be some way in which we can change the fruits of this labour for the many things we need in our everyday lives. This we can do by direct or indirect exchange.

Figure 9. Direct Exchange or Barter

Direct exchange, or *barter*, is illustrated in Figure 9 and involves the exchange of one good or service for another. Under this sytem, the village baker would need to exchange the bread he had baked for all the other things he needed. He might be able to arrange to supply bread to the shoemaker in return for a new pair of shoes or to the seamstress in return for a new nightshirt. Even in modern communities barter arrangements are sometimes possible, a lady for example allowing a neighbour to graze a horse on her land on the understanding that the fence and ditches are maintained properly in exchange.

But barter arrangements like this are clearly not possible for most of the many transactions conducted daily in a modern economy. Direct exchange on a barter basis has many disadvantages, which include:

Double coincidence of wants. Suppose you have baked a stock of loaves and want to exchange them for meat. You may find someone who wishes to exchange meat for another commodity but you discover that he will only accept wheat in exchange. As a result you are forced to exchange your bread for wheat and then to use the wheat to exchange for the meat you require. This complicated means of satisfying your requirements can only be avoided if you can find someone who not only wishes to possess what you have to offer but is also willing to give you in exchange the thing that you want, in other words there needs to be a double coincidence of wants.

Exchange values. Even when the problem of discovering this double coincidence of wants has been overcome and the two people concerned are ready to exchange the goods concerned, the problem of how much of one commodity is to be exchanged for the other arises. How many loaves should be exchanged for what quantity of meat? Every time a transaction is arranged disagreements are likely to arise about the exchange rate between the goods concerned and this is likely to lead to time-consuming haggling between the parties to the deal.

Difficulties of accounting. In the absence of a common unit to measure the values of large numbers of goods and services, accounting is difficult, indeed probably impossible. Thus a farmer producing wheat, cattle, and pigs could only compare his output this year with that of another by listing the change in the amount of each thing produced. There is no way in which tons of wheat can be added to cattle or pigs and the only way of measuring their respective values would be in terms of the many goods and services for which they could be exchanged.

Future value. A system of barter raises a number of problems when transactions take place over a period of time. Someone wishing to save now in order that increased consumption could take place in the future would either have to store durable goods or to agree to part with goods now on the understanding that he would receive goods in return at some future date. Clearly this is not very convenient, in particular as disagreements could arise over the amounts and quality of the goods to be received in the future. Similar problems would be faced by borrowers and lenders. Thus a farmer might borrow seed and agree to return it at the end of the growing season when the crop was harvested. Obviously it could not be the same seed and arguments might arise over the quality of the seed being used to repay the debt.

Because of the difficulties faced by a community operating a pure barter system of exchange, the use of an intermediate commodity is customary. This commodity – called 'X' in Figure 10 – enables *indirect exchange* to take place. The commodity 'X' in Figure 10 is *money*. Its use in enabling indirect exchange to take place will continue for as long as members of the community know that other members will accept it willingly in return for any good or service. Producers of goods and services will happily accept 'X' in return for the work they have done because they know that with 'X' they will be able to obtain now or in the future any commodity or service that they require.

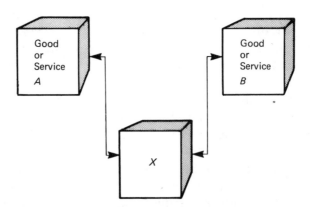

Figure 10.   Indirect Exchange

The Functions of Money

The major characteristic of money is therefore its acceptability in the community. Any commodity that has this characteristic will be money. If for some reason confidence in it were lost and it ceased to be generally acceptable, then it would cease to be money.

Money is of course of major importance to banks and bankers since it is the main commodity in which they deal. An understanding of the functions of money is therefore very important, and these functions are more complex than they might at first sight appear. This is because the functions of money are both varied and interconnected. Consider the coins used by a community. Clearly they are money. They will 'roll' and they can be 'stacked'. When they 'roll', or circulate, they are used in exchange for other goods; when they are 'stacked', they are saved for future use and at any time can be used for exchange with other goods. But not only can we spend or save our money; we also use it as a measuring rod. We know the value of a packet of cigarettes because we know how many coins we have to give in exchange. We know the value of the work we have done by the amount of money we receive in return for it.

Money has four specific functions, each of which solves the problems arising from a system of pure barter. The first two are sometimes called primary functions, the third and fourth derivative functions because they are derived from the other functions. They are as follows:

Medium of exchange. As we have seen, the use of money enables exchange of goods and services to take place more easily than under a barter system. A double coincidence of wants is no longer needed, the receipt of money in return for the work a person has done enabling that person to acquire the mixture of goods and services he needs to obtain the maximum satisfaction from his income. No longer does he have to synchronise his wants with those of other people.

The existence of money therefore gives the consumer a generalised spending power which is absent under a barter system. He no longer has to carry out two transactions at the same time. He can sell his goods or services to one person and obtain goods or services from someone else. The two transactions can also be separated by time, the money received by selling being used later when it is convenient to buy.

Unit of account. Money provides a standard measure of value or common denominator which enables a value to be placed on goods and services. It enables us to compare the costs of all the things available for our consumption, to decide what pattern of expenditure will yield the greatest satisfaction, and to measure the value of our work and of our savings. Accounting records are made possible since the unit of account enables the value of different types of commodity to be added together: the farmer, for example, can say that the value of his output is so many pounds or dollars instead of having to list all the things he has produced.

Standard for deferred payments. When a commodity performs the functions of both a medium of exchange and a unit of account it can be used for expressing the terms of future payments and contracts. No longer need a farmer borrow seed on the understanding that he will repay it at a later date. Instead he can borrow money to buy the seed and when he has sold his resultant crop he can use the money he has received to repay the loan. The convenience of money for providing finance becomes even clearer when you consider an example such as the difficulties which would be faced under a barter system by a business wishing to install new machinery in a factory. It would be difficult to find a supplier of machinery who would be prepared to lend it for a number of years and to take it back at the end of the loan period. Many transactions in a modern economy are conducted on the basis of credit, payment for the things purchased being spread over a number of future years. Buying a car by instalments would prove very difficult without money; buying a house would probably be impossible.

Store of value. Money provides an easy way in which the fruits of current labour can be saved and used in the future. The holder of money can use it now or at any time in the future to purchase anything he needs. Without money saving could only take place by storing tangible goods. Provided the thing chosen as money is durable there will be less chance of losses arising through deterioration or by theft.

It is because of these functions that money plays an indispensable role in a modern economy. Without it the productive processes we take for granted would not be possible. It acts as a lubricant, making it easy for people to specialise because the process of exchange is simple. It enables saving and lending to develop so that resources can easily be accumulated and put to productive use. By making the formation of prices possible it assists producers to know what to produce and in what quantities. It enables consumers to indicate clearly their desired pattern of consumption, a rise in demand for one good leading to a rise in its price which encourages increased production.

The Forms of Money

We have seen that the essential feature of money is that it is generally acceptable to the community it serves. Its origins pre-date earliest written history but it seems likely that people living under a barter system developed the habit of measuring the value of a commodity in terms of a standard article and that this came to be used as a medium of exchange. It seems unlikely that money was invented, suddenly introduced as the result of a brilliant brain-wave.

Many things have been used as money. Homer in the *Iliad* describes armour as worth 100 oxen, indicating that oxen in those days were regarded as a measure of value. Our word 'pecuniary' is derived from *pecunia*, the Latin word for money which in turn came from *pecus*, the word for cattle. The word 'fee' comes from the Anglo-Saxon *feoh* meaning both money and cattle.

Not only cattle has been used as money; at different times and in different places many commodities have performed this function. Cowrie shells, blocks of compressed tea, sugar, dried cod, elephants' teeth and even blocks of rock salt have all been acceptable as a community's money supply.

In order for a commodity to be used as money it needs to have certain characteristics which include:

Acceptability. The acceptability of a particular commodity as money depended largely on it having alternative uses. Cattle, tea, rum, and tobacco are obvious examples. Gold and silver, important money-supply materials, also possess this characteristic. Gold, for example, is in demand not only as jewellery but, beaten into thin sheet, is used as gold leaf. Valuable vessels are made from it, and it is used for commemorative medals as well as by dentists.

Durability. If a commodity is to be used as a store of value it is obviously desirable that it be durable. Gold, particularly when mixed with other metals, has this quality – unlike cattle, which die, or tea, which deteriorates over time.

Portability. It is desirable that money materials be easily carried to make it possible for purchases to take place easily and quickly. Gold's popularity as a money material was in part due to the fact that it has great value in relation to its bulk.

Divisibility. Gold, like silver, can be easily divided or united simply by melting. A problem with barter and with some money materials arises when there is a need to obtain a relatively low value good. For example someone with a cow to offer has a problem if he wishes to acquire a bar of soap in exchange. Clearly the cow is more valuable than the soap, but the cow is not divisible – at least when alive – and as a result it will probably be impossible to make this transaction. Gold's popularity as a money medium was enhanced by the fact that because it is divisible it can be used for small as well as large purchases.

Homogeneity. Units of some commodities used as money are not always alike. One cow can be fat, another skinny. Gold and silver however can be produced with a fixed quality and this quality can be checked by *assay*, a procedure used to test the purity of a metal.

Cognisability. Gold, and to some extent silver, is easily recognisable. Counterfeiting is difficult and can be easily detected.

Stability in value. Clearly if money is to perform its various functions, particularly as a store of value, it is desirable that the commodity chosen should enjoy a stable value. Certainly over short periods gold, when it was popular as a community's money supply, had a fairly stable value largely because the annual production of gold was small in relation to the total stock of gold used as money.

Notes and Coin

When metals first came into use as money people had the inconvenience of having to weigh the metal when undertaking a transaction. They also found it difficult to know whether the quality of the metal was really what it was supposed to be. These difficulties were overcome by the introduction of coins, which date from early times, at least from 2250 B.C. when the Chinese are said to have produced them. In making coins, metal was divided into pieces of different value, thus enabling transactions of differing values to take place easily. Stamping the coin, often with a picture of the ruler, provided a guarantee that the metal it contained was of a certain weight and purity. The production of coins takes place in a *mint* and our word 'money' is derived from the Temple of Juno Moneta where the Romans minted their coins.

The obverse side of a coin is that which bears the head or some other important device; the other side is the reverse side. Milling of the edges of the more valuable coins was introduced to make it more difficult for people to clip and collect metal from a coin whilst at the same time using it at its face value. Until the First World War U.K. coinage consisted of gold, silver, and bronze coins. But it became clear that the precious metals used were expensive, amongst other disadvantages. It is for that reason that in modern times various alloys have come into use such as nickel brass, bronze and cupro-nickel. The use of these coins is supported by law, which makes them *limited legal tender* – that is they must be accepted in discharge of a debt within the limits prescribed by the law.

Notes, however, are *unlimited legal tender*. Thus a purchase of goods for £1,000 creates a debt of this amount which can be discharged either immediately or at some future date. The creditor can legally be required to accept payment in notes but because the use of coin is limited sensibly by law he could refuse to accept coin in full payment of the debt.

The development of the U.K.'s note issue was traced in Chapter 3, and these notes together with coins constitute the currency of the country. Paper has a number of advantages as a money commodity. Its status as unlimited legal tender helps to make it generally acceptable as a medium of exchange, it is easily portable, homogeneous, and combines a high purchasing power with a low intrinsic value. Unlike gold it is not divisible; however, it is easy to produce in a range of denominations which make it acceptable in everyday use. It lacks durability but can be replaced quickly and easily when it wears out, although this process generates costs and may lead to coin being substituted for lower denomination notes. Intricate patterns of printing in special inks as well as the paper used make notes easily recognisable and these and other devices ensure that forgery is difficult to accomplish.

Money and Near Money

In a country with a developed economy many payments are made without the use of currency, in particular by using cheques and other means to transfer ownership of bank balances from one person to another. A cheque is not money because it lacks general acceptability. A person selling a second-hand car for £1,500 would be very foolish to accept a cheque for this amount in exchange for the car and the log book. He should wait until he is sure the cheque had been paid before parting with his property, otherwise he might find that the person giving him the cheque had either instructed his bank not to pay it or that the bank refused to pay because there was not enough money on its customer's account.

This does not mean that accounts with banks upon which cheques can be drawn – current or chequeing accounts – are not money. Clearly they are and in many countries balances on these accounts make up a large part of the money supply. Thus at the end of 1984 notes and coin in circulation in the U.K. amounted to £12.6 billion whilst deposits with the banks that could be withdrawn on demand amounted to £38.9 billion.

Whilst notes and coin and bank accounts on which cheques can be drawn clearly form part of the country's money supply since they serve as a medium of exchange, a range of other assets may be regarded as a 'temporary abode of purchasing power' and act as *quasi money* or *near money*. For example, the seven-day deposits of U.K. banks strictly require the customer to give the bank notice that he wishes to withdraw money from his deposit. In practice, however, he can do this without notice and at very little cost so that money on these accounts is almost as useful for medium of exchange purposes as notes and coin. In a similar way much of the money placed with building societies can be withdrawn on demand and is thus very close to serving as a medium of exchange. A variety of other assets possess a high degree of liquidity and also come close to being regarded as money.

The Value of Money

Thus although at first sight it appears easy to define the term money and to measure how much exists in a country at a particular time, in practice it is more difficult and can be the subject of expert disagreement. Likewise measuring the value of money is not as simple as might be expected.

There is no way in which we can say that a country's money is worth X or Y. The value of money is determined by what it will buy. If prices rise, the value of money falls because less can be bought with it. A general fall in price levels means that the value of money has risen. The only way to consider the value of money within the domestic economy is by measuring the change in prices over a period of time.

In order to measure changes in the value of money we use *index numbers*. This is a statistical device which involves selecting a *base date*, measuring prices at that date, and comparing them with prices at later dates. Thus if the price of bread was £0.25 a loaf at the base date and is £0.50 now, we know that the price of bread has doubled and that if we call the price of bread at the base date 100 we can say that it is now 200. This last figure is the *index number* for the price of bread in an index based on a particular date.

Whilst this index might be useful to someone interested in changes in bread prices, it is clearly not very helpful for determining the change in the value of money, since bread is only one of a large range of commodities and services that we buy. We need a more general measure of price changes and the more commodities and services we take into

Table 27 *Retail prices. Price in pence*

	Base date	Current prices
1 lb of bread	50	55
1 lb of butter	120	150
1 lb of tea	90	115
1 lb of sugar	30	50
1 lb of salt	10	30
Total cost	300	400

account, the nearer we shall be to this general measure.

Suppose we measure the prices of a basket of goods at the base date and at the present time in order to improve our index of prices. We may obtain the result shown in Table 27. Dividing the total cost of the basket of goods at each date by three gives us a current index number of 133, showing that prices have risen by thirty-three per cent above the figure of 100 at the base date. But a little thought will show that this result is misleading since clearly people do not buy equal quantities of the five goods we have considered.

Table 28 *Retail prices*

	Quantity consumed (lb)	Price in pence per lb Base date	Current prices	Cost in pence Base date	Current prices
Bread	3	50	55	150	165
Butter	$1\frac{1}{2}$	120	150	180	225
Tea	1	90	115	90	115
Sugar	$2\frac{1}{2}$	30	50	75	125
Salt	$\frac{1}{2}$	10	30	5	15
		Total cost		500	645

In Table 28 we attempt to be more realistic by assuming that different quantities of each good are purchased in the weekly shopping basket – twice as much bread as butter and so on. Dividing our results by five gives us the base figure of 100 and a current index number of 129, a more realistic result than the figure of 133 obtained in the previous example. We have now used *weights* in what is called a *weighted index*. The result is that although salt has trebled in price since the base date this is of less importance than the ten per cent rise in the price of bread because smaller amounts of salt are purchased than of bread.

Clearly it is important when constructing an index of retail prices not only to collect the prices of a wide range of goods and services but also to use appropriate weights when calculating index numbers. These principles must be applied when constructing any index, whether to measure prices – wholesale, import, export or retail – or other things such as the level of house building or industrial production.

Index numbers are of interest for a variety of reasons. An index of retail prices enables us to measure changes in real incomes by comparing changes in the amount of money earned with the change in the value of money. It also enables index-linked securities to be issued, thus ensuring that investments are not reduced in real value through rising prices.

Although index numbers provide a valuable guide to changes in an economy, they must be used with care. Thus with an index of retail prices the following points have to be taken into consideration:

1. The commodities and services whose prices are used to construct the index need revising from time to time. New products appear on the market and new services become available whilst some goods and services cease to be bought. Unless revisions are made the index will gradually lose its value.

2. Revision is also needed in the weights allocated to different commodities and services. People may reduce the proportion of their incomes spent on food and drink and spend more on motoring or entertainment.

3. The changing nature and quality of items included in the index must also be taken into account if the index is to provide a true picture of price changes. A colour television set giving access to a number of channels is clearly different from a black and white set with only one channel. In some cases changes are difficult to measure, for example in the quality of services or foodstuffs.

4. It must be remembered that a general index of prices does not show changes in the cost of living of any single person or group of persons. People spend their incomes in different ways and the index is only able to provide a general picture. The pattern of expenditure of young people is different from that of the elderly; single people differ

from those who are married in the way they spend their money.

5. A general price index is also unable to reflect regional or cultural differences in people's expenditure patterns. People living in the north of a country may spend more than people in the south on certain foodstuffs. The consumption patterns of one section of the community may differ sharply from that of other sections, perhaps because of religious differences or ethnic backgrounds.

Money Creation

The supply of notes and coins in most countries is under government control. Notes in the U.K. are produced by the Bank of England at its printing works and coins are made in the Royal Mint, a government department. Banks in Scotland and Northern Ireland issue their own notes but in England and Wales the Bank of England has a monopoly of the note issue.

More important is the way in which banks are able to increase the money supply by creating new deposits for customers in the banking system. Consider a very simple example. Let us suppose that Bank A has just commenced business and that new customers deposit £3,000 cash with it. Its balance sheet would look like this:

Bank A

Liabilities	£	Assets	£
Deposits	3,000	Cash	3,000

The bank knows that to leave all its customers' money in its vaults as cash would be unprofitable and that in any case it needs to maintain (say) only thirty per cent of deposits in cash and other liquid assets to meet any demands for withdrawal by its customers. It may decide to invest ten per cent of the deposits it has received in government securities and use the remaining sixty per cent for advancing money to borrowing customers. When these decisions have been carried out, its balance sheet will be as follows:

Bank A

Liabilities	£	Assets	£
Deposits	3,000	Liquid assets	900
		Investments	300
		Advances	1,800
	3,000		3,000

Now let us suppose that Bank A obtains its investments by purchasing government stock through the Stock Exchange from sellers who maintain their accounts with Bank B. Let us also suppose that the money it lends is spent on purchases from those who also conveniently are customers of Bank B. Bank B's balance sheet will now appear as follows:

Bank B

Liabilities	£	Assets	£
Deposits	2,100	Liquid assets	2,100

If we assume that Bank B wishes to have the same asset structure as Bank A, it will purchase government stock and make advances in a similar way and will then have a balance sheet like this:

Bank B

Liabilities	£	Assets	£
Deposits	2,100	Liquid assets	630
		Investments	210
		Advances	1,260
	2,100		2,100

What has happened therefore is that the total deposits of the two banks now amount to £5,100, banking operations having increased deposits and therefore the supply of money by £2,100.

But the story does not end there. The purchase of investments and the granting of advances by Bank B will increase deposits somewhere else in the banking system and the bank that receives them will itself be in a position to create more deposits by acquiring investments and lending to its customers. In practice, this process of deposit and money creation is continuous, since every day banks are lending money and increasing investments. Also every day the opposite is happening and some deposits are being destroyed.

The power of banks to create money is not, however, unlimited – a fact which can be illustrated if we consider the following balance sheet for all the banks making up a country's banking system:

All Banks

Liabilities	£	Assets	£
Deposits	10,000	Liquid assets	3,000
		Investments	1,000
		Advances	6,000
	10,000		10,000

It will be seen that if we assume that banks generally follow the same asset structure as Bank A, the amount of deposits created will be £7,000 – that is £10,000 less the £3,000 originally deposited. On the assumption that the banks all wish to keep thirty per cent of their deposits in liquid assets and that the total liquid assets available to them is £3,000, the total deposits they can maintain must be £10,000. If they can obtain more liquid assets or if they lower their liquidity ratios then they will be able to create more deposits. Ultimately it is their liquidity which determines the size of their balance sheets and the level of deposits. Closely associated with this is the amount of capital the banks have obtained from their owners, for clearly a bank cannot indefinitely increase its lending and the size of its other assets if it has an inadequate capital base. To do so might be unsafe and would undermine people's confidence in the bank.

In practice, a number of other factors also limit the banks' money creating activities. Clearly a bank can only increase its lending if there are people willing to borrow from the bank at the rates of interest and on the conditions that the bank is prepared to offer. Prospective borrowers must have acceptable reasons for requiring finance and must meet the lending criteria established by the bank.

Very often banks are constrained in their lending activities by action of the state authorities. These constraints form part of a country's monetary policy, a subject considered in more detail in the next chapter.

PERSONAL ASSIGNMENTS

1 Explain what would happen in a country if it decided to replace the total supply of notes and coin with cigarettes.

2 What forms of money in your country have the status of unlimited legal tender?

3 By what means can alterations in the value of money be measured? Show how the value of money in your country has changed during the last five years.

4 Are cheques money?

5 What factors limit the amount of money banks can create?

6 Explain the meaning of 'near money' and give examples.

CHAPTER 7

MONETARY POLICY

Most governments today recognise that they have a responsibility for the soundness of their country's economy. In some cases, this responsibility is reflected in quite detailed control or interference in specific economic matters. Even when this is not the case, however, attempts are made to influence major economic aggregates. Thus a government may see its task as moderating or reducing the rate at which prices are rising or as taking steps to reduce unemployment and to increase the level of production. Concern with matters like these forms the subject of *macroeconomics*.

Economic Objectives

Governments usually have a number of objectives when framing economic policy. These include:

Economic growth. The aim is to raise the standard of living so that people are able to consume more goods and services each year. This implies policies that will stimulate investment and increase the efficiency of productive units.

Full employment. It is clearly advantageous if all those who are able and willing to work can do so. If factories are not producing to full capacity and workers have nothing to do, then the country's resources are being wasted since generally speaking production lost in one year cannot be made good in other years. A high level of unemployment of the workforce can also lead to social and political problems.

Price Stability. Whilst a slight annual rise in prices may act as a stimulus to the economy because money incomes are rising, rapid inflation can be highly destructive. Money ceases to be a good unit of account and store of value and distortions occur as those with fixed incomes and savings suffer whilst borrowers and those in a strong enough position to win income increases benefit as prices rise. Inflation feeds on itself and an inflationary spiral can lead to *hyperinflation* and a breakdown in the monetary system.

Because it is not easy to predict rates of inflation, it becomes difficult to plan for the future and investment and production may suffer. Balance of payments problems may also arise if a country's exports fall because prices are rising more quickly than those of other countries. Imports too may be affected as it becomes cheaper to buy foreign goods than those made at home.

Balance of payments. Whilst fluctuations in the balance of trade with other countries is likely to occur, it is desirable that over a period of years payments should be in equilibrium. Countries like the U.K. which are heavily dependent on imports need to export to pay for these imports and must therefore be able to supply goods and services overseas. Failure to do so may lead to a fall in the country's reserves of gold and foreign currencies, to unfavourable movements in its rate of exchange with other currencies, or to the imposition of direct controls probably self-defeating as other countries retaliate by likewise imposing controls.

These aims of government policy are interconnected and it is never easy to achieve all the objectives at the same time. For example, by taking measures to increase output, employment may be increased and standards of living raised but this may be accompanied by rising prices and a deterioration in the balance of payments. On the other hand, a policy which reduces inflation and helps the balance of payments may lead to unemployment and to a reduction in economic growth. Sometimes a country experiences *stagflation*, when inflation occurs at the same time as stagnation is faced by industry, a condition difficult to remedy.

Economic Weapons

In seeking to achieve these objectives a government can use a number of weapons which can be classified broadly as follows:

Direct controls. These can take many forms and the extent of their use will depend on the political stance of a government and the nature of the problems faced. Thus in war time, a government may impose food rationing on consumers and control the allocation of supplies to industry in order to maximise weapon production. In peace time such controls may be unwelcome, although quite extensive controls are often imposed. For example, restrictions may be imposed to limit the amount of money people can spend or invest abroad, licences may be required to import goods, and banks may be subject to constraints on the amounts they can lend and the purposes for which lending is permissible.

Fiscal policy. Governments need to ensure the defence of their countries and maintain police forces to keep internal law and order. These and other services cannot be left to private enterprise. But often there is a choice. For example, a government may provide health and educational services and operate schemes to help the unemployed, the handi-capped, and the elderly. All these services cost money and can be paid for in part by those who benefit from their provision. Thus people may be required to contribute towards a national pension scheme or to pay prescription charges for the medicine they need. However after allowing for these payments, further income has to be raised either by the imposition of taxes or by borrowing. Taxation can be indirect or direct, depending on whether the person who pays the tax can pass it on to someone else. Thus a tax on imports is an indirect tax because it can be passed on to the consumer in the form of higher prices. A tax on income cannot be passed on in this way and is thus a direct tax. Governments in many countries have invented numerous ways of taxing people, raising revenue not only by taxing incomes and expenditure but also by taxing capital accumulated from past savings.

The structure of a country's system of taxation has important economic implications, encouraging or discouraging enterprise and saving, and redistributing income from one section of the community to another. The amount of money that needs to be borrowed to meet any expenditure not covered by taxation is also very important and in the U.K. is known as the *Public Sector Borrowing Requirement.*

Monetary policy. Separate from but closely associated with fiscal policy, monetary policy is concerned with levels of interest rates, of bank lending, and of the money supply. It is because of this that current monetary policy is of vital interest to banks. But it is also the reason why bank operations are of interest to the authorities and why an under-standing of how banks work is needed by observers of the economic system.

Monetary Theory

Just as the main objectives of economic policy have varied over time, so too have the weapons chosen by the authorities for achieving these objectives. At certain times monetary policy has been regarded as very important; at others less attention has been paid to monetary conditions. These policy changes have resulted partly from the current economic problems to be solved and partly from changes in the views of economists.

These views have largely been concerned with the part that money plays in the economy. The general view during the nineteenth and the first part of the twentieth centuries – the classical view – can be best understood by the following *quantity theory of money* equation:

$$M \times V = P \times T$$

In this equation 'M' represents the quantity of money and 'V' its velocity of circulation, that is the number of times it changes hands. This can be best understood by a simple example. Imagine that the money supply consists of six million £1 notes and that these are used once only during a month. Now suppose that there are only one million £1 notes but they are used six times a month. In both cases 'M × V' is the same. In the second part of the equation 'T' stands for the number of transactions taking place over the same period of time as that used for 'V', whilst 'P' represents the average price level of these transactions. Supporters of the quantity theory felt that in the short run the velocity of circulation ('V') and number of transactions ('T') did not change, thus the level of prices ('P') was determined by the money supply ('M'), an increase in the amount of money available leading to a rise in prices.

In the years before the Second World War high levels of unemployment were reached during a period of deep recession. The great economist Keynes, writing with these problems in mind, questioned whether the quantity theory could be used to stimulate the economy and so reduce the numbers out of work. The conclusion was that increasing the supply of money would be largely ineffective, for if people's holdings of money increased they would not buy more goods and services but rather would use the money to buy government bonds and other securities. Whilst these purchases might lead to a fall in interest rates which in turn could encourage investment, this would have only a weak and indirect effect on the economy. Monetary policy therefore came to be regarded as a poor weapon for controlling the economy and greater reliance was placed on fiscal policy.

Keynesian views generally dominated economic thinking until the

1960s when research by Professor Friedman led to the development of *monetarist* views which although controversial have led to much greater attention being given to pre-Keynesian theories, similar in some ways to those of the monetarists.

Monetarists generally distinguish clearly between the short- and long-term effects of increasing the money supply. Thus they believe that although the immediate effect may be to stimulate production and thus reduce unemployment, this effect will soon wear off and prices will begin to rise. In the short run, people will discover that their cash and bank balances have risen above their normal requirements and they will purchase more goods and services as well as securities, thus driving down interest rates, another stimulant to output. Unfortunately this situation does not last. Increased demand pushes prices up, interest rates rise again because of inflation, and people need to hold more money because of higher price levels. The result is that in the long run the increased money supply is reflected in increased prices, the level of production and employment being determined, according to monetarists, by the efficiency of industry and its ability to supply the goods that are wanted at home and abroad.

As will be seen, monetarist thought has been a strong influence on government policy and it is now quite usual for the authorities to attempt to control the growth of a country's money supply, the usual aim being to keep this in line with the growth of output so that prices remain stable.

The Money Supply

A major problem for a country attempting to control the money supply is the definition of what exactly it is trying to control. A major difficulty arises because money can be used both as a medium of exchange and a store of value. Thus it can be assumed that people's holding of notes and coin is required for medium of exchange purposes and that most people will avoid hoarding them because they may be stolen and no interest is obtainable on money so held. Money placed in a current account with a bank can be treated in the same way because it can be used on demand by drawing cheques to pay for goods and services. Even in this case there is a slight difficulty if people maintain a minimum balance so as to avoid paying bank charges, for it can be argued that such balances should not be regarded as a medium of exchange. However, as this cannot be measured, all current account balances are regarded as part of the money supply.

In the U.K. the measure of money known as M_1 includes notes and coin in circulation with the public as well as *sight deposits*, that is current account balances and other deposits in sterling which can be withdrawn on demand.

A broader measurement of money supply used in the U.K. is the aggregate known as *sterling M_3* ($£M_3$) which consists of notes and coin and sight deposits, that is M_1, together with sterling *time deposits* with the banks – that is deposits other than sight deposits for which nominally at least a period of notice has to be given before they can be withdrawn. These deposits can be regarded as a temporary depository of purchasing power and are included in $£M_3$ for this reason.

The deposits included in M_1 and $£M_3$ are all sterling deposits. However deposits can be made in currencies other than sterling and when these are added to $£M_3$ a larger aggregate is obtained which is called M_3.

It has been recognised that various short-term assets with a high degree of liquidity can also be used as temporary resting places for money until they are used as a medium of exchange. The U.K. authorities therefore have a measure of private sector liquidity known as PSL_1, which strictly speaking is not a monetary aggregate but a measure of liquidity, since the total includes items additional to cash and bank deposits. It is also recognised that deposits with building societies perform functions similar to those with banks and when these are added to PSL_1 a second measure of private sector liquidity, PSL_2, is arrived at. PSL_2 is the largest aggregate published by the U.K. authorities.

The difficulty of measuring aggregates useful for monetary control purposes is illustrated by the variety that exists in the U.K. – M_1, $£M_3$, M_3, PSL_1, and PSL_2. The addition of another aggregate – M_2 – figures for which were first published in June 1982, is a further illustration of the difficulties of definition. M_2 is an attempt to provide a measure more closely related to transactions in goods and services than some of the other aggregates and is designed to overcome difficulties in distinguishing between money as a medium of exchange and as a store of value.

Controlling the Money Supply

Even when monetarist theories are accepted, difficulties remain in deciding what measures of money should be controlled – hence the plethora of aggregate figures. But another difficulty also exists – how to control the money supply. No tap exists to regulate the flow of money into the economy in the way that one can control the amount of water in a bath. Instead it is necessary to attempt to control the things that lead to the creation of money.

As we have seen in Chapter 6, money is created by the banking system through its lending activities, an increase in bank lending resulting in general in a corresponding rise in bank deposits. Later in this chapter we shall consider how these banking activities can be controlled. But money is also created by government action, a simple example of which is when more notes are printed to pay for government expenditure. However, if taxation is increased to meet this expenditure the notes will be paid back to the government as taxes and there will be no increase in the notes in circulation. Likewise, there will be no increase if the notes are returned to the government as loans from the general public. The money supply will increase only if the government finances expenditure by borrowing *and* if that borrowing is from sources other than the general public.

The reality is somewhat more complicated than this, although the same principles apply. Firstly, we are concerned only with that part of government expenditure that is not met out of taxation, and other government income. Secondly, it is more convenient to consider borrowing by the public sector as a whole and include both central and local government and the nationalised industries owned by the state. We speak therefore of the *Public Sector Borrowing Requirement* or PSBR for short. Thirdly, we divide the private sector of the domestic economy into two parts, the banking sector and the non-bank private sector.

Table 29 *Sterling M_3 Counterparts (1984–5)*

	£ millions
Public Sector Borrowing Requirement	+10,274
Public sector borrowing from non-bank private sector	−12,486
Sterling lending to U.K. private sector	+18,607
Other counterparts	− 4,452
Increase in Sterling M_3	+11,943

Source: *Bank of England Quarterly Bulletin*

An examination of Table 29, which shows the counterparts to $£M_3$, will help to illustrate why the money supply grew in 1984–5. It shows how the PSBR raised the money supply (as measured by $£M_3$) in

1984–5, how this was more than offset by government borrowing from the general public (the non-bank private sector), and how bank lending was largely responsible for £M$_3$'s increase. These figures provide a clue to what must be controlled by the government if it is seeking to limit the growth of the money supply.

The increase in £M$_3$ and its components during 1984–5 are shown Table 30. These figures show how £M$_3$ increased in 1984–5; those in Table 29 show the reasons for the increase. Increased government expenditure makes £M$_3$ rise whilst an increase in government income leads to a fall. When expenditure exceeds income the government will need to borrow from the private sector, the effect of this borrowing on £M$_3$ depending on where this borrowing is from. If it is from the banks, an increase in their customers' deposits will be matched by a rise in bank assets resulting from increased lending to the government. If however the banks' customers lend to the government, deposits will be restored to the level existing before excess government expenditure took place. If the government borrows more from the non-bank private sector than it needs to cover the PSBR, this will have the effect of reducing £M$_3$. The *policy of over-funding* shown in Table 29 ceased in October 1985.

Table 30 *Increase in Sterling M$_3$ (1984–5)*

	£ millions
Notes and coin in circulation with the public	+ 750
Private sector sterling sight deposits	+ 6,456
Private sector sterling time deposits	+ 4,737
Increase in Sterling M$_3$	+11,943

Source: *Bank of England Quarterly Bulletin*

The Role of Monetary Policy

As we saw at the beginning of the chapter, governments attempt to achieve a number of economic objectives by using a variety of weapons. These include monetary policy, which has various objectives which can vary from country to country and which can change from time to time. These include:

    1. Controlling the growth of money and credit.

2. Establishing a satisfactory level of interest rates.

3. Seeking to obtain a desirable rate of exchange with other currencies.

4. Ensuring that government borrowing is financed as efficiently as possible.

These aims are interconnected. Thus to control money supply it is necessary to influence those things which affect it, the sterling M_3 counterparts shown in Table 29. If as a result of government fiscal policy the PSBR is rising, an increase in borrowing from the non-bank private sector will be needed to prevent money supply growth. People will have to lend more money to the government and to achieve this interest rates may have to rise. Higher interest rates may encourage an inflow of investment funds from overseas, leading to a strengthening of the exchange rate. This could be unwelcome, particularly if a fall in the exchange rate had been hoped for in order to stimulate the flow of exports.

Bank lending, as we have seen, has a very important influence on the level of money supply. Restraints on bank lending may enable the government to have a higher PSBR – the result either of increased spending or of reduced taxation – and thus to reduce the importance of funding this borrowing from the non-bank private sector. On the other hand, banking restraints may distort the financial markets and lead borrowers to seek funds from outside the domestic banking system. The banks may seek to meet this competition by finding ways to avoid the restraints and thus the authorities will have to counter this by improving the operation of restrictive policies.

Monetary policy in the U.K. since the Second World War has often been concerned with attempting to curb the activities of the banking system. The mode and scope of this policy has changed over time and broadly speaking can be distinguished by three main periods: 1945 to 1971, 1971 to 1981, and 1981 to the present time.

The period immediately following the Second World War was one in which controls were imposed largely on the clearing banks who were required to maintain a fixed proportion of their deposits either as cash in their vaults or as balances with the Bank of England. That these requirements were inadequate to obtain the results sought by the authorities is shown by the fact that *quantitative and qualitative controls* were also imposed. These controls required banks to limit the amount of their lending in line with requests made to them and also, from time to time, required that their lending should be to sectors of the economy believed by the authorities to be of particular importance to the country's welfare. In addition in 1958 a *special deposit* system was announced which meant that banks could be called upon to place money with the Bank of England in accounts which, whilst paying a modest rate of interest linked to Treasury bill rate, had the effect of reducing the banks' liquidity thus put tiny pressure on them to restrict the level of their advances.

As the years went by it became clear that these arrangements were distorting the banking system and restricting competition between banks. Those who were subject the control of increasingly sought ways by which they could circumvent them; those not subject to controls were able to undertake business which the controlled banks were prevented from carrying out. As a result, a new arrangement was introduced towards the end of 1971 known as *competition and credit control* which had as its objective, as the name implies, the control of the supply of credit whilst at the same time removing barriers to competition between different banking groups. Under this system all banks were required to maintain a prescribed level of *reserve assets* in relation to their *eligible liabilities*, a term broadly meaning those sterling bank deposits with an initial term of two years or less. Problems with the operation of the reserve-asset ratio system led to the introduction of *supplementary special deposits*, popularly known as the 'corset', which effectively was a direct quantitative control over the level of interest-bearing eligible liabilities (IBELS) that banks could acquire.

Difficulties in operating the monetary control mechanism remained, and the abandonment of exchange-control regulations in 1979 finally led to the system now in force. The Bank of England now largely operates in the bill market to maintain short-term interest rates within an undisclosed band agreed with the Treasury. In order to strengthen the bill market the number of banks whose acceptances make bills eligible for discount at the Bank was increased but such banks are required to keep prescribed proportions of their eligible liabilities as secured loans in the money market. The corset has been abandoned and the reserve-asset ratio system terminated. The sole requirement is that recognised banks and licensed deposit-takers with eligible liabilities averaging £10 million or more must keep ½ per cent of eligible liabilities as non-interest-bearing deposits with the Bank of England in order to provide it with an income to conduct its operations. Strictly speaking this requirement is not part of the system of monetary control but is in effect a tax on the banking system.

From the monetary control point of view, banks in the U.K. are now probably the least regulated in the world. However the Bank of

England is potentially able to exercise considerable control through the supervisory arrangements it can now employ following the passage of the 1979 Banking Act, details of which are considered in Chapter 12. Despite this, the freedom of U.K. banking has been a factor in attracting many overseas banks to London and other major British cities.

PERSONAL ASSIGNMENTS

1 Examine the cause of the change in the size of the figure for the U.K.'s monetary aggregate $£M_3$ during the last twelve months.

2 Consider the various measures that can be taken to control the level of bank lending.

3 By what means does the Bank of England relieve shortages of funds in the London money markets?

4 Explain the methods used by the authorities to influence the level of U.K. interest rates.

5 What do you understand by the term 'overfunding'?

6 Examine the sources of revenue of the U.K. government and show the ways in which it is spent.

7 What is the PSBR and why is it important?

CHAPTER 8

BANK LENDING

One of the main tasks of a bank is to lend money. As a financial intermediary one of its roles is to reduce lending risks. A large part of the deposits received by a bank is used to finance other people's activities and borrowers of many types seek assistance from it in financing a wide range of projects.

As professional lenders, banks provide finance in a variety of ways – by discounting bills of exchange, by advancing money to customers by loans in various forms, and by overdrafts. When a loan is granted, the customer's current account is credited with the agreed amount and a loan account for the same figure is opened in the customer's name. When the advance is by overdraft the customer can continue to draw funds from his current account despite the fact that the credit balance is exhausted. The balance becomes a debit or negative balance and can be increased to the overdraft limit agreed with the bank. In the days of hand-written ledgers these overdrawn balances were recorded in red ink thus accounting for the expression sometimes heard that a customer is 'in the red'.

Balances on both loan and overdrawn accounts appear as advances among the assets recorded in a bank's balance sheet and the interest received forms an important part of a bank's income. Overdrafts are often attractive to customers. They can reduce the amount of interest paid since this is computed only on a debit balance outstanding at the end of the day. Someone involved in an undertaking where income and expenditure are subject to daily fluctuations or change from season to season needs a variable borrowing requirement which can be met most cheaply through the overdraft system.

Lending Principles

Bank lending is an art as well as a science. Success depends on technical knowledge and on an aptitude to assess both the credit-worthiness of a potential borrower and the merits of the proposition to be financed. Lending principles are thus general guidelines which a lending officer should keep in mind when judging an advance application.

A bank lends other people's money, not its own, and a lending officer should always remember that he is effectively acting as a trustee for the bank's depositors. He needs to be aware of his bank's attitude towards risk-bearing. If he is too cautious, the bank's earnings may needlessly suffer; if he takes too many risks the bank may be faced with an unacceptable level of bad debts.

The Borrower

The *integrity* of a potential borrower is obviously of key importance as also is his *contractual capacity* to borrow. It would be foolish to lend to someone you cannot trust or without a legal obligation for him to repay his debt.

In deciding whether a customer is a good credit risk it is helpful to try to answer a number of questions:

1. How long has the customer had an account with the bank?

2. Has it been properly conducted? – have there been unauthorised overdrafts? – have cheques had to be returned through lack of funds?

3. Have there been previous borrowings and were repayments made on time and without difficulty?

If the customer is in business:

1. Has the business been a success and for how long?

2. Is he fit and energetic and prepared to work hard for the success of his firm?

3. Has he an extravagant lifestyle?

4. Has he made excessive drawings from the business or has a reasonable part of the profits been ploughed back to help it expand?

5. If the customer is about to start a business or to commence new activities, what technical expertise does he possess and what business experience does he have?

If the borrower is a company:

1. What is the quality of the firm's management?

2. Is it properly controlled?

3. How good are its production operations?

4. Is it good at marketing its products?

5. How does it plan future operations?

As with other aspects of lending, it is important to adopt an objective and constructive approach to an advance application. A well-known and successful businessman may appear to be over-confident and likely to take risks greater than the bank would like. On the other hand, a bank may be prepared to lend to someone who is innovative and who has a good idea for a new product or process as well as the technical experience to develop it provided he is joined by someone with sound business experience, able to look after the financial and marketing aspects of a business.

The Proposition

Only when it is known why a customer needs finance is it possible to consider a proposition in detail. The main consideration is whether it is in the interests of the customer and the bank. If it seems likely that a business proposition will fail, there is little point in going ahead. To do so would not be in the customer's interest and even if security were taken, the bank could be faced with the cost and possible problems of realising the security. Again, a number of questions can be asked:

1. Do the facts of the case make sense? For example does the customer's estimate of the future demand for his product appear realistic?

2. Is he over-optimistic?

3. Will the project yield sufficient income to enable interest to be paid and the advance to be repaid by the agreed date?

It is very important for the bank to know the source of repayment. This accounts for the attractiveness of an advance that is *self-liquidating*. Thus a bridging loan to enable someone to buy a house should be repaid when the existing property is sold. An advance to enable a trader to build up stocks before Christmas should be repaid when the goods are sold.

Other questions which should be asked include:

1. Is the amount to be borrowed sufficient for the purpose required? The banker may feel for example that the maximum amount he is prepared to lend is £30,000. If it becomes apparent at a later date that the cost of completing the project is £40,000 the banker has an uncomfortable choice. If he refuses to lend the additional sum the project may fail and the customer may be unable to repay the advance. Alternatively, if he provides additional funds this will raise the level of the advance above the figure he felt was prudent.

2. What amount of the customer's own money is to be used for the project?

It is usually unrealistic for a bank to accept all the risk of loss. It is desirable that some of the risk should be borne by the customer for a project he feels is sound. This will provide an incentive for him to make it a success.

Security

A decision to lend is based upon the banker's opinion of his customer and of the proposition he is asked to finance and not upon the value of assets owned by the customer and available as security. Even when ample security is available a banker should not lend if he is unhappy about the reason for the advance.

Security should be taken as a safeguard against unforeseen problems with an advance, as an insurance designed to protect the bank and its depositors. The London clearing banks have said that the greater part of their lending is unsecured. Lending to large companies is often on this basis since they usually have the resources to provide reliable and regular information about their affairs. This enables a bank to monitor an advance and to have early warning if things are going wrong. In the case of smaller companies, limited administrative resources make this too burdensome and thus the provision of security is likely to be more usual in order to offset the greater risk of loss.

When security is taken by a bank it is important that it can be realised easily and with the minimum of expense. The nature of securities which can be used by banks is examined in Chapter 14. It will be seen that it is important that a bank obtain a good title to the security so that it can be converted easily into cash. It is important that the value of the security can be ascertained without undue difficulty. Normally the amount of an advance will be less than the value of the security, this margin being required to allow for fluctuations in the security's value and any costs likely to be incurred in realising it.

Personal Borrowing

Lending to personal customers can be by means of a loan or an overdraft or in the case of the London clearing banks by a finance house subsidiary making finance available through a hire purchase or conditional sale agreement (*see* Consumer Durables, Chapter 2).

The introduction by the London clearing banks in the late 1950s of *personal loans* opened up an additional channel for assisting customers, particularly those wishing to buy a car or consumer durables or anxious to finance a home improvement scheme, for example the installation of double glazing. Personal loans are for fixed periods and at fixed rates of interest. They are usually unsecured and available for amounts up to

£5,000 for a period of three years. Where the loan is for home improvement it is often possible to borrow up to £10,000 for periods of as long as ten years.

Interest is computed at the time the loan is granted and depends on the sum borrowed, the period for which the loan is required, and the bank's current rate of interest on personal loans. The amount of interest due is added to the amount borrowed and the total sum is repaid by equal monthly instalments over the repayment period. Thus the monthly repayments on a personal loan of £2,000 for two years at 12 per cent would be:

	£
Amount borrowed	2,000
Interest	480
Sum to be repaid by 24 monthly payments of £103.33	2,480

The monthly payment is in part a repayment of the capital sum borrowed and in part a payment of interest on the loan. It follows that the average amount borrowed is less than the amount of the loan on which the interest charge is based, and thus the effective rate of interest is much higher than the nominal rate charged. This effective rate, the *annual percentage rate*, must be disclosed to borrowers as explained in the section dealing with the Consumer Credit Act 1974 in Chapter 12. It could be about double the nominal rate, the exact figure depending on the period of the loan.

Banks have developed a number of variations on the personal loan. *Revolving credit loans* enable customers to borrow to a prescribed limit whenever they wish. A fixed monthly payment is made and if in credit the customer receives interest on the balance. *Budget accounts* enable customers to spread household and other expenses evenly through the year. An estimate is made of the total amount of bills to be paid and the customer makes equal monthly payments into the account, drawing cheques on the account to pay bills when they are received. Extended credit facilities available through the use of credit cards also provide a source of borrowing for the bank's personal customers who may now also obtain loans for house purchase from banks by arrangements similar to those made by building societies.

In recent years banks have increasingly used *credit scoring* techniques to decide whether to lend to a personal customer. From previous experience, the bank defines what characteristics of borrowers seem most indicative of credit-worthiness and a potential borrower needs only to complete a form designed to enable the bank to measure these characteristics. For example, it is important to discover the stability of a potential borrower. Those who have held a job for some years are therefore usually regarded as a better risk than those who have changed jobs frequently. The occupier of a freehold home is likely to be regarded more favourably than someone living in a mobile home. From the information given a bank can prepare a score sheet similar to that in Table 31. The bank may decide that personal loans will only be granted to applicants scoring 600 points or above. In this case, the score is well above this figure, and provided other information is satisfactory (for example income, the amount of other borrowing, and previous lending experience), the loan will be granted.

Table 31 *Score Sheet*

	Maximum possible points	Points scored
Age	75	50
Marital status	100	100
Number of dependants	75	70
Type of living accommodation	250	200
Occupation	200	180
Length of current employment	175	100
Number of years at present address	125	25
	1,000	725

Credit scoring is an objective way of measuring risk and can be used by relatively inexperienced lending officers. It is a system often used when deciding the amount of credit to be allowed to a credit card holder or to someone asking for hire purchase finance.

Company Borrowing

The criteria used when considering a company's borrowing request are the same as for other kinds of lending: the integrity, competence, and credit-worthiness of the borrower and the purpose for which the advance is required.

All London clearing bank lending to companies is made on a '*going concern'* basis, that is on the assumption that the firm will continue in business. The current financial and trading position of the firm must be sound enough to indicate that it will be able to repay the advance within the agreed time and service the debt by paying interest when this is due. If the bank is satisfied that this is the case, it will usually supplement its appraisal by considering the risk it would face if things were to go wrong, if the assumptions made proved to be over-optimistic, and the company were to run into serious difficulties. This entails considering the company on a *'gone concern'* basis. In both cases the company's accounts need to be analysed and further information sought where necessary about particular items.

As we saw in Chapter 4, the main accounts of a firm consist of a balance sheet and the trading and profit and loss accounts. An appropriation account will show how the profit for a year has been dealt with and in the case of a manufacturing company there is also likely to be a manufacturing account showing the cost of the goods manufactured. Where possible the banker would expect to see accounts over a period of years, since changes over time are more revealing than figures for a single year. He should be able to discover how the firm's profitability has changed and the reasons for this change. He should also learn how much money is being taken out of the business by its proprietors.

From a set of accounts a large number of *accounting ratios* can be computed, changes in these ratios helping to reveal how the firm's business is progressing. Increasing profits may be a sign of strength but may also be associated with an increase in the proprietors' funds in the business. Thus if the *return on capital* (net profit divided by proprietors' funds) were falling the banker would need to know the reasons for this. Again, rising sales may indicate a healthy business but if the goods sold are under-priced this could affect profits. Comparison of the ratio of profits to sales (gross or net profit divided by sales) in different years may disclose trends which the banker may wish to investigate. Changes in the relationship between gross and net profits may be an important indicator of how a business is performing. If for example gross profits as shown in Table 15 are rising more quickly than net profits (Table 16) this may suggest that firmer control is needed over indirect costs. Again, an increase in the amount of goods in stock may indicate in the case of a manufacturing concern that production levels are too high in relation to the volume of sales.

An important aspect of a business for a banker is its liquidity. Current assets divided by current liabilities provide a *current ratio*, a measure of the firm's *working capital* or that part of the capital that circulates as a result of ordinary trading activities. Goods are sold, cash is received, and the cash is used to obtain more goods for sale, all part of a continuous process. However not all purchases and sales are for cash, for payment is delayed as credit is both received and given. Current assets therefore include money owing by debtors for goods purchased on credit. Likewise the amounts owing to creditors are included in a firm's current liabilities. The liquidity position is clearly strong when current assets are well in excess of current liabilities, that is when there is a high current ratio. A fall in the ratio could indicate that the company is seeking longer-term credit from its suppliers, possibly as a result of a cash shortage. This same shortage may mean that the firm has been forced to reduce the amount of credit it allows its customers. Reduced liquidity would again be shown by a fall in the liquidity ratio and sales may be depressed by the stricter payment terms imposed on customers.

In assessing a firm's liquidity, the '*acid test*' is often used. A *liquidity ratio* (or *quick ratio*) is obtained by excluding the value of any stock of goods or work in progress from the figure for current assets and dividing the result by the figure for current liabilities. It is assumed that the firm has ceased trading or at least is unable to realise cash for its stocks. It assumes also that it will be able to collect all the debts owing to it so that these, together with its cash reserves, will be available to repay all the firm's creditors.

A decline in the firm's liquidity indicates a shortage of working capital and suggests that the firm is *overtrading,* that is attempting to maintain a scale of operations beyond its resources. The size of the business may be impressive but the margin of safety is small and there is a danger of sudden collapse. The firm may find difficulty in paying wages or meeting tax demands, and suppliers may become worried and start demanding cash for deliveries. A bank overdraft in a case like this may be unwise since this would increase current liabilities and worsen the liquidity position. The proprietors should be advised to seek additional permanent capital for the business or, if this is not possible, to reduce the scale of their activities.

Unless care is taken some forms of bank lending can lead to a shortage of liquidity. Thus a medium-term loan to enable a firm to invest in additional equipment may need to be linked with additional working capital to meet the cost of additional wages and raw materials as the equipment is brought into production for otherwise cash shortages will be experienced. A *cash flow* forecast will help to prevent this happening for it is recognised that the generation of cash is essential if suppliers, employees, tax authorities, and others are to be paid on time. Earning profits is not enough. Goods may be sold at a handsome profit but until they are paid for cash flow is not affected.

A banker is likely to be very interested in a cash flow statement covering the years for which an advance is required. This will provide estimates of the flow of cash into and out of the business during a succession of time periods, perhaps of a month or a quarter depending on a particular situation. Inflows of cash will be estimated from the likely level of sales and the amount of credit given to purchasers. Outflows will depend on the cost of obtaining goods, the amount of credit allowed by suppliers, and on other payments the firm has to make in a particular period, such as rent and rates, heating and lighting, and advertising.

As well as indicating whether funds will be available at appropriate times to service and repay a bank advance, the cash flow statement may also show that in one or more time periods higher borrowing will be needed than the customer has realised. The banker will thus need to consider whether he is able to meet this demand. As we saw earlier, it is important that a banker should make sure that a customer has adequate finance for the purpose in mind.

A firm's *gearing*, that is the relationship between its loan and equity capital, is of great importance both to the firm and to a lending banker. If the amount of borrowed money is high in relation to the amount of proprietors' funds in a firm, it is said to be highly geared. This can often be attractive for a firm's owners, particularly if the business is doing well. The interest payable on loan capital is fixed with the result that increases in a firm's net income can be shared over the relatively small amount of proprietors' capital. The opposite happens when earnings are falling. Loan interest still has to be paid with the result that the profits to be shared by the proprietors fall sharply. In this case there is a danger that if earnings are insufficient to pay loan interest the firm could face failure.

A joint stock company raises capital from the public in two main ways: firstly by the issue of ordinary shares which together with retained earnings represent the value of the shareholders' equity in the business and secondly by the issue of debentures or loan stock to investors who receive fixed-interest payments and who are the company's creditors, not its owners. A higher degree of gearing is acceptable when a company enjoys a steady and fairly safe income flow than when risks are high and income is subject to wide fluctuations.

A banker is interested in a company's gearing because it affects not only the riskiness of the enterprise but also his position if the firm fails, that is when it is a 'gone concern'. If this happens, certain categories of the firm's creditors take preference over others when assets have been realised and money is available to pay its debts. Those who have provided loan capital will probably have obtained security on the company's assets and these will rank for payment before the bank if its advance is unsecured.

The 'gone concern' approach is designed to discover the bank's position should a firm fail. Assets are valued on a break-up basis assuming the worst possible events. For example, *goodwill* – representing the reputation of the owners and the skill of the managers of a business – is an intangible asset whose value is sometimes included in a balance sheet. If a firm crashed it would probably be worthless and so its value is usually ignored in a break-up valuation. Likewise the value of any *patents* or *trademarks* shown in the balance sheet are usually ignored on the basis that they probably could not be sold if their owners had failed. In this event some fixed assets may also have little value. A factory which has been used for producing highly specialised goods may be difficult to sell unless it can be easily converted to other uses. On the other hand, a retail shop in a main shopping area could be quite valuable if in good repair and well-maintained, although it might be overvalued in the firm's balance sheet.

Work-in-progress may be of little value when a manufacturing firm runs into difficulties. Other firms may be reluctant to finish the work, particularly if this would be costly and take a long time. The value of stocks of finished goods would depend on the ease with which they could be sold, but the firm's failure would probably indicate difficulty in selling quickly and at a reasonable price. The value of a firm's debtors will largely depend on the number of people owing money and who they are. Generally speaking their value is likely to be higher if a large number of people owe small sums than if the figures are large and only a few debtors are involved.

A bank would be most unlikely to base a lending decision purely on a 'gone concern' basis. Sometimes a 'going concern' assessment may be all that is required, although usually both methods are used since they are regarded as complementary.

Interest Rates

Interest rates charged for bank lending can be determined in three ways: by fixing the rate at a margin over either *base rate* or the *London Inter-Bank Offered Rate* (LIBOR), or by a rate fixed for the duration of the advance. Since 1971 banks have published a base rate which varies according to changes taking place in the general level of rates in the country and borrowers are charged interest at a rate linked to this base. Thus a first-class or 'blue chip' company may pay interest at a rate a little above base rate whilst smaller companies may pay two or three per cent above. A substantial part of bank deposits is received through the inter-bank market and a great deal of lending is now conducted at interest rates linked to LIBOR – that is the rate a bank needs to pay to obtain funds in the market. A fixed margin above LIBOR is charged, the rate to be paid usually changing at specified intervals rather than on a day-to-day basis. Movements in LIBOR are a main determinant of base rates. Such a link is important since failure to raise base rates may mean that bank customers indulge in *'round tripping'*, that is borrowing from banks at a rate only a little higher than base rate and relending the money in the market at a profit. Lending at fixed rates of interest can be dangerous when market rates are erratic for if these rise the advance could be unprofitable. Usually when a fixed rate of interest is charged it is substantially higher than would be the case with a variable rate.

A number of factors will be considered by a banker when fixing the margin above base rate or LIBOR to be paid by a borrowing customer. Risk is an important factor and, as has been seen, the margin is likely to be less for a 'blue chip' company than for one of lower standing. In determining the degree of risk, any security taken in support of an advance will also be taken into account. The term of the advance is another factor for consideration, and in fixing a rate the banker may also be influenced by other factors such as the profitability of other transactions with the customer and any important connections that may exist which are of importance to the bank.

International Lending

The development in the 1960s of the sterling inter-bank market (*see* Wholesale Money Markets, Chapter 3) was largely responsible for the growth of medium-term lending by the London clearing banks, a growth which continued in the 1970s and which included the development of syndicated lending – a process enabling banks to share with others the risks involved when granting large medium-term advances. The development of the eurocurrency markets (*see* The Eurocurrency Markets, Chapter 5) in the late 1950s made it possible for banks to meet increasing demands for international finance with the result that the growth of international banking occurred at the same time as the development of domestic medium-term lending.

International banking has a long history which can be traced back to the Middle Ages. By the nineteenth century, the London merchant banks were active in arranging finance for overseas governments and after the Second World War banking gradually developed into an industry with a variety of international features. Thus some clearing banks have followed an active policy of establishing wherever possible a full banking presence in other countries, either by opening branches or by acquiring existing local banks. Where lending is directed at local people and institutions, the principles of sound lending are applied in ways similar to those of the home country with account being taken of local conditions, differences in the law, and possible differences in accounting conventions.

However, the post-war growth of multinational corporations manufacturing and trading on a world-wide basis has led to developments aimed at meeting these corporations' needs. As well as short-term finance to support their international trade and to help them carry stocks and meet current expenses, these needs also include medium- and long-term finance for the construction of manufacturing plant and the purchase of various types of equipment.

Another source of growing demand for finance was overseas countries and government agencies. This demand grew strongly in the 1970s and international banks came to play a significant part in assisting countries facing balance of payment difficulties. This was particularly marked after the substantial oil price increase of 1973 which had the effect of increasing the income of oil-producing countries whilst at the same time creating balance of payment difficulties for others. Banks were able to recycle funds left with them by oil producers to countries facing payment deficits – an activity for which they were often praised but which has recently created serious problems.

Foreign currency needed by British banks for international financial transactions is received either as deposits from at home and abroad or by borrowing in the eurocurrency markets. These funds are used for lending to U.K. residents, to multinational corporations, and to overseas governments and their agencies. Frequently lending is on a syndicated basis, risks associated with large loans often being shared by 100 or more banks from different countries. By this means a borrower is able to obtain a larger loan than would normally be possible from a single bank. He has the advantage of having to explain his requirements to one bank only and this bank arranges the terms of the credit and organises the participation of other banks. When the loan is large, this bank will act as *lead manager* and work with a group of *managers*, that is banks who underwrite the loan, help prepare the loan documents, and obtain signatures of other participating banks to the loan agreement made with the borrower. The lead manager usually acts as *agent* with responsibility for operational aspects of the loan, for example determining the rate of interest to be paid under the terms of the agreement, collecting payments when due, and distributing them to the participating banks.

Some banks have become members of banking clubs or have formed *consortium banks* by joining with banks from other countries to conduct international operations, sometimes directed at particular regions of the world. These arrangements facilitate the formation of lending syndicates when these are to be established.

International lending presents problems which are not found when purely domestic transactions are involved. A clear understanding of the political and economic situation of other countries is often needed. For example, there may be difficulty in obtaining repayment of a foreign-currency loan to a company domiciled abroad when exchange control regulations are introduced which prevent it obtaining the currency it requires. Lending to overseas countries has often led to considerable problems due to their inability to meet interest payment deadlines or to keep to repayment schedules. A major principle of sound bank lending is that the finance provided should be used for an enterprise capable of yielding an income sufficient to service the debt and to permit repayments at the agreed times. Sometimes when finance has been provided for specific projects overseas this has not happened – sometimes due to initial over-optimism, sometimes because of economic changes which had not been foreseen. When lending has been for the general purpose of meeting a country's balance of payments deficits the problems can be much worse unless the country has so ordered its affairs as to improve its payments position.

High interest rates coupled with world recession are among the reasons which in recent years have prevented countries from meeting their obligations. Banks have been forced to undertake the onerous task of *rescheduling*, that is arranging for interest payments and debt repayments to be delayed on the understanding that steps are taken to improve economic performance. Large numbers of banks from different countries are often involved in the rescheduling process, but speedy improvement in a country's economy is often not possible because of world conditions or the unwelcome political effects of the changes needed. Whilst it is true that a country, unlike a company, cannot go out of business, there is always a danger that it will default and no mechanism exists to enable banks to seize and realise a country's assets. The assessment of *country risk* is difficult and whilst banks in the 1970s were often praised for their assistance in recycling oil money, the difficulties faced in the 1980s have largely arisen because sound lending principles have been ignored.

Risk Capital

There is a belief that unemployment levels can be reduced and economic growth achieved by encouraging the growth of small businesses and the provision of *risk or venture capital* for companies formed to develop new products, processes, or services. For prudential reasons, British banks are willing to provide only a limited amount of long-term finance and their need to protect depositors' funds makes it difficult for them to provide risk capital, the returns on which may take a long time in accruing. Nevertheless, clearing banks have established special units which seek to overcome some of these problems. An important source of equity finance for smaller companies is provided by the *Industrial and Commercial Finance Corporation* (ICFC) founded by the banks in 1945 at the same time as the *Finance Corporation for Industry* (FCI) was established. Both corporations were brought together in 1973 and now form *Investors in Industry* (3i) in which the clearing banks at present have a major stake.

Often people wishing to start a new undertaking lack the resources to put into the business and have difficulty in persuading friends and relations to help them. It is clearly unwise for a bank to shoulder all the risk of failure, particularly as many new businesses fail after a very short time. Government help has been provided by means of a guarantee scheme which protects a bank against some of the losses that may arise, but difficulties remain because customers are often unable to provide part of the start-up capital or the necessary assets as security for an advance. A further difficulty is often a customer's lack of business experience and banks have therefore established small business advisory services designed to provide professional financial management both to help owners develop a successful business and to maintain a check on its performance.

Lending Supervision

A bank's senior management needs to establish a clear lending policy. It needs to ensure that it has a well-spread loan portfolio in case a particular sector of the economy or a particular industry creates unwelcome difficulties – for example, an unduly high proportion of lending to property developers could cause problems if house prices fall; a preponderance of loans to farmers could lead to difficulties if agriculture becomes depressed. Decisions have to be taken about the proportion of advances that can be made on a medium-term basis and how much can be lent long term, for example for house purchase. In international operations, country risk has to be assessed and decisions taken regarding the amount of credit to be granted to particular countries.

Each bank needs a system for dealing with applications for an advance, the usual arrangement being for lending officers to be granted discretionary limits within which they have authority to take decisions. The level of these limits usually depends on the lending officer's experience and seniority, and the position he holds in the bank. Thus a branch manager may be empowered to grant advances up to a certain size, different figures sometimes being given for secured and unsecured advances. Applications for an advance in excess of a branch *manager's discretionary limit* (MDL) may need to be forwarded to a regional or district office where lending officers have greater discretionary powers. Applications for larger amounts usually require the sanction of head office's lending officers. Very large or difficult applications may need to be sanctioned by a committee of general managers or in some cases by an advance committee of the board of directors or by the board itself.

A branch manager faced with a difficult advance application is usually encouraged to discuss it with more senior staff before coming to a decision. Often he is not allowed to reject an application, even one within his discretionary limit, without reference to higher authority. When putting forward an application outside his discretionary limit he is required to set out his customer's requirements on the bank's internal form adding his own comments and recommendations.

Once an advance is granted the position needs to be regularly monitored, responsibility for this usually resting on the lending officer who sanctioned the advance. In the case of a small overdraft, the branch manager will probably keep a watchful eye on how the customer's current account is operated, ensuring that the overdraft limit is not exceeded and that there are no signs of activities likely to operate to the bank's detriment. In the case of medium-term company loans, the bank may require regular reports so that current figures may be compared with those originally estimated to ensure that the progress of the firm is satisfactory and action can be taken if it seems that the bank's position is likely to be damaged.

PERSONAL ASSIGNMENTS

1 Mr Jones, a 19-year old plumber employed by a local building firm, has asked for a personal loan of £450 for two years to enable him to buy a van costing £650. His father will lend him the rest of the money he requires. He is paid by cash weekly and lives at home with his parents. He has had a deposit account at your branch since he began work with his present employers three years ago: present balance £300. Would you grant this loan or refuse the request? Give your reasons.

2 Mary Smith is a 32-year old journalist who has rented a flat in London since taking up her present job with a national newspaper three years ago. She has had a current account at your branch for five years, her monthly salary payment being made direct to this account. She wishes to sell her existing typewriter for £250 and to buy a new electric machine for £800. To do this she has asked for a two-year personal loan of £550. She maintains a balance on her account just sufficient to prevent her having to pay bank charges. What is your decision regarding this application? Give reasons.

3 Miss Torvill calls at your branch with a Mr Dean to seek financial advice and assistance. They explain that they are professional ice skaters and that they are going to establish a company which will produce video cassettes for sale to members of the public interested in viewing ice-skating events. What information would you seek from them?

CHAPTER 9

PAYMENT MECHANISMS

In Chapter 6 we looked closely at money, what it is, what it does, how its value is measured, and how it is created. We saw that its prime function is to act as a medium of exchange, providing the means for payment to be made for the goods and services we buy, whatever their value. In this chapter, we consider the mechanisms which exist to provide channels for different types of money to be used, for making it possible for money to be transferred from one person or organisation to another.

Currency

Banks play a vital part in providing these mechanisms. Notes and coin provide a flexible and easy way for payments to be made and despite much talk of a 'cashless society', these forms of money are likely to remain very important in the years ahead. It is the banks who make this possible. Largely through their branch networks, they receive cash from those with a surplus to their requirements and make it available to those who need it.

Shopkeepers, supermarkets, post offices, and building societies pay their takings into a bank for the credit of their account, sometimes using the *night safe* facilities provided by the bank. This service is particularly useful for a trader who receives large sums of cash after the banks are closed and who for security reasons does not wish to keep it on his own premises. The money is simply placed in a wallet and delivered through a chute accessible from the outside of the branch. A customer can either arrange for the bank to open the wallet and credit his account or he can call at the bank, open the wallet himself, and pay into his account in the normal way.

Some branches regularly receive more cash than they need to meet customer demand whilst others regularly have a cash deficit. Physical movement of cash between branches and bank cash centres therefore takes place, necessitating strict security arrangements. Similar movements occur as banks withdraw torn and worn notes from circulation and replace them with newly printed notes. Seasonal fluctuations in the needs of the public are also met through the banking system. Demand for notes is highest during holiday periods and for Christmas shopping, and bank customers draw more cash than normal from their accounts during these periods. Notes and coin in circulation (part of M_1) therefore show marked seasonal fluctuations.

Probably about ninety to ninety-five per cent of all payments are still made in cash. The clearing banks maintain over 100 cash centres and draw notes from the Bank of England in London and from several large provincial cities. Coin is delivered free of charge to these centres by the Royal Mint, the body responsible for minting the coinage. Scottish banks draw notes from the Bank of England's Newcastle branch whilst in Northern Ireland the Bank of Ireland issues Bank of England notes under an agency agreement. Large value notes are set aside at the Bank of England in London in partial cover of the note issues of banks in Scotland and Northern Ireland.

Cheque Clearings

We have seen that bank deposits form an important part of the money supply. The traditional means for enabling these deposits to be used as a medium of exchange has been by drawing a cheque and handing it to the recipient for payment into a bank for the credit of his account. Assuming both accounts are in credit, the use of the cheque effectively transfers deposits from one person to another. About sixty per cent of all non-cash payments in Great Britain are made in this way and very often the process involves the transfer of funds from one bank to another.

This is not the case if the cheque is paid into an account in the same *branch* as that on which it is drawn. In this case the branch simply credits one account and debits another. In the same way, a cheque paid into an account in the same *bank* as that on which it is drawn leads only to a transfer of funds from one branch to another; another bank is not involved. If, however, the recipient of a cheque has an account with a bank different from that of the drawer, then a transfer of funds has to be made between the banks.

A cheque is an instruction to a banker to pay a sum of money to some person or organisation, that is to a payee. When this payee gives it to a bank for the credit of an account, that bank has to collect the proceeds from the bank on which it is drawn. In the early days, a representative of the collecting banker would present the cheque for payment to the paying bank, settlement being made in cash. As the use of cheques increased, however, it was realised that cash could be saved and put to profitable use if banks struck a balance between the amounts they owed and the amounts due to them so that only *differences* had to be settled in cash.

In due course the banks hired a room in which the exchange could take place and in 1833 a Clearing House was built on its present site in the City of London. The clearing was founded by private bankers in the City and West End and only after a struggle were the new joint stock banks given admittance to the clearing in 1854. The premises in which the Bankers' Clearing House operates belongs to the Bankers' Clearing House Limited which is owned by Barclays, Coutts, Lloyds, Midland, National Westminster, and Williams & Glyn's. Although owned by National Westminster, Coutts operates as a separate bank whilst Williams & Glyn's is part of the Royal Bank of Scotland group. The owners of the Bankers' Clearing House Limited, together with the Bank of England, the Central Trustee Savings Bank, the Co-operative Bank, and the National Girobank, constitute the ten members of the Clearing House.

It is somewhat ironic that the difficulties faced by the joint stock banks in gaining admittance to the clearing in the early nineteenth century have been repeated in recent years as other banks have sought to become members of the Clearing House. By December 1984, the ten existing members had agreed to accept the conclusions and recommendations of a report which opened the way both for other banks, including those from abroad, and institutions such as building societies to become members subject to a number of conditions. These included a willingness to meet the costs involved and an ability to meet minimum volume requirements. The proposed arrangements related not only to cheque clearings but also to other clearings and money transmission systems dealt with later in this chapter.

The report did not cover the cheque and credit clearings of Scotland and Northern Ireland, where separate clearing arrangements operate. Membership of the Scottish clearings comprises the three Scottish clearing banks – Bank of Scotland, The Royal Bank of Scotland, and Clydesdale Bank – and the Trustee Savings Bank Scotland. In Northern Ireland, membership comprises the four banks who form the Belfast Bankers' Clearing Committee – Allied Irish Banks, Bank of Ireland, Northern Bank, and Ulster Bank – and the Trustee Savings

Bank of Northern Ireland.

The Bank of England plays an important part in the Clearing House, for nowadays amounts owing by one bank to another are settled by means of a transfer from one bank's account at the Bank of England to that of another. Banks who are not members of the Clearing House need to use a clearing bank as an agent. Thus an overseas bank or a merchant bank maintains an account with a clearing bank which credits or debits its account in a way similar to those of its other customers.

Until 1858 the only clearing was the *town clearing*. Now there is a *general clearing* as well. The town clearing deals only with cheques of £10,000 and over drawn on City branches within easy reach of the Clearing House. Other cheques pass through the general clearing. Although the *number* of cheques passing through the town clearing is much smaller than that entering the general clearing, the total *value* of cheques dealt with each day is much greater because of the number of financial institutions with large payments to make between them. Because of the large sums of money involved, speedy clearing of cheques is very important.

The town clearing enables cheques to be cleared on the same day. Almost 100 branches of the banks participating in the clearing deliver bundles of cheques to the Clearing House early in the afternoon and once their total value is agreed they are taken to the branches on which they are drawn. Cheques unpaid by paying banks are returned later in the afternoon and the Bank of England credits or debits the banks' accounts for the net amounts due between them for that day.

All other cheques must pass through the general clearing. Cheques due for collection are sorted into bank order and unless drawn on the same branch are sent to the bank's own clearing department. Here all cheques drawn on other banks are amalgamated and exchanged for those drawn upon the bank itself. These cheques, together with those received for collection from its own branches, are then sorted into branch order and sent to the branches on which they are drawn. Each branch therefore receives cheques for payment in the morning – its *in clearing* – and despatches cheques for payment at the end of the day in its *out clearing*. Any unpaid cheques are sent direct to the collecting bank and a claim on it for the amount of the unpaid cheque is transmitted through the general clearing.

The physical movement of cheques around the country, their sorting into bank and branch order, and the reconciliation of their total value and the amount due from one bank to another is clearly an onerous task. In 1977 the London clearing banks estimated that about sixty per cent of their U.K. staff was employed in money transmission services and that the value of the capital resources employed approached £1,000 million. In 1984 the annual cost to the clearing banks of processing domestic payments was estimated at over £2 billion.

A large proportion of non-town clearing cheques are now sent direct to the banks on which they are drawn. Those cheques going to and coming from the Clearing House are carried in small electric vans containing trays full of cheques with dockets attached showing their value. Whilst no doubt this has helped to restrain rising costs, the main saving has been achieved through automation enabling cheques to be sorted and their value computed by electronic means.

This automation has been achieved by the use of magnetic numbering. Cheque books issued to customers are pre-coded using a system of *magnetic ink character recognition* (MICR). At the foot of each cheque, reading from left to right, are characters showing the cheque number, a sorting code number, and an account number. Each branch of each bank has a code number which appears in ordinary print on the top right-hand side of the cheque. When a customer has made out a cheque it is possible to encode the amount of the cheque in magnetic ink in the space left for this purpose on the right-hand side of the cheque. It then becomes possible to use electronic equipment for the clearing process and for debiting customers' accounts through a bank's computerised accounting system. Unfortunately cheques at present have to be sent to the branch of the paying bank since it has to be sure that its customer's signature on the cheque is authentic and that no other defects exist to prevent its payment.

Credit Clearing

The transfer of funds by cheque involves the movement of a debit. But a payment can also be made by a credit. For example, if I have to pay my butcher it has always been possible to pay money into a bank for the credit of his account instead of giving him a cheque. A similar arrangement existed for many years for those with a large number of payments to make, for example an employer making regular salary payments to a large number of employees. Every month the employer would complete credit slips for each of his staff and hand them to his bank. His account was then debited with the total amount to be paid and the credit slips were sent to the branch of the bank where each employee kept his account. Clearly when a credit is used for transferring funds rather than a debit the need for a bank to check that a signature has not been forged is obviated.

In 1960 the banks established a credit clearing so that it would no longer be necessary to send a credit slip individually to each branch concerned. Under these arrangements credits are dealt with in a way similar to cheques. Bundles of credits are despatched by a bank's branches to its clearing department which amalgamates all those for other banks, exchanges them, and receives in return bundles of credits for its own customers. A magnetic code at the foot of a credit enables it to be dealt with by electronic equipment. Settlement of balances between banks takes place each day, that for the town clearing on the day the exchange of cheques took place, that for the general clearing and credit clearing on the following day.

Many accounts can be settled easily by means of a credit slip. For example, a householder receives a quarterly account for telephone services from British Telecom attached to which is a credit slip which he can use for payment by handing it to a bank accompanied by cash or by a cheque drawn on his account.

The National Girobank

A credit slip like that used to credit the account of British Telecom is known as a *bank giro credit*, a name introduced by the banks following the establishment of the National Girobank in 1968. Organisations similar to British Telecom often attach Girobank transfer forms to their accounts for use by customers of the National Girobank. These forms have to be sent to a centre where accounts are maintained on a computer, the transfer of funds simply involving the reduction of a balance on one account and an increase in the balance on another.

The National Girobank operates through branch post offices and not through a separate branch system, although a number of regional centres are being established to help develop closer links with customers. It is managed as a separate business by the Post Office Corporation and pays the Corporation for the use of its 20,000 U.K. post offices and for mailing services. All customers' personal transactions apart from depositing and withdrawing money at post offices are handled by post.

The provisions of the Banking Act do not apply to the National Girobank which is supervised by the Treasury and not by the Bank of England. In many ways the services are the same as those provided by other banks. Both current and deposit accounts may be held but no overdrafts are permitted although current accounts are maintained free of charge. Personal loans, bridging loans to provide finance between the time one house is purchased and another sold, and flexiplan loans are available. Cheques received by a customer of the Girobank are sent to its centre where they are placed to the credit of the customer's account; facilities are also available for a non-customer to pay money into a post office for the credit of a Girobank account. Cheques can also be obtained from the Girobank centre so that payments can be made to someone not holding a Girobank account.

Periodic Payments

National Girobank competes with other banks in providing customers with a standing order or direct debit service. Both are methods for making periodic payments, the first involving the transfer of funds by means of a credit, the second by means of a debit.

A *standing order* is simply an instruction from a customer to a banker to pay a sum of money to another party at stated times for a stated period or until further notice. For example people saving through the national savings yearly plan (page 18) are required to complete a standing order mandate under which their bank makes a monthly payment to the Director of Savings. Each month on the required date the customer's account is debited with the amount due and a credit is passed to the Director's account. If there are no funds on the customer's account and no overdraft arrangements exist then the bank may decide not to make the payment.

The standing order system is satisfactory if the amount to be paid remains unaltered over a period of time but is unsatisfactory if this varies. For example, a person wishing to pay a supplier regularly each quarter for the goods or services he has received cannot use the standing order system as the amount payable is likely to alter each time. Instead, a customer may provide his banker with a mandate to accept *variable direct debits*, which simply gives the bank authority to accept debits to the customer's account for varying amounts. The system is particularly useful for clubs and societies who need to collect a large number of subscriptions each year but who from time to time, particularly when prices are rising, may wish to increase the amount of the annual subscription. If payments are made by standing order it is necessary for each member to instruct his bank to change the amount payable. If payments are made by variable direct debit, however, this is avoided and thus time and expense is saved for the body concerned and its members.

Some bank customers are reluctant to enter into direct debit arrangements feeling that they lose control over the amount being debited to their account. Others may feel that the system is open to abuse. The banks seek to prevent this in two ways: an organisation wishing to use the direct debit system to collect payments can only do so if sponsored by its bankers and it also has to provide an indemnity against any losses arising from debits incorrectly made.

BACS and CHAPS

Two systems have been developed to improve money transmission systems. In the late 1960s the banks introduced a system for making payments by electronic means, thereby obviating the need to use paper. *Bankers' Automated Clearing Services Limited* (BACS), a company owned by the banks, enables customers to transfer funds electronically using a large main-frame computer installation in north-west London.

The types of transactions handled by BACS include wage payments for firms with large numbers of employees, the collection of funds from a multitude of sources under direct debit mandates, and the settlement of bills by an organisation on a regular basis. BACS accepts instructions to make payments and to collect debts by means of magnetic tape, cassettes, or diskettes. Until recently it was necessary for these to be physically delivered to the BACS computer centre but now it is possible to provide transfer instructions by telecommunication links from anywhere in the U.K.

To use the BACS system, a prospective customer must have the facilities for preparing payment information through its own computer system. This can be used to compute the salary payments due to staff or payments to pensioners. An insurance company can collect premiums from policy holders, a firm can make monthly payments of varying amounts to its regular suppliers. Local authorities, government departments, and banks themselves can use the system in the same way as a company. As with other clearing systems, BACS' operations lead to payments between banks. The amounts owing and owed are included in the daily settlement together with the amounts due from the other clearings.

CHAPS, the *Clearing House Automated Payments System*, introduced early in 1984, is a computer-based system allowing payments and settlements to be made on the same day. In due course the new system is likely to replace the town clearing and perhaps in the future may lead to same-day clearing throughout the U.K.

Plastic Cards

Pieces of plastic are now a recognised way of helping payments to be made. A *cheque card*, the simplest example, guarantees payment of a cheque when presented for payment. Banks issue these cards to customers who use them when paying for a purchase by cheque. Provided that the code number on the card is the same as the branch code number on the cheque, that the signature on the cheque agrees with that on the card, and that the card has not passed its expiry date, the cheque will be paid even if funds are not available on the customer's account or the cheque is irregular in some way. The card does not give a customer the right to draw cheques on an account in excess of the balance or of any agreed overdraft limit.

Cheque cards can also be used to cash cheques up to the guaranteed limit. The complete cheque book has to be presented to the bank's cashier and the cheque signed in front of the cashier. Ordinary cheque cards are not available for use outside the U.K. For safety reasons they should be carried separately from the cheque book and the payee of the cheque must write the card number on the back of the cheque.

A *credit card* enables a payment to be made without the use of a cheque. The purchaser of goods or services presents the card in payment and signs a voucher confirming the purchase and the amount due. Those providing the goods or services are reimbursed by the bank issuing the credit card and the customer receives a monthly statement showing details of his purchases and the amount owing. A minimum sum is payable when payment is due but the card holder then has the option of paying the balance immediately or of spreading payments over future months. Interest is charged on any balance outstanding. Credit cards may also be used to obtain a cash advance, interest being charged from the date of the advance until full repayment has been made. When the credit card is received, the holder must sign it so that the signature on sales vouchers can be verified. The card holder may not exceed the credit limit notified at the time the card is issued and may use it only whilst it is valid.

The first credit card was introduced in the U.K. in 1966 by Barclays Bank, this card, the Barclaycard, acting also as a cheque card. Other banks decided to cooperate by introducing the Access card which was issued by the Joint Credit Card Company Ltd, a company established for this purpose by the banks. Both types of card are linked to international systems, Barclays and other U.K. banks to the Visa organisation and Access to MasterCard and Eurocard, both of which have a large number of world-wide affiliated banks thus enabling the cards to be used outside the U.K.

An additional credit card can be issued to any person who is at least 18 years of age providing of course that the credit card account holder agrees. Thus a husband and wife may both have cards. Likewise a company can arrange for employees to be issued with credit cards. In this case, a credit limit is fixed for each card holder as well as an overall limit for the firm. A statement of account is sent to each card holder every month and the company is charged for the total amount due on a monthly basis. The scheme is very useful for a company whose employees incur expenses for which it is responsible. Both the staff and company are provided with a regular record of these expenses and there is no need for the company to provide staff with a cash float. Staff morale may be raised when a company recognises that a member of staff is a suitable person to be a holder of a company credit card.

Cheque cards and credit cards both underwrite to a fixed amount and for a fixed period the credit of a card holder. *Charge cards*, for example those issued by American Express and the Diners Club, are unlike Barclaycard and Access in that an enrolment fee and an annual subscription are payable but no credit limit is specified. Payment of the monthly account has to be made in full and there are no interest charges. Sometimes there are fringe benefits, American Express for example offering free travel accident insurance and a cheque encashment service to its card holders.

Plastic cards are used also for *automated teller machines* (ATMs), which are pieces of equipment designed to perform the work of a bank cashier or teller. The basic function of these machines, which operate under different names in different banks, is to allow a customer to obtain cash. This is done by inserting a plastic card and tapping in a *personal identification number* (PIN). Often these machines can be used for ordering a new cheque book or for asking for an up-to-date statement of account to be supplied. Some machines give the balance of the account and details of recent transactions, others provide a paying-in service.

By the end of 1985 about 7,000 ATMs are expected to be in use in the U.K. A large number are placed in outside walls of bank branches and can thus be used twenty-four hours a day. Some are placed in a special lobby and others in the customer area of a banking hall. Others are installed away from a bank's branches, for example in factories and large stores, thus making it possible to service bank customers at a distance from a branch. Machines are being developed to give a friendly service, to greet a user by name, and to say 'good morning' or 'good afternoon'. There seems no reason why they cannot be programmed to address foreigners in their native language.

By using terminals at the point of sale – *electronic funds transfer at the point of sale* (EFTPOS) – it is possible for goods to be paid for at the time of purchase by an immediate reduction in a balance held on a computer. Schemes enabling banking operations to be conducted from the home are now in existence and these and other developments are undoubtedly changing the nature of banking systems. ATMs and automated processing are often less costly than traditional methods and are being actively developed by many banks. Often these changes are reflected in the scales for bank charges, an automated debit on a current account for example frequently being charged at a lower rate than a cheque drawn on the account.

Building societies, anxious to extend their services, particularly for those without bank accounts, have also introduced ATMs and credit cards, often in cooperation with a bank. British Rail offers a charge card designed for travellers which provides discounts for card holders at hotels, for meals in restaurant cars, and in some cases for car hire charges. Plastic cards every day play an increasingly important part in the transfer of funds.

The Trustee Savings Bank

Trustee Savings Banks developed during the nineteenth century following the establishment of the world's first savings bank in a Scottish village in 1810. Their aim was to encourage thrift by providing a safe home for small savings. Increasingly in recent years the nature of the movement has changed as services have been developed to compete with other banks. Individual banks have been formed into groups and the absence of a legal owner may cease in 1986 and shares may be issued to the general public so that the bank can compete with other banks as a joint stock company.

The Trustee Savings Bank now offers a range of services similar to other banks. Current account facilities are available on which cheques can be drawn and payments made by standing order or by direct debit. Cheque cards are available as well as credit cards linked to the Visa organisation. For travellers abroad foreign currency can be supplied and travellers cheques issued.

International Payments

Travel facilities form part of the banks' services. Notes issued by many overseas countries can be supplied subject to any restrictions on their import imposed by a country. *Travellers cheques* in sterling or other currencies are available in a variety of denominations. These are paid for at the time of purchase and have to be signed in front of the issuing banker. When cashed, the holder countersigns the cheque and the two signatures are compared to check their similarity before payment is made. Travellers cheques provide greater safety than currency. If notes are lost or stolen, little can be done about it. Banks issuing travellers cheques, however, are usually prepared to replace them or to refund the face value of those missing.

Letters of credit can be issued to a traveller to enable him to cash cheques up to an agreed amount and within a prescribed time at overseas banks and both credit cards and special cheque cards can also be used overseas. An alternative arrangement is for a convenient overseas bank to be instructed to pay cash to the traveller or to credit funds to an account for his use.

Instructions are given to overseas banks and received by British banks by mail or telegraphic transfers, the method used depending upon the degree of urgency involved. Nowadays most instructions pass between banks by teleprinter and increasing use is being made of S.W.I.F.T., the *Society for World-Wide Interbank Financial Tele-communications*. This is a cooperative society owned by member banks and registered in Brussels. Members are charged an entrance fee and pay for the use of the service. S.W.I.F.T. is a computer-based system which allows banks to transmit messages quickly. Funds are transferred in this way, and the system can be used for other types of message as well. Many large banks now have computer systems and these, like S.W.I.F.T., have reduced the amount of paper generated.

Large numbers of transfers are made to pay for trade between countries. For example, a bank overseas can be instructed to pay an exporter on application or his account can be credited, the bank advising the exporter when this has been done. Alternatively the bank can provide a draft drawn on a local bank which the recipient can deal with in the same way as he would cheques received from people and firms in his own country.

In order to make transfers possible, banks maintain accounts with *correspondent banks* in other countries. A British bank for example is likely to have accounts with different banks in the U.S. A draft in U.S.

dollars drawn on one of these banks or a S.W.I.F.T. instruction to it to pay someone dollars would result in the reduction in the British bank's dollar balance. The reverse process would occur when the British bank acquired dollars either itself or for its customers. As well as having correspondents overseas, a British bank will also act as a correspondent bank for banks abroad. These accounts are known as *vostro accounts* and correspond to the current accounts of customers held at a branch, the difference being that they are the accounts of overseas banks. Records of the British banks' holdings of currency abroad with its correspondents need to be maintained and the accounts it keeps for this purpose are known as *nostro accounts*. A British bank's nostro accounts are therefore the counterpart of other banks' vostro accounts. A bank needs to keep a careful watch on the currency levels shown by its nostro accounts. For example if holdings of dollar balances become too low because it has sold more dollars to its customers than it has purchased it may need to purchase more dollars in the Foreign Exchange Market, whilst if the balances become too large losses could be suffered if the level of exchange rates moved adversely.

1 What is the maximum sum currently guaranteed by a cheque card in the U.K.?

2 Explain the difference between a cheque card, a credit card, and a charge card.

3 Consider the methods likely to be used by customers when transmitting funds in the year 2000.

4 What risks are involved by banks when dealing in foreign currencies?

5 Give the names of banks currently using general clearing facilities.

6 Explain briefly the current arrangements for clearing cheques and making credit payments in the U.K.

CHAPTER 10

BANKING SERVICES

The essential features of a commercial bank are that it safeguards people's deposits, grants advances to those wishing to borrow, and provides a money transmission service. Traditionally the British commercial banks, notably the London clearing banks, have considered their role to be that of dealing in short-term finance. Deposits were received almost exclusively through current account balances and by seven-day deposits, both of which are effectively payable on demand. Lending, whether by loan or overdraft, was essentially for short periods and the discount of bills of exchange was looked upon with favour since these are self-liquidating, merchandise financed by the discount, for example, being sold to provide funds to meet the bill on maturity.

During the last twenty to thirty years, however, the business of banking has changed and developed. For example, the source of bank deposits has broadened: large sterling deposits are now received from overseas; a high proportion of deposits is taken on a time basis rather than at sight; a large sum is received against certificates of deposit; the inter-bank market provides an important source of deposits. The growth and development of the eurocurrency markets has meant that the figure for sterling deposits of banks in the U.K. is significantly smaller than that for deposits in other currencies.

No longer do the commercial banks consider that short-term lending is their main task. From the early 1970s the clearing banks began to increase greatly their medium-term lending and in recent years long-term finance for house purchase has been offered. Personal-loan schemes were introduced in the late 1950s and have increased in importance since the early 1970s. Providing funds for the finance of specific projects such as the development of North Sea oil and gas, often in foreign currencies, has been of great importance in recent years, as has lending to overseas countries. Banks have developed special units to help specialist needs to be met, for example the needs of small businesses or of those wishing to develop a new enterprise.

As we saw in Chapter 9, developments in the ways in which banks acquire funds and make them available have been accompanied by important changes in the payment mechanisms introduced in recent years. At the same time other services have been introduced and developed with the result that major banks are now often described as financial supermarkets in which a wide variety of financial services can be purchased.

Executor and Trustee Services

In Chapter 1 we saw that a bank is a system for delivering financial services to customers, services involving the granting of credit and services where no credit is involved. Income from the provision of non-credit services is now of great importance for the large banks and is obtained by direct commission or other charges rather than from interest payments on outstanding advances.

What appears to be the oldest of these non-credit services dates from the early years of this century when banks began to establish trustee departments, the purpose of which was to deal with the administration of people's estates. When someone is making a will he has to decide who he wants to deal with his affairs when he dies. He needs a *personal representative* to administer his estate, a person he can trust to carry out his wishes honestly and efficiently. This could be a friend or relation, a solicitor or a *corporate trustee* such as a bank. The advantage of appointing a bank to deal with one's affairs is that it has perpetual succession, that is, one can be sure it will still be there when one dies unlike an individual who could die or be killed before one's own death. The main disadvantage of using a bank for this purpose is that the cost is likely to be a good deal higher than if a solicitor were employed. However, bank trustee departments employ highly skilled staff whose experience is backed by specialist examinations conducted by The Institute of Bankers. It is highly unlikely that cases of fraud would arise or that the bank would fail to make good any loss suffered as a result of an employee's wrongdoing.

The person named in a will to administer an estate is called an *executor*. On the death of the *testator*, that is the person who has made the will, the executor is responsible for making the funeral arrangements and for winding up the estate. He has to collect the deceased's assets and pay any outstanding debts, see to the payment of all taxes owing and becoming due at the time of death, and distributing the balance to the beneficiaries in accordance with the terms of the will. Similar tasks are formed by *administrators* who have to be appointed by a court if there is no will or if there is nobody able or willing to act as executor. This situation might arise for example if the person named as executor in the will has already died or if for some reason he does not wish to act as executor.

Very often a bank will find it has a continuing responsibility as *trustee*, holding some or all of the dead person's property for the benefit of beneficiaries named in the will. For example, a man might wish his widow to receive the interest on the money he has saved, the capital sum being shared by his children when she dies. Again, he may wish to leave some of his money to children or grandchildren but may not wish them to receive it until they reach a certain age, 18, 21 or 25, for example. In these cases the effect of the will is to create a *trust*, the bank taking responsibility for looking after the property and dealing with it in accordance with the terms of the will. This may include the management of investments, a task involving the provision of an adequate income for the life beneficiary whilst protecting the overall value of the investments for the eventual beneficaries.

The provisions of a will are by no means the only ways in which a trust is established; this may be done within a person's lifetime for a variety of purposes. For example, funds could be placed with a bank to be invested in order to provide an income for a mentally handicapped child or for a member of the family or a friend, the objective being to provide an income whilst at the same time preventing the person using unwisely the money put aside for his benefit.

The expertise of the banks in managing trusts and in arranging the investment of trust funds has led them in recent years to develop comprehensive investment services. These can be a complete management service where a bank takes complete charge of a person's savings, arranges for their investment, pays the income direct into that person's bank account, and periodically reviews the *investment portfolio* to see whether changes should be made that will increase income, lead to better capital growth, or result in tax savings. Often the investments are transferred into the name of the bank and held on the customer's behalf. This relieves the customer of a great deal of paper work, since the bank receives notices from companies concerning shareholders' meetings and other matters such as takeover bids and rights issues and deals with them on the customer's behalf. The investment portfolio arranged by the bank takes into account the current needs of its customer – his need for present and future income, the desirability of seeking capital appreciation, and his tax position. For example, the need for income and the tax position of a person is likely to change quite radically upon retirement; a professional woman whose husband is working is likely to have quite different needs if she becomes a widow later in life. Once it has established its customer's requirements the bank will either make changes in the investments on its own initiative or after consultation with the customer.

Remuneration for the bank is likely to be by an annual fee calculated on the market value of the investments at the time the fee is payable. Value-added tax has to be paid in addition to the fee. Banks generally set a minimum figure for the investment portfolio they are prepared to manage, probably on an initial valuation of £25,000.

There are other advantages in allowing a bank to take on the role of executor. Executors cannot administer a person's estate until they have obtained a grant of *probate* and this is not usually issued until capital transfer tax has been paid. There is an obvious difficulty of having to pay tax before it is possible to use the deceased's assets and for this reason banks are frequently asked to make an advance to the executors to enable them to pay the taxes owing, to obtain probate, and then to realise sufficient assets to repay the loan. Where a bank has been appointed executor and investments are held in the bank's name this problem does not arise since the bank can immediately after death realise sufficient assets to pay capital transfer tax and obtain probate.

Some banks offer an extension of their investment management service which can be particularly useful to those in old age. If a person falls ill or is no longer able to manage his affairs, the bank will take over the payment of his bills, pay household expenses, and make any other necessary payments. The income from his investments is used for this purpose and if this proves to be inadequate the bank will arrange to realise the necessary capital.

A customer not requiring the complete management service outlined above can still obtain considerable assistance from his bank. For example, arrangements can be made for interest and dividend payments from a portfolio of stock exchange securities to be made direct to his bank account whilst the bank will hold the certificates of his holdings in *safe custody*. Purchases and sales of stock exchange securities may be made through the bank, which passes the customer's orders to its broker and takes a share of the broker's commission for its services. A bank will normally provide general investment advice but will seek the views of a broker about particular investments and pass these on to the customer. When required, the bank will pass details of a customer's investment portfolio to a broker who will value the investments and make recommendations about its composition, suggesting perhaps that some investments should be sold and replaced by new or increased holdings.

Returning to the role of a bank as a trustee, it should be recognised that the services discussed so far relate to private customers. But banks also act as trustees in other ways. This could arise when a company decides to raise funds by the issue of a *debenture* to the general public, a bank acting as trustee to protect the interests of debenture holders (*see* Debentures, Chapter 14). The duties of the trustee are contained in a *trust deed* usually entered into between the company and the trustee whose main task is to ensure that the company meets its obligations. Where the debenture is secured by a fixed charge over the company's assets, it is likely that the documents of title to these assets will be held by the bank as trustee.

Many of the large banks manage *unit trusts*, another way in which they provide an investment service not only for their customers but for the public at large. We have seen in Chapter 2 that the managers of a unit trust are responsible for the investment policy for each of the trusts they manage. They are one of the parties to a trust deed which is used to establish a trust. The other party is the trustee, who is responsible for holding the trust assets which are divided into units for the public to hold. The task of acting as trustee for unit trusts dates from the 1930s, but the entry of the clearing banks into management dates only from the mid-1960s.

A bank cannot act as trustee for an authorised trust of which it is manager. The role of trustee is laid down in the deed forming the trust, but certain tasks must be specified including that of requiring a unit trust manager to retire if the trustee feels this would be in the interests of the unit holders. The trustee also has to ensure that the requirements of the trust deed are complied with, to examine and approve advertisements and other material produced by the managers, to collect and distribute the income from the trust investments that it holds, and to supervise the maintenance of a register of unit holders.

Banks sometimes act as trustees for *private pension schemes*, receiving the contributions of employers and employees, investing the funds in accordance with the trust deed, and making pension payments to those who have retired. In come cases the bank will be responsible for making investment decisions; in others this will be the responsibility of an investment manager or investment committee.

Banks are frequently asked to act as trustees for a variety of bodies. These are often registered as charities because of tax advantages and sometimes the bank is responsible for the investment of trust funds. These funds are sometimes the result of endowments to universities, art galleries, and other bodies made by a person during his life or by a legacy at his death.

Taxation Services

The taxation services provided by large banks are closely allied to their executor and trustee services, for the way in which investments are made and the provisions made in a will can affect in many significant ways the amount of tax that has to be paid.

The structure of taxation in the U.K. is highly complicated and some people have no desire to spend time and effort dealing with the tax authorities. Sometimes they will ask an accountant or a solicitor to do the work for them, sometimes they turn to their bank. A bank will usually be prepared to give occasional tax advice and will also offer a more comprehensive service on a continuing basis. Usually this service is for the use of personal customers, although sometimes the needs of business customers are catered for.

Taxes are levied on incomes, on expenditure, and on capital. A range of allowances and reliefs can be claimed which reduces the amount of tax payable on income. One task of the bank is to check that the tax authorities have taken full account of all the allowances available and that sources of income have been correctly assessed, whether derived from earnings, property, investments, or other sources.

Capital gains tax is payable on the increased value of certain investments and assessing liability for this tax, taking account of investment losses, is a complex business. Judicious changes in an investment portfolio can reduce the amount of tax payable and there are advantages to a customer if the bank is both looking after his investments and dealing with his taxes.

Another area where a bank's advice can be valuable is with *capital transfer tax* which is payable during lifetime and at death on gifts and transfers to other people. Exemptions and reliefs are available and it is particularly important that the effects of this tax are taken into account when a will is being made. For example, although this tax is not payable when capital passes between a husband and wife, it might be sensible for capital to be left to the children when the first partner dies to reduce the size of the estate subject to tax on the death of the second partner. Likewise, it can be sensible for a person to give some of his capital to his children during his lifetime, again reducing the amount of tax payable after his death.

As well as giving advice on tax matters a bank will also complete and submit a customer's tax returns and will check that the assessment of the amount of tax payable is correct. It will deal with the tax authorities on his behalf in the event of queries or of an overassessment and where necessary will reclaim any overpayments.

Insurance

The insurance industry has a number of branches: life, fire, accident, marine and so on. A distinction can be drawn between the life branch where the term *assurance* is used because it is dealing with events certain to happen such as a person dying or reaching a certain age, and the other branches where the word used is *insurance* since the event insured against may or may not happen. The shouldering of insurance risk is in the main undertaken by *underwriters* at the Corporation of Lloyd's situated in the City of London or by insurance companies. Members of the public cannot deal directly with the underwriters but use the services of a Lloyd's *broker* who seeks the best terms for the client he represents, not only from Lloyd's underwriters but from companies also.

Of the many insurance brokers in the country only a few are Lloyd's brokers. The majority act on behalf of members of the public, giving advice on the best insurance available – not necessarily the cheapest – and arranging for a policy to be issued. The broker in effect is selling to his client the best policy obtainable and is remunerated for his services by commission received from the insurer.

Although the banks had been involved to some extent with insurance for many years, it was not until the early 1960s that the clearing banks took a serious interest in the field of insurance broking. Through subsidiary companies the banks now undertake to arrange insurance of almost every kind, from life assurance to insurance against inclement weather.

Life assurance is an important part of the banks' insurance business, not only because of their function as insurance brokers but also because of their entry into unit trust management. This arises through the existence of unit-linked life policies which, as we saw in Chapter 2, provide that the maturity and surrender value of a policy is determined by the market value of the units to which it is linked.

Instalment Credit

We have already seen the importance of finance houses as providers of credit and the notion of payments by instalments. Hire purchase, credit sale agreements, and conditional sale arrangements constitute the main business of these firms, although a number of them also grant personal loans and accept deposits. Finance is provided for consumers to make it possible for them to buy cars, caravans, motor cycles, and household and other goods. Industrial hire purchase had grown steadily in importance and provides firms with finance to buy fleets of company cars, machinery, and other equipment.

Towards the end of the 1950s the banks became worried by the competition they faced from the finance houses and began to take a financial interest in some of the leading houses whose business in some cases dated back to the nineteenth century. The banks' interest in the houses gradually increased so that today each of the clearing bank groups includes a well-established finance house amongst its subsidiary companies.

Leasing

Leasing is an alternative to the purchasing of assets by instalment credit. Ownership of the assets remains with the leasing company, the *lessor*, while the *lessee* has the use of the assets for which he pays a rental charge.

The banks' involvement in leasing began with the interests they acquired in finance houses which had developed this type of transaction in parallel with their other activities. Through their subsidiaries, the banks have played a leading part in leasing, the demand for which, encouraged by tax advantages, had grown strongly. Cooperation among the subsidiaries has led to the formation of consortia to provide leasing facilities for high-value assets such as ships and aircraft, computers, and even an oil refinery.

Factoring

Factoring is a good example of a bank's mixed service (one which may or may not involve the granting of credit). It involves dealing in some way with the book debts of a company, that is the money owing to it for goods it has sold, its *receivables*.

The service provided may be entirely administrative. The *factor* relieves the firm of the burden of sending out invoices, of keeping a record of the amounts owing to it by its customers, of making sure that the customers pay the firm by the due date, and when necessary of reminding them that they have failed to pay or even in some cases of taking action to recover the debt. This is the non-credit aspect of the service.

Another aspect is when the factor merely purchases the book debts of a company at a discount. This service, known as *invoice discounting*, provides the firm with cash in exchange for its receivables. In this case credit is being provided but the factor leaves all the administrative tasks to the firm concerned.

In a full factoring service, responsibility is taken for all aspects of this part of the firm's business. The factor not only relieves the firm of the administrative burden of looking after its receivables but also purchases the debts, thus shouldering the risk to the firm that payments may not be made. Since the factor is assuming the credit risk, he takes responsibility for credit control, assesses the credit risk, and decides what amount of credit will be allowed by the firm to individual customers by establishing a *credit intelligence service* for this purpose. It is likely that a purchaser of goods is a debtor to a number of firms for whom the factor is acting and he must therefore establish a system to measure the risk that this purchaser may not be able to pay a number of firms who are the factor's clients. The availability of computers to handle the factor's administrative tasks makes it easier for him to discover the extent of the risk he is bearing in each case.

The development of factoring in the U.S. encouraged the clearing banks to develop this service which is conducted by specialised subsidiaries within the banking groups. Since the late 1960s these subsidiaries have developed international factoring operations in a number of ways. For example, offices opened in other countries have sought to provide a local service for firms similar to that offered at home. Factoring of sales in overseas markets has been developed and operates in a way similar to that for domestic sales with the added complications of assessing credit-worthiness, dealing with import duties, and similar problems. Sometimes too a U.K. factor will provide a factoring service for a bank overseas. Thus it is possible for the receivables of a firm in the U.S. to be purchased or discounted through its own bank by the factoring house subsidiary of a bank in London.

A system of trade finance for exporters similar to a factoring service has also been developed in recent years. Known as *forfaiting*, it involves the purchase by a forfaiter of the trade debts of an exporter without any right of recourse against the exporter. In other words, the forfaiter assumes all commercial, political, and other risks that payment will not be received by the exporter. The exporter is able to compete in overseas markets by offering his goods on credit but by using forfaiting his sales are converted into cash transactions.

Merchant Banking

Following the clearing banks' move into merchant banking and the development during the 1970s of financial services not previously regarded as part of their business, the distinction between merchant and other banks has become less precise. We have seen in Chapter 3 how merchant banking developed from the provision of acceptance credit facilities into other areas of activity. The clearing banks, usually through subsidiary companies, now compete with the older merchant banks by providing financial advice to companies, assisting them in obtaining capital resources, and playing an active part in investment management. They help provide finance through the use of acceptance credits as well as through *loan syndication*, a technique used when a group of banks, often from different countries, come together to provide large loans on a joint basis.

In the past it could have been said that merchant banks were good at planning a financial package whilst commercial banks had the financial strength to supply funds to enable the package to become effective. This no longer applies to merchant banking arms of the clearing banks whose vast resources can be drawn on to back up the advice they have given. In addition, they can also draw upon the wide range of specialist services offered by other parts of the banking group. Business can be found not only by the direct efforts of the merchant banking subsidiary but also through the parent bank's introduction of commercial banking customers.

International Services

The development of banking as an international business has been recognised by The Institute of Bankers through the introduction of an International Banking Diploma containing three specialist inter-national banking examinations. Major banks now conduct their business in the major countries of the world and participate in the international capital and money markets. The range and complexity of international banking services have changed radically in recent years and would no doubt surprise those who established the clearing banks' foreign branches and departments in the early years of this century.

Many of the original services remain, for example, bills of exchange and shipping documents relating to the country's imports and exports are dealt with and the banks are major dealers in foreign currencies. Overseas travellers also enjoy extensive help from the services available – the banks supply travellers with foreign notes and coin and travellers cheques (also called travel cheques) and will obtain or renew their passports. Despite the introduction of cheque and credit cards available for use overseas, arrangements can still be made for the issue of a *letter of credit* to enable the traveller to cash cheques abroad. Funds can also be sent to a bank for the customer to draw on as he wishes.

Bank travel services are of value to both holidaymakers and business people. *Letters of introduction* provided by a bank are likely to be of particular use to the latter, enabling them quickly to meet members of the local business community including representatives of the Chamber of Commerce. Exporters can sell their foreign currency earnings to a bank for sterling whilst importers can satisfy their currency needs through a bank. Through its dealings in the foreign exchange market, a bank can arrange for these transactions to take place immediately or at a future date.

Where an exporter has a well-established and trusting relationship with an importer he may well be prepared to deal with him on *open account*, whereby payment at the appropriate time is received by means of a draft or the transfer of funds from the importer's bank. He may as an alternative draw a bill on the importer payable at a later date and, after acceptance, either hold the bill until maturity at which point he can arrange for the bank to collect the proceeds, or, if he requires funds immediately, sell the bill to the bank at a discount. For greater safety he may draw a documentary bill on the importer, specifying that the documents attached to the bill to enable the importer to have possession of goods will be released either when he accepts the bill or when he pays it.

As a greater safeguard, the bill may be drawn under a *documentary credit*. One way in which this might be used is for the importer to arrange for his bank to pay for the goods once it receives documents of title to the goods. The importer's bank notifies a bank in the exporter's country who will inform the exporter of the arrangement. The correspondent bank, acting as agent for the importer's bank, may *confirm* the credit, thus undertaking that it will pay the exporter for the goods when the correct documents are received. The exporter has the comfort of knowing that a bank in his own country has guaranteed payment against the documents for the goods he is exporting. The credit may be *revocable* or *irrevocable* and the safest means of safeguarding himself against non-payment by the importer is when the exporter is able to arrange for payment to be made by an irrevocable, confirmed documentary credit.

These payment and finance services provided by the banks oil the wheels of international trade through the help given to both exporters and importers. An additional service of particular help to exporters is provided by the close relationship that exists between the banks and the *Export Credits Guarantee Department* (ECGD), a government body established in 1919 to assist exporters. The ECGD has two main functions: firstly, it provides the exporter with insurance against loss arising from default by the importer, restrictions by a country on currency transfers, or the cancellation of import licences; secondly, it guarantees banks against loss arising through loans made either to the exporter (*supplier credit*) or to the overseas buyer (*buyer credit*). Amongst its other services is the insurance for new investment overseas against losses arising from war, expropriation, and restrictions on currency transfers.

ECGD also provides support for the issue of *performance bonds*. This is a bank guarantee provided on behalf of an exporter of capital goods, such as the provision of oil refinery facilities, that its customer has the financial resources to complete a contract and that he will comply with its terms. Sometimes when a customer is seeking a contract from overseas the bank will be required to provide a *tender* or *bid bond* guaranteeing that if the contract is awarded the customer will enter into it and comply with the terms of the tender. When the contract specifies that the buyer is to make advance payments to the bank's customer as different stages of the contract are completed, the buyer may require a *bank guarantee* to protect him from loss if the whole contract fails to be completed.

The development of the eurocurrency markets has given an added dimension to the banks' services. Lending to another bank is usually on a short-term basis, whilst that to commercial customers is normally for two to five years or longer. Medium-term loans are usually granted on a *roll-over* basis, the rate of interest charged being adjusted in line with market rates every three or six months. The rate charged is usually fixed in relation to the *London Inter-Bank Offered Rate* (LIBOR), thus protecting the banks against adverse movements in market rates.

During the 1960s and 1970s a market developed in *eurobonds* as a complement to the eurocurrency markets and which enables money to be lent for longer periods. Eurobonds are issued by the large international banks and held by investors or as part of a bank's investment portfolio. The bank responsible for the issue, the *management bank*, is joined by other banks who agree to participate in raising the finance and thus serve as underwriters to the issue.

Other Bank Services

The range of bank services is too large to be considered adequately in one chapter, or even in one book. For example, investment information is only one type that banks make available. All the clearing banks publish a regular review, often containing articles of interest to readers as well as up-to-date statistical information and comment on current economic conditions. Regular surveys of the economy are also published as well as reports on many overseas countries. Often banks are prepared to help customers by providing a special report on conditions in the home and overseas markets for a particular product. They will also obtain status reports in response to enquiries about the financial standing of someone with whom a customer wishes to deal, a useful service to exporters as well as to those considering a domestic transaction. To answer such enquiries a bank normally seeks information from another bank, although sometimes it will use the services of a *credit reference agency*. Likewise, a bank will provide a status report on one of its customers if it receives a request from another bank.

We have seen some of the many ways in which a bank is able to reduce its customers' administrative burdens, for example by providing an investment or factoring service. In some cases the banks have used their investment in computers to help customers. Some of these services are related closely to their money transmission services, others are not. Thus a bank might provide a *payroll service* under which it calculates the amount of pay due to each member of a firm's staff after allowing for such things as tax and national insurance payments. The account of each employee is credited automatically at the due date and payslips are prepared for each employee showing the amount of earnings less deductions that has been paid to his account.

Bank *computer bureau* services can assist customers in other ways. Tapes can be produced showing details of credits received and cheques paid which a firm can then reconcile with its own accounting records. Arrangements can be made for the bureau to record all a firm's purchases and sales and to maintain stock-control records. Specialised services are often provided for stockbrokers, solicitors, accountants, building societies, and retailers.

Many banks act as *registrars* for companies. They maintain stock or share registers, dealing with transfers and keeping the register up to date. Certificates are issued by the bank to new investors, interest and dividend payments are made at the appropriate times, the firm's annual report and accounts are circulated, and the bank prepares the returns needed by law on the firm's behalf.

The clearing banks' aim of providing a large range of services has led one to acquire a travel agency and another to establish a chain of estate agents. More recently, links have been forged with stockbrokers and stockjobbers.

PERSONAL ASSIGNMENTS

1 What benefits can be obtained by a company and its employees from a bank's company credit card scheme?

2 Explain the advantages and disadvantages to a company of using leasing as a means of obtaining additional equipment for its factory.

3 In what ways has the development of hire purchase assisted U.K. residents to raise their standard of living?

4 How can a bank help a customer who has won £25,000 as a premium bond prize?

5 Why must probate be obtained when a person dies? What action would you need to take if a close relative died without having made a will?

6 Under what circumstances would you find a bank acting as trustee?

CHAPTER 11

MARKETING BANK SERVICES

A bank which believes that the way to increase its profitability is to discover the needs of its customers and prospective customers and which then sets about satisfying these needs as effectively as possible can be said to be *marketing orientated*. We saw in Chapter 1 that a bank may be regarded both as a system for delivering a range of services, usually financial, and as a system for earning profits. To produce an output of services, inputs are required which must be brought together as effectively as possible to maximise profits. Profits are determined by the difference between earnings produced from the services supplied and the cost of providing them.

Marketing and the Corporate Plan

A bank which year after year produces the same range of services is likely to be less successful than one which attempts to assess the likely change in demand for its products, to decide what new products might be a success, and perhaps sets about creating a market for a new service based on an original idea. Failure to adopt this type of approach may continue for many years with no noticeable bad effects on a bank's profits, although within a highly competitive system it would be unwise to rely on such an outcome. In any case, a more dynamic approach is likely to yield results superior to those that might otherwise have been achieved. *Marketing* needs to be seen as an integral part of management and hence of corporate planning. Marketing means more than *selling*, although selling is an important part of it.

A bank's corporate plan may include as an objective the introduction of a new service. But this is only the starting point. Decisions have to be made concerning the input of resources needed to commence and to develop this service. Who is to be responsible for its satisfactory introduction? What office accommodation and equipment will be needed? How many staff are required and where will they come from? What qualifications and experience do they need? What training programmes are needed to develop staff expertise so that the new service can be operated effectively? What is the precise nature of the system that has to be developed to produce the service? These questions and others have to be answered and may in turn lead to a series of other questions. New accommodation may be required: where should it be? Is existing space available and suitable? Should premises be hired or purchased? Will it be necessary to build accommodation and how long will it take? It may be necessary to recruit new staff to the bank: is it necessary to advertise for specialist staff? Can staff be selected from those normally seeking employment by the bank? Should universities and polytechnics be visited to recruit staff? Will it be necessary to attract experienced staff from other firms and how should this be done?

Marketing Strategy

Before considering its objectives, a bank needs to be aware of its current situation. For example, it needs to know how it compares with its competitors, whether its share of deposits is rising or falling, whether the level of its advances is changing in line with that of other banks, what changes in market share are taking place for each of the services it offers.

As part of this evaluation process, it may seek to assess its likely position at the end of the planning period on the assumption that its present policies remain unchanged. Some *market research* may be carried out to test the strength of demand for existing and new services. *Attitude surveys* may be conducted in an attempt to discover what people think about the bank, about its services in general, or about particular services.

A bank can then set about the task of defining its objectives based on this information. It may decide that a more active lending policy is needed or that a drive to obtain more deposits should be a prime objective. It may know that it is well ahead of competitors in providing a particular service and decide to build on this strength in the expectation that there are good prospects for increasing its market share. On the other hand, it may seek to improve its position in areas where it knows it has weaknesses.

In developing its strategy, it is essential for it to know which of its services are currently the most profitable. It may find that the cost of developing a particular service will be less than the additional revenue obtained from it and therefore decide to allocate additional resources to its development. If a service is generating low profits or even making a loss, its development is likely to be given a low priority or if possible it may even be withdrawn. On the other hand, a different view might be taken if it can be shown to contribute to the profitability of other services. Thus a bank may encourage people to use its executor and trustee services not because they are particularly profitable in their own right, but because they generate demand for another profitable service such as investment management.

Market Segmentation

One aspect of marketing strategy is to consider for whom a service is designed. For example, a drive to increase lending might be tackled in a number of ways: by attempting to increase the amount of money lent for house purchase, to raise the amount advanced by personal loans, or to raise the level of advances to the corporate sector. The market for each kind of advance is different, requires a different approach, and will vary in profitability and the risk involved. A decision to increase lending to the corporate sector will lead the bank to consider whether the best approach would be to tackle industrial concerns, the service industries, financial institutions and so on. If it wishes to lend more to industry it might well consider which industrial sectors offer the best prospects.

Only when the bank has established clearly what it wants to do can it decide how to set about doing it – where it will advertise, for example, and what form the advertising will take. A good example of marketing strategy is provided by the banks' desire to obtain the accounts of school-leavers. It is generally felt that a young person who opens an account with a bank is likely to continue as a customer in later years. Those entering higher education may be expected to earn good salaries in years to come and are particularly attractive as potential customers. Brochures advertising a bank's services are likely to start appearing just before the commencement of the college year; posters appear in student common rooms; press advertising commences. Special offers may be made such as free banking services, and sometimes free gifts of use to students are offered to those who open an account. Obviously, the services most likely to interest a young person, such as the bank's travel services, are emphasised. It would be silly to try to sell trustee, and investment services, factoring and leasing in this market.

Specialised packages of services are also offered to other markets – to the elderly, to women and so on. Many banks now employ specialist staff to look after different industries. For example, the clearing banks have established specialist units to help in understanding the needs of farmers, to assist them with their financial problems, and to give advice and help to branch managers and lending officers when required. The problems and needs of small businesses have also been recognised by the clearing banks, who have established special advisory units to service this segment of the market.

Delivering Bank Services

It is important that bank staff know what services they should be selling. There is little point in having a corporate plan which sets out a bank's policy unless those concerned with its implementation know about that part of the plan that directly affects them. For example, a bank may decide that a particular service is unprofitable and that whilst it is not possible to withdraw it, it would nevertheless like to see the service reduced. Obviously if a branch manager does not know this he could spend a large proportion of his time trying to sell the service, a situation which he might consider to be sensible but which in fact is operating to the bank's disadvantage.

Suppose that a bank has decided that its aim is to increase its advances by ten per cent during the following year. Targets may be set for each region in which the bank operates and although these might differ, overall the bank will expect to attain the desired increase. Regional targets may be broken down so that each branch knows what it is expected to contribute. A branch manager may then be completely free to decide how he is to achieve the desired increase – by seeking to raise the level of personal loans outstanding, or by trying to obtain the increase by a different path. The tactics to be adopted will probably be left to the manager since he is the person who should have an intimate knowledge of the area served by his branch. He will be best able to evaluate any changes that are taking place and to decide how he can best take advantage of opportunities offered for profitable development of the business in line with the bank's planning objectives.

The manager of a branch may have a more general target – possibly to increase the profits of the branch by a set amount. Even if no target is set for him, he may well wish to establish his own goal to work towards. He may know, for example, that a new building development near his branch will in due course be used for office accommodation with shops at street level. He will realise that here may be opportunities for new business, not only from the firms moving into the new premises but also from their employees. His skill as a good marketing person will be demonstrated by his success in devising tactics that enable him to generate higher profits from the opportunities now open to him.

In more general terms, a branch manager needs to be aware of the advantage of *cross-selling*. For this he must have good product knowledge. He must know as much as possible about the range of services the bank is able to provide. Whilst it would be unrealistic to expect him to have expert knowledge of each service, he should know enough to understand the circumstances in which it might be of interest to a customer or potential customer. Thus he should ensure that when somebody is enquiring about buying travellers cheques, the bank's other travel services are mentioned – for example travel insurance, or, if the bank has a travel agency the services it can provide. When speaking to a customer who is about to retire, he may raise the question of a will and point out the advantages of appointing the bank as executor. He may suggest that the bank would be happy to provide an investment service and suggest ways in which the bank could help by giving tax advice or taking over the problems of preparing returns and negotiating with the tax authorities. It might be appropriate to draw attention to the different unit trusts managed by the bank or to offer the bank's help if the customer is thinking of selling his house.

In many cases there is no direct contact between the manager and branch customers and it is important that staff generally are marketing orientated. Often the role of the manager will be to introduce customers to an expert on the bank's staff who can give detailed information about a particular service. Sometimes with a business enterprise it may be necessary for a meeting to be arranged with senior bank staff who are able to advise the company on financial matters such as the raising of new capital. In some banks, account executives have the task of looking after the financial needs of a number of companies, cross-selling the bank's corporate services whenever possible.

Although for normal purposes a bank customer has no need to visit the branch where his account is kept, the geographical spread of a bank's branch network is still important, convenience being a major factor in determining with which bank an account will be opened. The importance of the overseas branch network is clear, a base in one or more major cities of another country being necessary if a bank is to compete successfully with local institutions. In a number of cases clearing banks have purchased banks with established branch networks in other countries, the outcome of which, at least in the short term, has not always been very happy.

Sales Promotion

A good deal of thought must be given by a bank as to the best way in which it is to sell its services. Its *pricing strategy* is one aspect requiring careful consideration. For example, the practice of allowing current account customers a free banking service only if a minimum credit balance is maintained can lead to customer annoyance if too rigidly applied. If the balance falls below the required minimum by a small amount for only a day or two, the charge levied can be very high if a large number of items have passed through the account and the customer may well resent paying this charge, particularly if the average balance has been greatly in excess of the minimum required. Differentials in interest rates charged to different categories of borrowing customers are likely to reflect the risks involved as well as the cost of managing an advance. Thus the rate of interest charged on a small personal loan may well be higher than for a large advance to a major, well-established, 'blue-chip' company, despite the fact that no security has been taken. The granting of free account facilities to students is an example of a pricing strategy designed to capture new accounts – a strategy which might also be applied if a bank wishes to establish demand for a new service quickly.

In determining the price to be charged for new and existing services a range of factors has to be considered. A low initial price for a new service may be sensible if other banks are already providing that service and the aim is to penetrate the market. On the other hand if the new service faces no competition, a high price may be set to generate good profits even if at a later date emergent competition means that the price has to be lowered. In some cases a high price may be charged if the bank does not wish to develop a service; in others the strategy may be to charge what the market will bear. For example, a customer may be prepared to pay handsomely for a service which enables him to obtain big savings on his tax payments. A difficulty faced by banks is to differentiate their products. Thus the standard of service of one clearing bank is usually very similar to that of another and there are few obvious differences in the efficiency of a particular service offered. It follows that in framing a pricing strategy a bank needs always to consider how the other banks will react to the decisions it makes.

Another aspect of sales promotion to be considered is the bank's *advertising strategy*. Is a new service to be brought to the attention of customers only or of customers and non-customers alike? If *test marketing* to see how people react to the new service is planned, possibly in one part of the country only, is the advertising to be on a local basis or is there merit in letting a wider public know what is happening? Another point for consideration is what means are to be used. Are there to be advertisements in magazines, the daily, or weekly press? Are they to appear in the popular press, in quality newspapers, or only in financial journals and newspapers? What about radio and television? Are there to be posters on public hoardings or in the bank's branches? Will brochures be prepared and where are these to go?

Those responsible for the bank's advertising are likely to have a shrewd idea of the effectiveness of its various possible forms. They should know the best method of putting a message over to different groups of people. Almost certainly they will have to operate within a budget, possibly with sums allocated for particular purposes. Services with little growth or profit potential are unlikely to be allocated a budget but may perhaps benefit from general advertising designed to keep the name of the bank in the public mind and to present a desirable image: 'the friendly bank', 'the listening bank', 'the helpful bank', 'the caring bank', 'the action bank', etc.

Packaging, a term more likely to be associated with goods than services, is an important consideration for a bank anxious to promote its business. This is the 'silent salesman' aspect of marketing. For example, a credit card should be attractive to look at and easy to use. The same should also apply to the bank's cheques. Standardised, aesthetically pleasing headed stationery should be used and the bank's chosen symbol – its logo – should appear frequently inside and outside its branches and offices, on its promotional literature, and in its advertising material. Frequent and easy recognition of the bank will keep it constantly in the public mind.

Public Relations

Local branch managers and their staff play a key role in promoting a bank's image. A friendly, efficient service probably does more to enhance a bank's profitability than the largest of advertising budgets. The image is easily damaged. The person who calls at a branch to report the sudden death of his mother who had an account there is unlikely to be very impressed when simply asked somewhat brusquely the number of her account. A word of sympathy would help.

The way in which the telephone is answered and how the call is dealt with does much to affect a bank's image. Long queues are harmful and as a famous banker said many years ago, 'There are few things that try a man's temper more than to be kept waiting at a banker's counter'. Sensitivity to the differing views and attitudes of customers is an essential part of public relations. The ability to refuse an advance without upsetting a customer is evidence of a good manager. It is more tactful for a clerk to tell a customer that he will do his best to obtain the needed foreign currency in five days than simply to tell him that he will have to wait a week. The part played by a manager and branch staff in community affairs and the respect they have earned will go far in determining how that community regards the bank.

A bank's public relations can be improved in many other ways, for example by the way in which senior staff are regarded by national leaders – whether statesmen and politicians or leaders of the business community. Good working relationships with the press and television organisations should help to create an understanding of what the bank is trying to achieve, even if comment by the media is not always friendly. Well-prepared press releases will help to generate sympathetic understanding whilst openness about the bank's activities will help to earn it respect.

Sponsorship of sporting, artistic, and other events assists in keeping the name of the bank before the public and in promoting a favourable image. The provision of funds to enable higher education institutions to conduct teaching and research supports the drive to obtain students' accounts, an aim sometimes assisted by providing prizes, bursaries or scholarship awards.

Branches are often encouraged to participate in local community activities and at the national level some banks release staff, often on full pay, to assist voluntary charitable organisations or to serve on committees of enquiry. Bodies established to assist those wishing to start in business are sometimes assisted by staff seconded from a bank.

At both national and local levels speakers from banks frequently address meetings, whilst bankers are often interviewed on radio or television when financial or economic events are in the news.

Bank Marketing

In the past bankers rather disliked the notion of marketing, often regarding it as 'touting for business'. Some no doubt retain this attitude and would rather be regarded as professionals prepared to offer their services to those who ask for them. However, as we have seen, the selling function is only part of what is meant by marketing, although selling bank services is recognised as crucial to the success of a bank in today's highly competitive environment.

It is bad marketing if a commercial customer feels that his bank does not understand his business or appears not to be interested in his problems or in what he is seeking to achieve. The banker needs to be able to discuss intelligently with a customer his business accounts and how the business is likely to progress in the future. Sympathy and understanding are part of good marketing.

Some years ago the bank manager was seen as a general practitioner of the financial world, his role in the modern world being described as follows: 'Look at his job. He has long had to run an office efficiently, to advise on personal financial problems, to judge credit risks and to sort out companies' balance sheets. Now he is expected to act as salesman for the bank too. Yet he has virtually no training – bar experience – for the job.' (McRae, H. and Cairncross, F. *Capital City: London as a Financial Centre*, Eyre Methuen, 1973.) Since those words were written, big efforts have been made to improve the situation. Training programmes have been adjusted to take account of changing conditions and requirements and steps have been taken to provide branch managers with back-up facilities to make their job easier.

PERSONAL ASSIGNMENTS

1. A reporter from a local newspaper tells you he has been told to prepare 'profiles' of leading figures in the community for publication in his paper over the next three months. He is calling to see you next week. What would you do?

2. Which bank in your local High Street is most prominent? Why is this?

3. Provide a critical survey of bank advertisements appearing in the national press at the present time.

4. What is meant when a bank is said to be marketing orientated?

5. Prepare a report showing how a bank could best seek to obtain the business of school-leavers.

6. What factors have to be considered when deciding what to charge for a bank service?

7. Do you think that branch managers should be required actively to solicit business within the community?

8. What arrangements would you make when asked to provide an 'open day' for children from local schools?

CHAPTER 12

THE LEGAL FRAMEWORK

A bank, like any other business, operates within a legal framework and those responsible for its operation must ensure that its activities come within the law of the lands in which it operates. If incorporated in the U.K. under the Companies Acts, it must comply with rules governing the way in which meetings of shareholders have to be convened and registers of shareholders maintained. It must ensure that the required returns to the Registrar of Companies are made at the correct times and that the necessary disclosures are made when its accounts are published.

In addition to these and other rules derived from the way in which it is incorporated, a bank as an employer must also take account of legislation covering terms of employment, dismissal, and working conditions of employees including rules governing their health and safety. It will also need to be aware of what is required under the law covering taxation, national insurance schemes, and the operation of pension funds as well as under other branches of the law which impinge on its work.

In Chapter 1 we saw that a bank needs to take account of the law and of any changes that are taking place when it is establishing its corporate plan and deciding how it is to operate in the future. In particular, it must be aware of changes in the way the Bank of England supervises the banking system under the Banking Act.

The Banking Act, 1979

In 1975 the U.K. government announced its intention of introducing legislation to control the operations of institutions taking deposits from the general public or from the wholesale money markets. The Bank of England had operated for many years a system of prudential supervison and its supervisory role, although not deriving from statute, was for a long time accepted throughout the primary banking sector. However, the serious banking crisis which started in late 1973 and which led to the Bank of England's 'lifeboat' operation to safeguard deposits of the general public made it clear that the so-called secondary banks had largely escaped the supervisory net. Although the 'lifeboat' operation was effective in securing the viability of the banking industry and in preventing loss to depositors, the government felt that deficiencies needed rectifying. It was also necessary to meet an E.E.C. directive on bank supervision.

Until 1979 the U.K. was probably the only country with a highly developed banking system with no system of comprehensive supervision under a banking statute. Passage of the Banking Act in that year changed this. From now on it was no longer possible for banks or other financial institutions to accept deposits without the prior authorisation of the Bank of England. Building societies, the National Savings Bank, and local authorities were among those exempt from the Act's provisions. Non-exempt bodies were prevented from taking deposits unless they were *recognised banks* or *licensed deposit-takers* (LDTs).

To acquire the status of a recognised bank, an institution must have enjoyed for a reasonable period a high reputation within the financial community. It must provide in the U.K. either a wide range of banking services or a highly specialised banking service. The banking services offered fall into the following categories:

1. Current or deposit account facilities in sterling or foreign currency.

2. Provision of finance by overdraft or loan in sterling or foreign currency.

3. Foreign exchange services for domestic and foreign customers.

4. Finance through bills of exchange and promissory notes together with foreign trade and documentation in connection with foreign trade.

5. Financial advice.

The Bank of England has the power to decide whether an institution is providing a wide range of services, and in particular to disregard the fact that an institution is not providing one or two of the services in categories 3 to 5.

A recognised bank providing a wide range of banking services must have a minimum of £5 million net assets, that is its paid-up capital plus reserves. At least two individuals must direct the business of the institution which must be conducted with integrity and prudence and with those professional skills consistent with the range and scale of the institution's activities.

In the case of a licensed deposit-taker, the required minimum net asset figure is £250,000. Every person who is a director, controller, or manager must be a fit and proper person to hold that position and at least two individuals must effectively direct the institution's business.

A recognised bank is allowed to describe itself as a bank, whereas a licensed deposit-taker may not do so. However, if its principal place of business is overseas it may include the word 'bank' in its title providing that it is used in immediate conjunction with the description 'licensed deposit-taker'. Where the title appears in writing, these words must be at least as prominent as those of the title.

Passage of the Act resulted in the U.K. having for the first time a policy of deposit protection. In 1982, a *Deposit Protection Board* was established with power to levy contributions from recognised banks and licensed deposit-takers in amounts ranging from £2,500 to £300,000. The funds collected are placed with the Bank of England for investment and can be drawn on to compensate members of the public for loss of deposits due to failure of a supervised institution. The scope of the scheme is modest, compensation being limited to seventy-five per cent of the first £10,000 of any one deposit.

An institution seeking recognised banking or licensed deposit-taker status is required to answer a questionnaire which among other things requires a statement of aims and programme of operations including the types of business it plans to conduct. Balance sheet projections are required as well as details of the structural organisation of the institution. A list has to be provided of all directors, controllers, and managers indicating, by reference to the definition contained in the Act, the sense in which persons are controllers. Confirmation is required that at least two individuals effectively direct the business and their names and positions within the organisation have to be given. Directors, controllers, and manager are required to answer a personal questionnaire designed to discover their suitability for the posts they hold.

Apart from assessing the quality of management, the Bank of England's main method of supervision is to monitor the capital adequacy and liquidity of the institutions for which it is responsible. In the case of adequacy of capital, the need is to ensure that the capital position is acceptable to depositors and other creditors and that it is sufficient in relation to the risk of losses that could be sustained. The Bank assesses the capital adequacy of each regulated institution on the basis of the nature of the business conducted and its profitability record. No precise ratios are prescribed, but a view of each individual institution is taken and discussed with those concerned with its management.

The importance of liquidity for a banker cannot be over-emphasised and it is therefore not surprising that the Bank of England pays great attention to this aspect of banking business in its monitoring system. It does this on a cash flow basis (page 110), looking at a bank's possible inflow and outflow of money during different time periods, ranging from eight days onwards. Thus when it considers the next eight days in a bank's life the Bank of England will compare the amount of deposits that could be withdrawn during that time with the amount of cash that might be available to meet customers' demands.

The Bank of England's objective is to ensure that the management policies of the institutions for which it is responsible result in a prudent mix of various forms of liquidity appropriate to their circumstances and that management-control systems are able to ensure that these policies are sustained at all times. The Bank likes to work in cooperation with institutions to safeguard the banking industry. The main change since 1979 is that its authority is now backed by act of Parliament.

The Consumer Credit Act, 1974

The *Consumer Credit Act* is designed to regulate credit agreements where the amount involved is within prescribed limits. Under the Act's conditions, all agreements to advance money to individuals, sole traders, and business partnerships by means of hire purchase, a conditional or credit sale, or by personal loan must be in writing. A licence to do so is required from the Director-General of Fair Trading, the absence of which makes it a criminal act to trade in credit. This applies to banks, finance houses, money-lenders, and others who provide credit, as well as to those who introduce consumers to suppliers of finance.

The Act and the regulations made under its authority control the content of credit advertising, prohibit the unsolicited provision of credit cards, and make it an offence to send documents to minors (those aged under 18) inviting them to borrow money or to obtain credit facilities. It is an offence also for traders to call at people's home to sell goods or services on credit (unless this is permitted by the licence), or to call on potential customers to offer them loans unless invited. Moreover this invitation must be in writing.

'*Truth-in-lending*' is a central feature of the legislation and this applies in particular to the cost of borrowing. Borrowers must be in a position to know the true cost of borrowing as indicated by the *annual percentage rate* (APR), thus enabling them if they wish to compare borrowing costs from different sources.

The '*equal liability*' provisions of the Act means that a bank's credit card company can be liable for loss if a supplier of goods or services is guilty of misrepresentation or fails to complete an order either because it breaks the contract or goes out of business. The same principle applies if credit arrangements are made by means of a personal loan and it is clear therefore that the Act, often regarded as too complex, is of great importance to bankers.

The Fair Trading Act, 1973

This Act established the *Office of Fair Trading* and granted wide powers to its Director-General for consumer protection. It is the Director-General who is empowered to grant licences under the Consumer Credit Act and it is his office or a local authority's trading standards department which takes legal action when rules are broken.

However, the Office of Fair Trading is also concerned with other aspects of consumer protection, some of which may be of importance to bankers or their customers. For example, it may take legal action if a manufacturer tries to force retailers to sell his goods at a minimum price or if people try illegally to restrict competition, for example by agreeing to fix the prices of the goods or services sold. The Office has important functions regarding monopolies and mergers and may take steps to arrange for the *Monopolies and Mergers Commission* to investigate and report on whether or not a proposal is in the public interest.

The Bank's Customers

A banker has to deal with many types of customer varying from individuals to major international corporations. A number of things can happen to them, for example they may die, cease to be able to manage their own affairs, or become bankrupt. A firm may go into liquidation or winding-up proceedings may be brought against it. In these and other situations the banker has to know what to do, whether the customer has a credit balance on his account or has been borrowing from the bank.

When somebody opens an account with a bank a contractual relationship is formed, the bank and the customer having rights and responsibilities that have been established over many years. A *contract* is merely an agreement that is enforceable by law and may or may not need to be in writing. Thus, as we have seen, the Consumer Credit Act requires that consumer credit agreements must be in writing. In the case of the contract existing between a bank and its customer, however, this is not usually the case.

The nature of the banking contract has been defined gradually by the courts. An early case (Foley v. Hill, 1848) established that the basic relationship between a bank and its customer was that of debtor and creditor. Thus a customer with a credit balance on a current account is one of the bank's creditors, a position which is reversed if the account becomes overdrawn. The bank can deal with money deposited with it in any way it wishes but of course it must repay an equivalent sum when the customer wants it. If this were not the case, the bank would have to look after any notes a customer deposited and return the *same* notes when they were asked for.

The terms of a banking contract were summarised as follows in another case (Joachimson v. Swiss Bank, 1921). The bank undertakes to receive money and to collect bills for its customer's account, borrowing the proceeds and undertaking to repay them. The promise to repay is to repay at the branch of the bank where the account is kept and during banking hours. Repayment is for any part of the amount due against the written order of the customer to the bank at the branch. The bank must give a customer reasonable notice before closing his account and the customer must exercise reasonable care in executing his written orders so as not to mislead the bank or to facilitate forgery.

Subsequent cases have dealt with the rights and obligations of a bank and its customers. For example it was found that a bank has a duty of providing correct statements of account and a customer may not demand repayment of an amount exceeding the balance on the account. The bank must not generally disclose information about its customer's affairs (Tournier v. National Provincial & Union Bank of England Ltd, 1924).

This last requirement refers to the banker's duty of *secrecy*. However in the Tournier case it was established that a banker is entitled to disclose information about a customer's affairs under the following circumstances:

1. When disclosure is compelled by law. Thus a banker may be required to provide copies of entries in his books by a court of law or to give information to inspectors appointed by the Department of Trade.

2. When disclosure is in the public interest. This situation could arise when state security is threatened, for example in time of war.

3. When disclosure is in the interest of the bank. Thus if a bank is

taking legal action to obtain repayment of an overdraft it will clearly need to say how much money is owed to it.

4. When the customer consents to disclosure. Consent may be implied or express, for example when the banker is told to give information to an accountant dealing with the customer's affairs.

A bank may be required to disclose information about a customer's affairs if a *garnishee order* is served on it. This can happen when a creditor is trying to recover money owed to him by one of the bank's customers. The bank must not pay to its customer the sum mentioned in the order or any lesser amount in the account and in due course, when ordered by the court, must make payment of the sum involved to the creditor. When a garnishee order is made the banker should set off any debit balances on the customer's accounts against any credit balances. The banker is entitled to deduct debts owing to him from the amounts he owes the customer. If this results in a net debit balance then the customer is owed no money by the bank and the garnishee order is ineffective.

The right of *set-off* can be useful to a banker but must be exercised with caution. He has the right to set off balances on different accounts of a customer providing he has not agreed to keep them separate. The right can be exercised when accounts are kept at different branches and when they are held in the same right. Thus the balance on a customer's account designated 'household account' can be set off against another called 'private account'. On the other hand, if one account is clearly used to hold funds on behalf of other people, a solicitor's clients account for example, no right of set-off exists.

Banker-Customer Relationships

When a banker opens an account for someone not known to him it is prudent to enquire whether he is a suitable person who can be relied upon to act with integrity. The bank will usually take up references to ensure as far as possible that this is the case. Failure to do so could lead to loss if for example the new customer pays in a stolen cheque and withdraws the proceeds. The true owner of the cheque may try to recover from the bank the money he has lost and the bank may have to bear the loss unless it can show that it had opened the account in the customary way.

When an account is opened the bank will take a *mandate* from the customer dealing with the way in which the account is to be operated. A specimen signature will also be taken in order that instructions from the customer can be checked to be sure that his signature has not been forged. A *forged signature* is inoperative and a banker who pays away his customer's money under these circumstances would not be able to debit the customer's account. In some circumstances the *doctrine of estoppel* might apply if it could be shown that the customer had by his actions contributed to the loss. Thus if the customer knows that someone is forging his signature on cheques but fails to warn the bank, he would be estopped from denying the authenticity of his signature.

When a joint account is opened it is important that the mandate shows clearly whether cheques are to be signed by one, more than one, or all of those in whose names the account is held. If someone other than the account holders is to be allowed to sign, this must also be clear from the mandate. It is also important that the account holders agree to *joint and several liability* which allows the bank, should the occasion arise, to sue the account holders either jointly or one after another. Without the necessary clause in the mandate this would not be possible, since the account holders would have a joint liability which means that the bank has only one right of action, either against the parties jointly or against only one of them, but not both. If this action failed that would be the end of the matter whereas with joint and several liability the bank can claim against each party in turn.

Joint and several liability also means that the bank can exercise its right of set-off against the individual accounts of the joint account holders. It also means that if one of these parties dies his representatives will be liable for paying any debts outstanding on the deceased's estate. When liability is joint only this is not the case: a jointly owned asset passes to the survivors, likewise a joint liability is the responsibility of the survivors only. When an account is overdrawn and one of the parties dies it is necessary to *stop* the account by ceasing to place items to the debit or credit of the account. This is to preserve the liability of the deceased's estate and follows from the *rule in Clayton's case*. This rule, a very important one for bankers, means that if an account is overdrawn any credits paid in are deemed to reduce the existing overdraft whilst any further debits create a new overdraft. It follows that if an overdrawn account is not stopped (that is broken, ruled off or frozen) an overdraft at a particular date would be progressively reduced as credits are made to the account and thus the estate of a deceased joint account holder would be freed gradually from liability. Further cheques paid after the date of death might leave the account overdrawn but could not lead to a claim against the estate. Because of the rule in Clayton's case there are a number of occasions when an account should be stopped so as to fix the amount of liability at a point in time. For example, when a guarantor dies any payments into an overdrawn account which he has guaranteed will gradually reduce the liability of his estate. Cheques paid after his death by the bank's customer might leave the amount of the overdraft unaltered but the guarantor's estate would not be liable for this sum.

A banker if he wishes may lend with safety to holders of a joint account provided that the mandate provides this authority and that the account holders accept joint and several liability for their debt. This is not the position if an account holder is a *minor*, that is a person under the age of 18. Whilst the banker may with safety operate such an account whilst it is in credit he should exercise care if the minor seeks to borrow. Normally a minor cannot be forced to repay money he has borrowed and any security he has given in support of an advance is void. Obtaining a guarantee from an adult for a minor's debts must be avoided since a guarantor is only liable if the debtor is liable. If however an adult is prepared to give an indemnity to the bank he cannot escape responsibility for the debt even though this may be avoided by the minor.

As we saw at the beginning of Chapter 10, when someone dies leaving a will his affairs are dealt with by one or more *executors*. If there is no will or there is nobody to act as executor one or more administrators have to be appointed to wind up the deceased's estate. Before these personal representatives can dispose of any assets they have to obtain *probate* if they are executors or *letters of administration* if they are administrators. Once these are received the bank can allow the personal representatives to draw out any credit balance in the deceased's account. It can also lend money to the personal representatives in order that they can pay any capital transfer tax due from the estate. Banks often lend for this purpose since probate or letters of administration are not normally granted until after the tax is paid. Once a banker learns of a customer's death all transactions on the account must cease. Cheques must be returned unpaid and any credits placed in a separate account for use in due course by the personal representatives when they have authority to deal with the estate.

A *trust* is created when assets are held by *trustees* to be used for the purpose set out in a document creating the trust. Trusts are formed in a number of ways. For example someone in a will may direct that the income derived from certain assets is to be paid to a beneficiary during his lifetime and that on his death the capital sum is to pass to another person. It is likely under these circumstances that the executors will now become trustees charged with the responsibility of ensuring that the terms of the trust are observed. Their change of status is important. Executors can delegate authority among themselves so that if the mandate opening the account permits, not all the executors need sign cheques drawn on the executor account. Trustees in contrast must normally all sign cheques drawn on a trust account. The main exception to this rule is when the document creating the trust provides otherwise. Trustees have very limited powers to borrow whilst executors and administrators may borrow and use the assets of the estate as security to support this borrowing.

Bankers sometimes have difficult decisions to make when they believe a customer to be of unsound mind. When a person becomes incapable of managing his affairs a procedure exists under which an office of the Supreme Court known as the *Court of Protection* assumes responsibility for protecting and managing the property. A *receiver* is normally appointed by an order of the Court which sets out the powers that may be exercised by the receiver to carry out the day-to-day management of the patient's affairs. On the death of the patient the jurisdiction of the Court ceases, the receiver is discharged, and the estate is wound up by personal representatives in the usual way.

Directly the banker receives notice that his customer has been declared incapable of conducting his affairs the account should be stopped until he receives an order from the Court of Protection. When no such declaration has been received but the banker believes that the customer is suffering from mental incapacity he must seek the advice of the medical authorities. If a doctor or the medical superintendent of a hospital confirms the customer's incapacity, the account must be stopped since the banker might then become liable for any cheques or standing orders paid.

The banker needs to understand how to deal with the business accounts of customers. These will range from those of sole traders to those of partnerships or joint stock companies and the types of business conducted will include the wholesale and retail trades, farming, and manufacturing industries. Whilst no special factors have to be considered when dealing with the accounts of sole traders, certain points have to be watched when more than one person is conducting a business with partners.

When dealing with a partnership, a banker should obtain a mandate in the same way as with other types of joint account. He should obtain a copy of any existing partnership agreement if one exists and bear in mind that the provisions of the *Partnership Act* of 1890 apply unless excluded by a partnership agreement. Thus on the death or bankruptcy of a partner, the partnership is automatically dissolved and the partner's estate is not liable for any partnership debts that arise after his death or bankruptcy. It follows that the account must be stopped if the banker wishes to ensure that the estate remains liable for any debts due to the bank. In practice, a partnership agreement will usually specify the action to be taken on the death, bankruptcy, or retirement of a partner, probably providing that on death or retirement of a partner the remaining partners will buy his share in the business.

Many of a bank's business accounts are likely to be for companies formed in accordance with the Companies Acts and operating within the comprehensive framework of rules that these provide. Unlike a partnership, a company has a life of its own distinct from the lives of its members, the owners of the company. A company, a separate legal entity, is formed by filing *memorandum and articles of association* with the Registrar of Companies who registers them and issues a *certificate of incorporation*. Only then does the company have a legal existence.

The memorandum of association deals with the affairs of the company in relation to the outside world whilst the articles of association are concerned with the internal conduct of the company. The memorandum sets out the objectives of the company and any action by the company outside the scope of the memorandum is *ultra vires*, that is beyond the powers of the company and therefore not binding upon it. In a similar way any action by the directors of the company which is outside the scope of the articles is *ultra vires* the directors although such action can be ratified by the company at a later date.

It follows from this that when an account is opened for a company, the banker must be sure to see the memorandum and articles of association and the certificate of incorporation so that he knows he is dealing with a properly constituted legal entity. He must be particularly careful when lending to a company to ensure that this is within the power of the company and that the directors have authority to borrow on behalf of the company. A careful scrutiny of the memorandum and articles is necessary otherwise it may be found that the borrowing is *ultra vires* and that it will be impossible or difficult to obtain repayment of the debt.

The Liability of Banks

There are a number of ways in which a bank can incur liability to a customer or to someone else. Thus a banker may be liable to a customer for *negligence* if, for example, he has advised him to put money into a specific investment as a result of which the customer suffers loss and can show that the bank has been negligent in the advice it gave. Another possible instance of negligence can occur when accepting articles or documents from a customer for safekeeping. The banker in this case is a *bailee* and he would be unlikely to incur loss as a result of theft providing he had safeguarded the items in an efficient and prudent way. If however it could be shown that this was not the case – for example, if he had failed to place the items in the bank's strongroom – then the banker would be likely to suffer loss through negligence.

A banker has to be very careful when handling enquiries about a customer's financial position. The answering of status enquiries and the giving of banker's opinions are recognised banking practices but replies must be dealt with tactfully. It is usual for these to be given only to other bankers, and in general enquiries should likewise only be accepted from other bankers. If a report is too favourable, the enquirer may suffer loss and bring an action against the bank for negligence or *misrepresentation*. On the other hand if the report is too unfavourable he may face a claim from his customer for *libel* or *breach of duty*. Libel occurs when *defamation* is in writing whilst spoken defamation is referred to as *slander*.

Although the basic relationship between banker and customer is one of creditor/debtor it often happens that a banker acts as *agent* for a customer – that is, he carries out transactions on behalf of his customer, his *principal*. The banker must be careful not to exceed the powers given to him by this principal otherwise he may incur liability for the tasks he has performed. Thus if he is purchasing a company's shares on behalf of a customer he must ensure that he pays no more for them than any price limit that he has been given. The banker's risk of loss when acting as agent will be considered further when we deal with negotiable instruments in the next chapter. Here too the banker's liability in respect of *conversion* will be looked at. Conversion occurs when someone deprives a person of possession of property, whether innocently or on purpose. Thus conversion would take place if a banker handed property left with him for safekeeping to the wrong person.

Obviously the dangers faced by banks in conducting their affairs are also faced by other firms and obviously too they must obey the law in all its ramifications in the same way as other firms. If incorporated under the Companies Acts, they must ensure that they comply with the requirements of these Acts. They must obey the tax laws, the regulations regarding the health and safety of their employees, and those relating to the way in which they advertise their services.

PERSONAL ASSIGNMENTS

1 How does a recognised bank differ from a licensed deposit-taker?

2 Explain why the rule in Clayton's case is important for bankers.

3 Why would it be unusual for a banker to accept a guarantee as security for overdraft facilities granted to a minor?

4 Explain the significance of joint and several liability.

5 Explain the difference between a trustee, an administrator, and an executor.

6 What does the term *ultra vires* mean?

7 Explain briefly how a business is incorporated under the Companies Acts.

8 How does a banker's liability in respect of conversion differ from that of negligence?

CHAPTER 13

NEGOTIABLE INSTRUMENTS

In Chapter 3 we saw how written instructions given to a banker by a depositor ordering him to pay money to someone else developed into the cheques we use today. We saw also how the bill of exchange was used during different periods as a means of payment, as a means of borrowing, and as a channel for investment. Both cheques and bills are *negotiable instruments*, that is they enable a holder to obtain a *good title* to the instrument even if it has been obtained from a thief.

Suppose a tape recorder and a £10 note are stolen from my home and the thief sells the tape recorder and changes the note for ten £1 coins. If I can trace the tape recorder I can claim its return even if the person obtaining it was an innocent party and had given value for it. However I cannot reclaim the return of the £10 note even if I can trace it since it is a negotiable instrument and the new holder has a good title to it even though he acquired it from a thief. The note is one form of *promissory note*, which like a cheque or a bill of exchange possesses negotiability and is defined as an unconditional promise to pay made by one person to another.

An instrument may possess *transferability* but not negotiability. Thus a cheque marked 'not negotiable' is still transferable but a holder cannot obtain a better title to the cheque than that of the person who transferred it to him. Someone who cashes a stolen cheque, even if unaware that it is stolen, cannot claim its value from the drawer since the words written on the cheque have destroyed its negotiability and thus prevented him from obtaining a good title.

Cheques and Bills

In Chapter 3 it was explained that the Bills of Exchange Act of 1882 codified the existing law regarding bills of exchange and defined a cheque as a particular type of bill, one drawn on a banker and payable on demand. Cheques as well as other bills play a very important part in a bank's day-to-day operations and it is therefore essential that bankers have a sound grasp of the laws governing them.

A bill of exchange is an unconditional order in writing. Thus the drawee – in the case of a cheque, a bank – must be instructed to pay: it is not enough simply to authorise him to pay. The instruction must not be conditional on something else happening, for example on the receipt of funds for the credit of the drawer's account. Writing includes typing and printing but there is no legal requirement that this should be on paper, although in practice this is always used.

A bill must be addressed from one person to another and signed by the person giving it. 'Person' includes bodies which have a legal identity and thus the drawer and drawee of a bill can include a company.

A bill must require the person to whom it is addressed to pay on demand, or at a fixed or determinable future time, a sum certain in money. A bill is payable on demand when it is expressed to be so payable or when payment is required at sight or upon presentation. Since a cheque is defined as a bill drawn on a banker and payable on demand, it follows that it cannot be made payable at a future time. If a bill is not payable on demand, then the date for its future payment must be determinable. Thus it can be drawn payable upon the death of someone but not, for example, upon someone's marriage, since such an event may never take place.

The amount concerned must be a *sum certain* in money – not the same as a *certain sum*. A bill requiring payment with interest or at a stated rate of exchange is valid since these are regarded as sums certain. Although the Bills of Exchange Act stipulates that where the amount of a bill is in both words and figures and these differ, the sum payable is that denoted by words, the practice of bankers is slightly different when dealing with cheques. If the amount is in figures only, a cheque is normally not paid whilst if in words only the cheque will usually be paid. If the words and figures differ the amount in words will be paid if it is less than that in figures. In other cases, the cheque will be marked 'words and figures differ' and returned to the drawer for correction.

A bill must be made payable to a specified person, to his order, or to bearer. A cheque payable to Mr Smith or order simply means that Mr Smith may require the amount to be paid to another person. A cheque payable to bearer means what it says, that the person in possession of it is entitled to payment.

Paying Cheques

In Chapter 9 the importance of cheques as part of a country's payment mechanism was examined and we saw how the clearing system enabled one bank to present cheques to other banks for payment. In addition, cheques are received for payment over the counter of branch banks. It therefore follows that every working day large numbers of cheques are received by banks for payment. Cheques received in these ways are paid when the signature of the drawer is cancelled by a paying clerk or cashier placing his initials on the signature. After this, the cheque can be debited to the drawer's account.

Before paying a cheque, the paying banker must ensure that the cheque is in order. First and foremost he must make sure that the signature on the cheque is that of his customer. If it is a forgery he has no authority to debit his customer's account since he can only pay money away on his customer's instructions. The banker is in a similar position if he neglects to observe a customer's mandate. Thus if a joint account requires two signatures there could be trouble if only one person has signed the cheque.

Another important consideration for the paying banker, and a fairly obvious one, is whether or not the customer has enough money on his account to meet the payment. If not, the cheque can only be paid if the resulting balance is within an agreed overdraft limit or if the bank is prepared to make funds available to meet the cheque. If a cheque is not paid it must be *dishonoured*. If it has been presented over the counter an immediate decision has to be made; if it has come through the clearing, the banker has until the end of the day to decide whether to pay or dishonour the cheque. A cheque presented through the clearing which is dishonoured must be returned unpaid, the cheque being marked to indicate the reason for dishonour. Thus a cheque unpaid because of insufficient funds will be returned with the words 'refer to drawer' written on the front.

Another reason for dishonouring a cheque is when the drawer has *stopped* the cheque or countermanded payment. This may happen if a cheque has been lost or if the drawer decides against paying a trader for defective goods. As soon as a paying banker receives notice that a cheque is stopped, his authority to pay it ceases and he thus cannot debit his customer's account. The customer must give full details of the cheque to be stopped and if it is presented the banker must return it unpaid, usually with the answer 'orders not to pay'.

The paying banker must also ensure that the cheque is in order technically before paying it. He must examine the date of the cheque and the amount payable as well as considering any endorsement or crossings on the cheque, matters which we shall come to later. As regards the date, the cheque must not be paid if it is *stale, overdue*, or *postdated*. There is no precise legal definition of when a cheque is stale or overdue, but it is customary to refuse payment after six months from the date on the cheque, which is then returned unpaid with the answer 'out of date'. There is no legal reason to prevent a person giving someone a cheque dated at some future date, but a banker pays such a cheque before the stated date at his peril. The drawer of a postdated cheque does not expect payment to take place ahead of time and the banker would be in a difficult position if the cheque were stopped or another cheque returned through lack of funds because the postdated cheque had been paid. Postdated cheques should therefore be returned with the answer 'postdated'.

The position regarding cheques whose amount is unclear because the words and figures do not agree has already been considered as well as the circumstances in which the cheque should be returned marked 'words and figures differ'.

Endorsements

Since the passing of the *Cheques Act* in 1957, the exemptions contained within it have greatly reduced the number of cheques needing endorsement. Before the passage of the Act, the payee of a cheque had to endorse it by signing the cheque, usually on the back, before he could pay it into a bank for the credit of his account. This simple signature is known as an *endorsement in blank* and has the effect of making the cheque *payable to bearer*. After endorsement in this way, the cheque can be passed to someone else by the payee in payment, for example, for goods he has purchased. The new holder if he wishes can pay it into his account or use it again for another purchase. The cheque, effectively payable to bearer, can circulate and be used for settling a number of transactions in much the same way as a bank note.

The payee may be concerned that once he endorses the cheque it may be lost or stolen and may therefore name the party to whom he is passing it. Thus Mr X the payee may endorse the cheque as follows:

Pay Miss Y or order

Signature of Mr X

This is a *special endorsement*. Mr X the payee is the *endorser* and Miss Y is the *endorsee*. As soon as Miss Y endorses the cheque in blank it becomes payable to bearer. Thus the bearer of a cheque is any holder of a cheque which was made payable to bearer or on which the only or last endorsement is an endorsement in blank.

As a general rule, only those who have signed the cheque can be held liable on it, that is the drawer and all those who have endorsed it. Thus in our example if Miss Y pays the cheque into her account and it is returned unpaid because the drawer has no money, Mr X is liable to Miss Y for the value of the cheque and he has to look to the drawer for recompense.

The Cheques Act's main effect was to make an endorsement unnecessary on a cheque which is being paid into the account of the payee. Thus a cheque payable to Mr X which is being paid into a bank for the credit of Mr X's account no longer needs endorsement. Probably the majority of cheques are dealt with in this way, and the Act thus saves a lot of time and effort for banks and their customers. Sometimes, however, endorsement is required. For example, if Mr X decided to pay the cheque into his account with a building society he would be asked to endorse the cheque since the building society will pay the cheque into its account with a bank. In this case, the cheque is being credited to an account which is *not* that of the payee and is thus outside the exemption contained in the Cheques Act.

Crossings

Crossed cheques should only be paid by a banker if they are presented to him for payment by a banker. Thus the payee of a cheque can not present it for encashment to the bank on which it is drawn but has to pay it into a bank account or arrange for another person to do so for him. If, for example, he pays it into a building society, the building society has to pay it into its own bank account.

Most cheques are now crossed cheques, a crossing consisting of two parallel lines across the face of the cheque with or without the addition of the words 'and company' or an abbreviation of these words. This is known as a *general crossing*. If the name of a bank is written on the face of a cheque this is known as a *special crossing* and only that bank is entitled to receive payment from the paying banker. A banker must be sure when he is paying a crossed cheque that he pays to a banker if it is a general crossing and to the named bank if it is a special crossing.

Risk and the Paying Banker

The risks a paying banker faces are in respect of his customer and of third parties. If his customer's signature on the cheque has been forged, then the account cannot be debited since the banker has no authority to pay the cheque. Likewise, if the cheque has been stopped but has been paid, the banker faces loss because again he had no authority to debit his customer's account. Similar loss may occur if he pays a cheque after he has received notice of the customer's death.

Sometimes protection may arise through the *doctrine of estoppel* (*see* Bank-Customer Relationships, Chapter 12), a doctrine which comes into play when a person by his conduct leads another person to suffer loss. Thus if a customer knows that her husband has forged her signature on three cheques but has not told the bank she will probably be estopped from denying that the fourth signature is hers and from preventing the forged cheques from being debited to her account. In a similar way, a customer has a duty to draw cheques in a reasonable way so as to prevent forgery or wrongful alteration of the amount payable. If for example he has drawn the cheque in such a way as to make it easy for someone else to alter it, he will not be able to hold the banker responsible for any loss incurred.

Liability to a third party can arise in a number of ways. If the true owner of the cheque has suffered loss, possibly because the cheque has been stolen, and the banker has paid the cheque contrary to the requirements of the crossing, he will be liable to the true owner of the cheque. However, providing the banker pays a cheque in accordance with the crossing, in good faith, and without negligence, he is placed in the same position as if payment of the cheque had been made to the true owner.

It might be expected that a paying banker will be in trouble if he pays a cheque which has been stolen and which, after the thief has forged the payee's endorsement, is presented to him for payment. However, a little thought shows that it is normally impossible for the paying banker to know whether or not an endorsement is genuine. Both the Bills of Exchange Act and the Cheques Act recognise this and protect the banker when he has paid a cheque in good faith and in the ordinary course of business. In particular, the Cheques Act provides protection both when a cheque is not endorsed and when an endorsement is irregular.

Collecting Cheques

When the payee of a cheque pays it into his account with a bank, the bank has to collect the proceeds from the bank on which it is drawn.

Normally no problem or risks are likely to be faced by the collecting banker who, when he passes a cheque through the clearing, expects it to be paid automatically. Likewise, if the customer for whom he is collecting the cheque is not the payee but the cheque has been correctly endorsed, no problems should normally arise.

If, however, the banker collects a cheque from someone who is not the true owner, possibly because the cheque has been stolen, he may, despite the fact that he has acted innocently be accused of *conversion* – that is, of acting so as to deprive the true owner of possession of his property. In practice, large numbers of cheques are collected daily by bankers on behalf of their customers and the law recognises the impossibility of checking the true ownership of every cheque collected. For this reason, the Cheques Act protects the banker from loss provided:

1. That he acts in good faith and without negligence.
2. That he receives payment of the cheque for a customer.

Banks can be assumed to act in good faith but negligence is difficult to define. However, a bank would be judged as negligent if it collected without enquiry a cheque for a private customer where, for example, the payee were the Inland Revenue or a company.

Care must be taken when opening an account for a customer not known to the bank, for it could be held that the bank had been negligent in failing to obtain adequate references or in failing to act prudently and in accordance with current banking practice. For example, the protection of the Cheques Act could be lost if a cheque were collected for a thief who used it to open an account and about whom adequate enquiries had not been made. Although the words 'account payee' or 'account payee only' written on the face of a cheque are not strictly part of a crossing, it is probable that a banker would be deemed negligent in collecting such a cheque on behalf of someone other than the payee.

Since the passing of the Cheques Act, bankers can no longer be regarded as negligent by reason only that an endorsement is missing from a cheque or that it is irregular. If, however, there are any circumstances which raise doubts about a transaction and the bank failed to make enquiries, it is likely that it would be held negligent and thus lose its legal protection as a collecting banker. However, circumstances may arise whereby any loss can be mitigated, as for instance when the banker can show that there has been contributory negligence.

The Holder in Due Course

At the beginning of this chapter, we considered the difference between transferability and negotiability, the latter quality enabling an innocent party to obtain a good title from a guilty party. A cheque is a negotiable instrument unless it is marked 'not negotiable', in which case it remains transferable despite the fact that it has lost its quality of negotiability.

A *holder* is the payee or endorsee of a cheque who is in possession of it or the bearer of it. If he has given value for the cheque, he is known as a *holder for value* and has the same title as the person from whom he obtained the cheque. If, however, he can show that he is a *holder in due course* he has an indefeasible title, he can sue on the cheque in his own name, and he is not affected by defects in the title of prior parties.

In order for a holder of a cheque to be a holder in due course, he must have taken it in good faith and for value and without notice of any defect in the title of the person from whom he took it. The cheque must be complete and regular on the face of it, it must not be overdue, and the holder must have taken it without notice that it had previously been dishonoured. For example, suppose that Miss Smith (the drawer) gives Miss Jones (the payee) a cheque for £50 and it is stolen after she has endorsed it. The thief persuades a friend, Mr Richards, to cash the cheque for him but it is returned unpaid because Miss Smith stopped the cheque when she heard that it had been stolen. In this case Mr Richards, who cashed the cheque, is entitled to receive £50 from Miss Smith because he is a holder in due course. If however the cheque had been marked 'not negotiable', Mr Richards would not be entitled to the money since this would destroy the cheque's negotiability and it would not be regular on the face of it. Mr Richards would then be a holder for value but not a holder in due course.

A banker who cashes a cheque in the same circumstances as those of Mr Richards would be in the same position as Mr Richards depending on whether or not the cheque was crossed 'not negotiable'. In some cases, being a holder in due course may be to the banker's advantage. As a collecting banker, he is protected by law only if he can show that he has not been negligent. For a holder in due course, negligence does not arise since he has to show only that he acted in good faith. Thus as a collecting banker he may lose his legal protection against the charge of conversion because he has been negligent, but still be able to put forward the claim that he is a holder in due course. In order to succeed he must, as we have seen, satisfy a number of conditions, in particular that he has given value for the cheque he holds.

The *giving of value* for a cheque by a banker can take place in three ways. The most obvious is when he cashes the cheque, but he is also held to have given value if he can show that he has allowed a customer to draw against the proceeds of the cheque which he is collecting on the assumption that it will be paid. A third way in which he can claim to have given value is if he credits the cheque to his customer's account with the specific intention of reducing or eliminating an overdraft.

Cheque Cards

Since a cheque card guarantees the payment of a cheque up to a specified limit, the drawer cannot countermand payment by instructing his bank to stop the cheque. Thus if he has purchased goods which for some reason he finds unsatisfactory he has no way of preventing the seller from receiving payment for the goods. Normally cheques used in conjunction with a cheque card will not be returned unpaid if they have been completed incorrectly.

Other Negotiable Instruments

A banker is likely to deal in his business with instruments which, while negotiable, are neither cheques nor other types of bills of exchange. A *promissory note* for example is not a bill of exchange or a cheque because it is an unconditional *promise* to pay rather than an unconditional *order*. However, it is covered by the Bills of Exchange Act and is fully negotiable unless otherwise stated. By far the most frequent form of promissory note in use is the bank note. If one of these is stolen, the thief has no title, but a *bona fide* transferee for value has a good title against all the world and the note cannot be claimed by the true owner.

A bank note is payable on demand to bearer and thus does not need endorsement. The person writing a promissory note is known as the *maker* (unlike a cheque where he is the drawer) and if he makes the note payable to his own order he must endorse it if it is to be recognised legally as a promissory note.

A *bankers draft* is drawn by a bank on itself and is used when complete confidence is needed that it will be paid on presentation. Thus a customer may need such a draft when purchasing a car, for example, the seller being reluctant to part with the vehicle and the log book unless he is quite certain that he will be paid. Since the bank is both drawer and drawee, a bankers draft is probably neither a bill of exchange nor a cheque since it is not drawn by one person on another. However, bankers drafts are recognised in the Bills of Exchange Act and a holder has the option of treating one either as a bill of exchange or as a promissory note. Bankers drafts cannot be drawn payable to bearer on demand since they would then be bank notes and would contravene the legislation giving the Bank of England the monopoly of the note issue in England and Wales.

Cheque forms made payable to 'cash' or 'wages' are not cheques, since the Bills of Exchange Act definition says a cheque must be payable to the order of a specified person or bearer. If the payee is a fictitious or non-existent payee, a bill or cheque may be treated as payable to bearer, but clearly this does not apply in this case. A 'cheque' payable to cash or wages is usually drawn to enable cash to be drawn from a bank. Clearly, the banker paying such an instrument is not entitled to legal protection from the Bills of Exchange Act since the 'cheque' does not fall within its scope. Although the Cheques Act provides some measure of protection for some types of instrument that are not cheques, the safest procedure is to cash these 'cheques' only for known customers or their recognised agents.

Bills of Exchange

Bills of exchange other than cheques are frequently dealt with by banks and in the section on Bills of Exchange in Chapter 3 we saw that in addition to providing a means of payment, bills can also be used as a source of finance. This comes about when the bill is payable at a future date. Once the bill has been accepted, it can be discounted immediately, thus enabling a seller of goods to receive funds at once whilst the purchaser can delay payment until the maturity of the bill. A bill not payable on demand should be presented as soon as possible to the drawee for acceptance. Only then is his liability on the bill secured, this liability to a holder in due course remaining even if the drawer's signature has been forged. Acceptance is also necessary to fix the maturity date of a bill payable after sight, the term of a bill being calculated from the date when it was presented for acceptance. Bills are used both as a source of domestic finance and as a means of financing international trade. When goods are sent by ship, a number of documents are required before the consignee can claim them. To provide security it is clearly desirable that these documents are not released until the seller is assured that payment will be made, and it is for this reason that arrangements are often made for this release only when the bill has been accepted or when it has been paid.

A simple example would be when an exporter draws a bill on an importer payable to himself and stipulates that shipping documents are to be released only when the importer (the drawee) accepts or pays the bill. Documents attached to the bill, called a *documentary bill*, are released only at the appropriate time. A bill unaccompanied by documents is called a *clean bill*. The shipping documents will include a *bill of lading* which is signed by the master of a ship or his agent acknowledging receipt of the goods and giving the consignee the right to take possession of the goods under prescribed conditions. Other documents are likely to include an invoice, certificate of origin, and an insurance certificate.

In Chapter 3 (Merchant Banking) we saw that an *acceptance credit* is an arrangement by which a bank accepts bills on behalf of a customer. Thus a foreign importer may arrange for a bank to accept a bill enabling the exporter to arrange for it to be easily discounted. When documents have to be handed over at the time of acceptance, the credit is known as a *documentary credit*; when no documents are involved it is called a *clean credit*.

Bills of exchange used in international trade are sometimes drawn in *sets* that is in two or three parts on different pieces of paper. This is done in order to reduce any loss arising from delay when the bill is sent from one country to another. Acceptance may be written on any part of the set, but on one part only otherwise the acceptor would be liable to holders in due course of each part of the bill.

The whole of the parts of a set constitutes one bill. Each part must be identical except that each must be numbered: 'First of exchange', 'Second of exchange', and so on. Steps can be taken to obtain early acceptance of the first part and once this has been done the other parts are marked accordingly. A holder then brings all the parts together so that he has one bill which has been accepted and which can be presented for payment at the due date.

PERSONAL ASSIGNMENTS

1 Explain the difference between negotiability and transferability.

2 Under what circumstances would a bank pay a crossed cheque payable to 'cash'?

3 List the circumstances under which a banker dishonours a cheque by non-payment.

4 Explain the difference between an endorsement in blank and a special endorsement.

5 What do you understand by the doctrine of estoppel?

6 Explain the circumstances under which a bill of exchange needs to be presented for acceptance. Why do cheques not need accepting?

7 How does a general crossing on a cheque differ from a special crossing?

CHAPTER 14

SECURITY FOR ADVANCES

In Chapter 8 we considered the ways in which banks assess risks and under what circumstances they are prepared to lend only with the backing of adequate securities. In this chapter, we consider the ways in which bankers protect themselves when lending on a secured basis and what forms of asset a borrowing customer can offer to satisfy the banker's lending requirements.

There are various legal processes enabling a banker to obtain rights to other people's assets. A *lien*, for example, is the right of someone to retain property of another person until a debt due to him is repaid. With an ordinary lien, the borrower remains legal owner of the property and the creditor in possession of it has no right of sale. A *particular lien* is when there is a transaction relating to the property; a *general lien* arises out of the overall transactions between the parties concerned.

A *banker's lien* is a general lien over that part of a borrowing customer's property which has come into the banker's hands in the ordinary course of business. Whilst he has no lien over property given to him for a particular purpose, this does not apply to property passing through his hands in the usual way. For example, while no lien could exist over a company's shares delivered to a banker for sale or for safe custody, he might have the right to retain the proceeds of a cheque received from the customer for collection. The lien of a banker has been described as an implied pledge and for this reason he is generally regarded as having power to sell securities over which he has a lien, a situation not applying to other liens. The power to sell when a customer defaults can only be exercised if the customer has reasonable notice of the banker's intentions.

A *pledge*, which is implied in the case of a banker's lien, arises as the result of an express agreement and gives the pledgee a power to sell the property pledged if a debt has not been repaid at the agreed time or when there have been unsuccessful attempts to obtain repayment.

Whilst a lien merely gives the right to retain something, a pledge involves the delivery of property or the title to property by the pledgor to the pledgee.

As with a lien, the ownership of the property is retained by the pledgor but the pledgee is entitled to possession of the property until the debt is repaid. Unlike a lien, property not owned by the borrower can be pledged, provided that this is done with the owner's consent. Physical delivery of property pledged is not necessary provided that there has been legal delivery of the title to the property or that this can be implied, for example by delivery of a key to the store where the property is held.

A third method by which a banker can obtain security for an advance is by mortgage. A *mortgage* is a conveyance of an interest in property as security for an advance or as a means of discharging an obligation. The best known example of a mortgage is probably that of a person who buys a house and obtains a mortgage from a building society. The house is the property of the buyer, who as the borrower of funds mortgages the property. This borrower is the mortgagor, the building society is the mortgagee.

A mortgage may convey a legal or equitable interest in real or personal property. Real property consists of freehold land; personal property can be *choses in action* (things in action), in which case the right of ownership has to be contested in court, or *choses in possession*, that is, property which can be handed over simply by delivery such as a picture or a television set. When there is a *legal mortgage*, the mortgagee is placed in the position of a true owner with a right to sell if the borrower defaults. In the case of an *equitable mortgage*, ownership remains with the borrower and the mortgagee has no automatic right to sell and no right to possession without a court order.

In some cases, a banker can secure his lending by an *assignment*. This is simply the transfer to the bank by a borrowing customer of his rights to receive money. Thus a life assurance policy can be assigned to a bank giving it the right to receive any money payable under the policy.

Hypothecation is a term used by bankers when taking a charge over goods or documents of title to goods when it is not possible for the goods to be pledged. Neither the ownership nor possession of the goods is passed to the bank, but the borrowing customer signs a *letter of hypothecation* giving a charge over the goods and agreeing that if the bank wishes to sell the goods he will execute the necessary documents to give ownership of the goods to the bank.

Life Assurance Policies

A useful way of taking security for an advance is by securing a mortgage on a life assurance policy by means of assignment. Such policies are of two main types: *whole-life policies*, under which the sum assured is payable on the death of the life assured, and *endowment policies* which mature at a specified time or on death, whichever happens first. Both types of policy can be with or without profits. A *'with profits'* policy is one whose value is increased periodically when the profits made by the insurer are shared among holders of this type of policy. The holder of a policy pays a single premium or regular premiums to the insurer up to the time that the policy matures and these premiums form a life fund which is invested and out of which are made the payments on maturing policies. The profits of this fund enable the insurer to pay bonuses on 'with profit' policies – usually every three or four years and often with a terminal bonus when the policy matures. Not surprisingly, the amount of premium payable is higher with policies that have the benefit of these bonuses.

If a policy holder wishes to cease paying premiums, he can leave the policy as a *paid-up policy*, receiving a reduced amount at maturity based on the premiums already paid, or he can seek to surrender the policy, receiving its *surrender value* from the insurer. This surrender value is likely to be small or non-existent in the early years of a policy's life but will increase regularly in later years. The surrender value of a policy can easily be obtained from the insurer, so the banker knows the value of the security he is taking and against which he can lend. The banker must ensure that premium payments are made at the due time otherwise the policy will lapse; providing these payments continue, however, he knows that the value of his security is increasing. He also knows that realising the security is easy since all that is necessary is for the policy to be surrendered, the money received being used to repay his customer's borrowing.

Assignment of a policy is straightforward. The bank's form of assignment is signed by the policy holder, sealed, and notice of assignment sent to the insurer. This procedure constitutes a legal assignment and allows the banker to sue on the policy in his own name. An *equitable assignment* can be easily obtained by the deposit of the policy accompanied by a written promise to assign the policy to the bank if called upon to do so. This type of assignment is likely to be less attractive to a banker because his customer may not cooperate and because the banker cannot himself claim either the proceeds at maturity or the surrender value of the policy. Another disadvantage is that an insurer will not accept notice of an equitable assignment.

When a bank or other lender no longer needs the security of a life assurance policy it is reassigned and the insurer informed. The banker taking a policy as security should always make sure that it has not already been assigned. The insurer will provide this information and if there has been an earlier assignment the banker must ensure that reassignment has taken place otherwise his title to the policy may be defective.

A contract of life assurance is a contract *uberrimae fidei* (the utmost good faith) and an insurer could avoid the policy and thus refuse to pay sums due if accurate and full information had not been provided. The banker should bear this in mind when accepting the policy as security and he should make sure that the age of the assured has been admitted, that the insurer has seen the assured's birth certificate, and that a note to this effect has been received from the insurer.

The banker should also make sure that the insurer, probably an insurance company, is financially sound and reputable and that there are no special clauses in the policy that could lead to future difficulties. He should also ensure that there is an *insurable interest*. This arises when someone insures the life of another person: for example, a policy of assurance covering a wife or husband is permissible but normally a parent has no insurable interest in the life of his children and such a policy could be declared void.

Stocks and Shares

There is little difficulty in securing an advance against the security of stocks and shares. Those issued in bearer form are negotiable instruments and a bank obtains a good title simply by taking possession of them. At the same time, the banker will take a *memorandum of deposit* from the customer as proof that the intention is for the bank to hold them as backing for present and future advances.

The title to registered stocks and shares is obtained by entry in a register; the transfer of title being achieved by notice to the company's registrar. To obtain a legal mortgage, the banker will arrange for shares to be registered in the bank's name or that of a nominee by sending the share certificate to the company registrar together with a transfer form signed by the present owner. A memorandum of deposit will be taken from the customer showing that the shares in the bank's name are deposited as security and stating that the bank has a right to sell the shares if the customer does not repay the advance to the bank at the required time. The memorandum must state that the shares are charged as a continuing security in order to prevent the rule in Clayton's case from operating (*see* Banker-Customer Relationships, Chapter 12).

An equitable mortgage can be obtained by the deposit with the bank of the share certificate together with a memorandum of deposit. This will contain the same provisions as that for a legal mortgage with an additional clause by which the customer undertakes to complete the necessary documents to allow the bank to sell the shares if this becomes necessary. Clearly the disadvantage of this is that when the appropriate time comes it may be difficult to persuade the customer to do this. However this difficulty can be overcome by obtaining a *blank transfer* from the customer at the same time as the memorandum of deposit is signed. A stock transfer form is completed and signed by the customer but left undated. Should the bank need to realise the security, it simply has to date the transfer and sell the shares, the name of the purchaser being entered on the form which is sent to the company's registrar who amends the share register to show the name of the new owner.

Merchandise

A pledge is used when negotiable instruments such as bearer securities are taken by a bank as security. A more common use of a pledge arises when goods or documents showing a title to goods form the security for an advance. Usually it is the title to goods which is pledged, often to goods imported into the country and awaiting sale. In such cases, the goods are likely to be in a warehouse in the name of the bank's customer who will arrange with the warehouse keeper to hold them in the name of the bank. When goods are stored in a warehouse, the warehouse keeper will issue a receipt. Whilst this does not act as a title to the goods, it can be sent to the warehouse keeper together with a *delivery order* signed by the customer asking him henceforth to hold the goods on behalf of the bank. In due course a new warehouse receipt will be issued in the bank's name.

A bank customer using goods as security for an advance signs a *letter of pledge* as well as the delivery order. This letter will state that the security is a continuing one, that the bank has a right to sell the goods, and that the customer will insure the goods and pay all warehousing expenses. Lending against merchandise is likely to be made only to customers of undoubted honesty. There is always a danger that goods may be fraudulently sold without the banker's knowledge, that they may not be of the correct quality, or that deterioration will affect their value. The banker must also ensure that the goods are fully insured at all times.

Land

The term 'land' includes anything on the land (such as a house), in the air above the land, or in the ground underneath. It may be held in two ways. *Freehold* is where an owner has an interest known as a 'fee simple absolute in possession', which in practice gives him full rights to the land for all time. A *leasehold* is where ownership of the land is for a 'term of years absolute', that is, the owner has full rights to the land but for a limited period only, usually known as a lease.

Compared with the other assets a banker can take as security, land has the advantage of permanency and cannot be lost or physically moved. As with other assets the banker needs to be sure that he has a good title to the property, evidence of which depends on whether the land is registered or unregistered. In the case of *unregistered land*, this evidence is contained in the *deeds* of the property, a bundle of documents which together trace its legal history. Many of these documents are likely to be *conveyances*, the method used for transferring the title to unregistered freehold land. There may also be mortgages and their discharges and *assents*, that is, documents used to transfer property to a beneficiary on the death of an owner of land. When deeds are deposited with a bank it is important that a solicitor examine the documents to make sure that the customer has good title to the property, a title established by ensuring that there is good *chain of title* – that the chain has not been broken at an earlier date by perhaps a mortgage which has not been discharged.

Registered land is land whose title is registered by the Chief Land Registrar. When land is first registered the deeds are examined and if these are satisfactory a certificate is issued. Thereafter the deeds do not need to be checked to see that the holder has a good title. If the land is sold, the Registrar is informed, a new certificate replacing the old one is sent to the new owner, and the Land Register is amended to show the new owner. The intention is that all land will in time become registered in order to simplify and speed up the process of transfer from one person to another.

The usual way of taking a legal mortgage over land is by a *form of charge* which thereafter will be one of the documents included in the deeds of unregistered land. The form will state that the security is a continuing security, that the borrower will repay all sums owing, and that he will keep the property in good repair and fully insured. An equitable mortgage leaves ownership of the land with the customer and means that if the bank needs to realise its security it will need the cooperation of the customer in order to do so. One solution is to include a *power of attorney* clause in the form of charge which gives the bank power to perform all the legal formalities needed for sale.

A banker taking land as security needs to arrange for *searches* of various registers to be carried out. Local authorities maintain registers of local *land charges* containing information likely to affect the value of the land. It may be found for example that a road-widening scheme is about to take place or that building development is planned for adjacent land. The property may be found to be listed as of special historical or architectural interest or it may be about to be acquired by the authorities under a compulsory purchase order. Obviously the banker will wish to know and to take account of anything he can discover likely to affect the value of the land and its acceptability as security.

As well as keeping registers recording the title to registered land, the Chief Land Registrar also maintains a series of other registers dealing with matters likely to affect the usefulness of a particular parcel of land as security. The most important of these is the *Land Charges Register*, a register divided into different classes which deals with such things as *restrictive covenants* which prevent the owner of the land from doing certain things – for example keeping pigs in his back garden or building another house on his land. Mortgages not protected by the deposit of deeds, known as *puisne mortgages*, can be registered and if this is the case then the banker will know that the customer has already borrowed against the security of the land.

When registered land is taken as security local searches must be carried out in the same way as for unregistered land. However, there is usually no need to search the Land Charges Register. A search of the Land Registry so as to obtain an up-to-date disclosure of entries on the register will be required and this can be accomplished by sending an appropriate form for completion by the Registrar.

Valuation

It is clearly important for a banker to be able to value the security against which he is lending. When deciding how much to lend against security, account has to be taken of the likely fluctuations in value during the period of the advance and the ease with which the security can be realised to repay a bad debt.

In the case of a life assurance policy, the value may be discovered quite easily by obtaining the surrender value from the company issuing the policy. In other cases, reference will have to be made to the market price. In the case of stocks and shares dealt in on The Stock Exchange, the current value can easily be discovered from the press or from the Stock Exchange Daily List. In the case of land, much will depend on the property involved. If a customer wishes to use his house as security probably all that is needed is a valuation by a local bank officer who has a clear idea of prices in his area. In the case of a large or unusual property such as a block of flats or a parade of shops, a professional valuer may be asked to value the property. Merchandise valuation is likely to be at the purchase price rather than the selling price unless of course the market price is lower than the cost of the goods.

The amount of money lent on a secured basis will depend on the type of asset involved, its likely future fluctuation in value, the ease with which it can be sold, and any costs involved upon realisation. If lending is limited to eighty per cent of valuation the bank is said to have a *margin* of twenty per cent. The bank would seek a higher margin in the case for example of a company's shares subject to speculative demand than in the case of other shares where the demand was less volatile.

Debentures

A debenture is an acknowledgment of indebtedness by a company, the only type of customer able to offer this form of security for an advance. This type of debenture is known as a *naked debenture* unlike a *mortgage debenture*, which provides a charge over a company's assets and which is the usual type taken as a security by a banker. A *fixed charge* is one given over specified assets; a *floating charge* covers the remaining company's assets. A company cannot deal with assets covered by a fixed charge without the agreement of the bank whereas this does not apply to other assets covered by a floating charge since these vary from day to day. The company's stock of finished goods, its raw materials, and work in progress are constantly changing and can be disposed of as required. Once the debenture *crystallises*, however, these assets can no longer be dealt with. This occurs when a receiver is appointed for the debenture holder, the company ceases trading, or winding up commences, in which case the receiver is given power to administer the assets and to use them to repay the company's debt to the bank.

When a bank has taken care to ensure that borrowing by a company is within its powers, it will take the debenture under seal, that is by a *deed*. It is likely that the debenture, known as an *all-moneys debenture*, will contain both fixed and floating charges. The debenture has to be registered with the Registrar of Companies otherwise it is likely to be void against the company's liquidator and other creditors.

Debentures can be issued to the general public and if quoted can be bought and sold on The Stock Exchange. A holder of this debenture stock has the right of receiving a fixed rate of interest on the investment at regular intervals. A trust deed is drawn up and a trustee appointed to look after the interests of the debenture holders. The debenture is a loan secured by a charge over the company's assets and a debenture holder is a creditor of the company who if the company fails is entitled to payment of his loan ahead of shareholders. Debenture stock is the safest form of stock issued by a company and can be taken by a bank as security in the same way as other stocks and shares.

Guarantees

A *guarantee* is somewhat different from other forms of security for an advance considered in this chapter. It is simply an undertaking by one or more people to take responsibility for another person's debt, people to whom a banker may turn if his customer does not repay an advance.

A guarantee is made simply by the *guarantor* signing the bank's usual form of guarantee. To be of any value, it must obviously have as its guarantor a person of means, of good character, and who is able to honour his commitment without too much difficulty if called upon to do so. Unless the guarantee is supported by some form of security taken from the guarantor it is probably best to regard an advance as unsecured. Security provided by another person as backing for a customer's borrowing is known as *collateral security*.

Two difficulties can arise when an attempt is made to enforce a guarantee. Firstly, the guarantor may lack the capacity to give the guarantee because he is a minor, mentally ill, or an undischarged bankrupt, or secondly the banker may not be in a position to claim repayment from the customer. As we saw in Chapter 12, a minor cannot normally be forced to repay a bank advance and because of this a guarantee is of no help because a guarantor cannot be forced to pay an unenforceable debt. The same position would arise if money had been lent to a company beyond its borrowing powers. The company could not be forced to repay the debt and neither could its guarantor. It is for this reason that a bank will attempt to protect its position by an *indemnity* clause in its guarantee form since an indemnity does not presuppose that another person is liable.

In cases where a guarantee is given by more than one person, their liability must be joint and several so that if necessary each or all of them may be sued. This should be stated in the form of guarantee which should also make clear that it is a continuing guarantee. There should also be a provision that the release of one or more guarantors from liability does not act as a release of the remaining guarantors.

A guarantor has a number of rights which a banker is bound to observe. The banker has a duty not to mislead the guarantor and must therefore provide all relevant information about the customer's account before the guarantee is signed. Whilst answering any questions truthfully, he should take care not to volunteer information in case he is in breach of his duty of secrecy to his customer. It is usually desirable that a prospective guarantor meets the banker together with the customer to answer any questions before the guarantee is signed.

Once the guarantee is signed, the guarantor has a right to know the extent of his possible liability, how much he would have to pay if called upon by the banker immediately. He has the right to pay off the customer's debt once repayment is due or to require the banker to demand repayment from the customer. He can sue the customer in the name of the bank for money he has paid under the guarantee and he also has a right to any security that the customer has lodged as backing for an advance. Unless otherwise agreed, a guarantor has a right to revoke his guarantee at any time. He remains liable for any debts outstanding and within the amount of his guarantee up to the time of giving notice and also for any obligations incurred by the bank prior to notice. Once notice is received, the banker should inform his customer and rule off his account in order to prevent the rule in Clayton's case from operating.

Unlike an insurance contract, a guarantee is not a contract *uberrimae fidei*, and a banker need not therefore disclose facts which might influence someone deciding to give a guarantee. However, the banker must guard against the risk that the guarantor may seek to avoid liability by a claim of *undue influence*. This could occur between a husband and wife or between a solicitor and client. If the guarantor is a customer of the bank and it could be shown that it was to the bank's advantage that he should guarantee a debt of another customer, the bank could have trouble in showing that undue influence had not arisen. If such a problem is likely to arise it is a sensible precaution to arrange for a prospective guarantor to receive independent advice, possibly from a solicitor, who would witness the guarantor's signature and confirm that the advice had been given and understood.

Safe Custody

It is convenient at this stage to consider the position of a banker who receives boxes, parcels, and documents for safe custody. As we saw at the beginning of the chapter, a banker does not usually have a lien over items received for safe custody and these cannot therefore be regarded as security for an advance. Only if it could be shown that documents are held by the bank in the ordinary course of business could a lien exist. An example might be the holding of a bearer bond which had to be produced in order to collect interest payments for the credit of a customer's account.

The act of leaving property with someone for safe custody is known as *bailment* and when a banker provides this type of service he is a *bailee*. There are two types of bailee: *paid bailees* (bailees for reward) and *gratuitous bailees*. A gratuitous bailee is expected to look after property in his care in the same way as a reasonably prudent person would look after his own property. A paid bailee is expected to use every means available to protect the property. Normally a banker does not levy a specific fee for looking after a customer's property, although it can be argued that he provides this service as part of his agreement to open an account for a customer. There is thus some doubt as to which category of bailee a banker comes within and therefore as to the standard of care required. It is clear however that in the case of theft a bank would not be liable for the loss of its customer's property. The customer should be urged to insure property against loss or damage since the bank cannot be regarded as an insurer. Probably all that is needed is the standard of care expected of a banker. If, however, the banker delivered property to the wrong person he would be liable for conversion. Likewise he might suffer loss if he had been negligent, forgetting for example to lock the property in a strongroom.

Items lodged by customers are often in locked boxes or sealed envelopes. Where frequent access is required, as in the case of stocks and shares, however, they may be held in unsealed envelopes or in other ways which would facilitate their ease of use. Customers' wills are often held in this way. When a customer dies, his executors or their solicitors will be allowed to inspect the will – it may contain funeral instructions –

and to remove it. No other property should be released until probate has been granted and exhibited to the bank.

PERSONAL ASSIGNMENTS

1 A banker's lien has been decribed as an implied pledge. What significance does this have for a banker?

2 When more than one person gives a guarantee they are usually required to accept joint and several liability. Why is this?

3 A bank's form of charge usually states that the guarantee shall be a continuing one. Why is this?

4 Consider the action that must be taken by a banker when taking as security unregistered land which the customer holds in 'fee simple absolute in possession'.

5 What does a solicitor have to do when he is asked to tell a bank whether or not a customer has a good title to unregistered land?

6 What must be considered by a banker when he is offered shares in a company as security for an advance?

7 Name the various registers that have been referred to in this chapter and briefly explain their use.

CHAPTER 15

BANK STAFF TODAY AND TOMORROW

The wide range of financial services offered today by the major banking groups means that a large number of different tasks are performed by bank employees. In evidence to the Wilson Committee, the London clearing banks reported that at the end of 1976 they had a staff of nearly 278,000, of whom almost 204,000 were employed by the parent banks with a further 25,000 in subsidiary companies, and 50,000 wholly or mainly working overseas. About 155,000 staff worked in domestic branches and nearly 35,000 were involved in head office services and support functions such as cheque clearing and computer operations. Some 13,000 worked in the banks' various international subsidiaries, departments, and branches in the U.K.; over 7,000 were in trust subsidiaries and divisions; and about 7,000 were involved in providing leasing, factoring, and instalment credit services through the banks' subsidiaries. The balance of nearly 12,000 staff were occupied in providing the banks' merchant banking, insurance, travel, and credit card services.

Of parent bank staff, seven per cent were managers and eleven per cent appointed officers without managerial status. Clerical staff accounted for about seventy-seven per cent of total employees and non-clerical staff for about five per cent. At the end of 1976 about one-third of the staff worked in London, mostly within three miles of Charing Cross. Women accounted for about fifty-five per cent of the total workforce.

Whilst a high proportion of U.K. banking staff are employed by the clearing banks, a sizeable number work in other banks including foreign and overseas banks, the Bank of England, the National Savings Bank, the Trustee Savings Bank, and the National Girobank. At the end of 1984 it was estimated that over 39,000 staff were employed by foreign banks and securities houses in London.

Bank Operations

In Chapter 1, banks were described as systems for providing a range of financial services, systems which themselves consist of many sub-systems designed to achieve certain objectives. There has to be a system for receiving deposits, another for making advances. There is a cheque-clearing system and one for dealing with direct debits. Systems are required for issuing travellers cheques, for making payments abroad, and many more. From the figures quoted it can be seen that bank staff are involved in a wide range of activities from highly complex and skilled merchant banking operations to routine tasks within the money transmission systems.

No doubt most members of the general public have a picture of banking derived from their knowledge of their local branch. Whilst perhaps about twenty-five per cent of those employed in U.K. financial service industries work for the clearing banks, it seems likely that about one-third of these banks' U.K. employees are not engaged in domestic branch banking. It follows that modern banking is more diverse and complex than many people realise.

Even the tasks performed in a typical branch in the High Street of a medium-sized town vary quite widely. This branch might have a staff of between twenty-five and thirty people headed by a manager and an assistant manager responsible for branch activities, mainly lending activities and customer relations. There will probably be one or two appointed officers with responsibility for day-to-day administration and perhaps five senior staff dealing with such matters as the technical aspects of lending control, taking and releasing security for advances, safe custody, stock exchange transactions, and foreign services. There might be six cashiers and eight other staff dealing with money transmission. The branch might also have two secretary-typists and a messenger. In smaller branches staff have to combine a number of these activities whereas in a large office work tends to be more specialised with perhaps a group of staff engaged in foreign work or in a section responsible for securities.

Staff Planning

In order to provide an output of financial services, a bank needs a variety of inputs of which undoubtedly the most important is its staff.

People are needed to plan, organise, and direct the bank's work. It needs people to coordinate and control the work of other people. Other forms of input into a bank system have to be organised by people. It follows therefore that to be successful a bank must recruit staff sufficient both in quality and quantity to provide as effectively as possible the services it currently gives to its customers, as well as those which it proposes to offer in the future. Part of the corporate plan of a well-managed bank is likely to deal with recruitment policy – the number of staff to be recruited, the proportions of male and female staff, the educational standards needed, and the personal qualities required.

When recruiting new staff the bank is likely to have in mind its future mangement needs and will often select a proportion of entrants on this basis. Often targets will be set for the number of graduates to be recruited. Usually there is less interest in the subject read than in the personal qualities of the applicant. A highly successful merchant bank offering investment and corporate services to an exclusive group of customers may be more interested in the intellectual and cultural qualities of new staff than the bank recruiting many more graduates, largely for service overseas. In this case, the bank may be more interested in selecting people able to meet the rigours of unfavourable climates and to live and work in places with limited amenities and far removed from large towns.

It is fairly obvious that a bank is particularly anxious to recruit staff of undoubted honesty and integrity and who can be trusted to treat as confidential the affairs of both the bank and its customers. It is likely to seek staff with a balanced approach to life whose backgrounds indicate that they are able to establish good relations with other people and who are likely to become reliable and conscientious members of the bank staff.

Staff Development

The effectiveness of staff can be improved in three main ways: by experience, through job rotation, and by training. Often those selected with management positions in mind receive accelerated training, spending relatively short periods in different parts of the bank's organisation. Other staff may be moved from one branch to another or to a new section in a head office department in order to gain additional experience and to enable them to bring a fresh approach to their work.

Many banks provide a variety of training courses for staff at varying levels of seniority. Large banks often have fine training facilities, sometimes in a staff college with residential accommodation. Often new staff will attend an induction course where they will learn a little about the bank's history and its organisation, how to deal with customers, the types of account that depositors may use, and a general description of their likely duties. They are also likely to be introduced to the bank's book-keeping system, be told how to clear cheques, and be shown how to use the telephone and simple machines. Additional courses may be available, dealing perhaps in more detail with day-to-day operations or with instruction on the operation of computer terminals and an explanation of the information provided by computer.

Staff about to undertake cashiering duties will probably attend a course involving practical training in a model branch where they will learn how to handle cash and to balance a till. They will learn how to deal with the various items that pass over a branch bank's counter, the way in which night safe facilities operate, and how to deal with customers. Other courses are likely to deal with the foreign services provided by the bank or with various aspects of security work, in particular the way in which various types of security have to be handled when supporting a bank advance.

Courses at a variety of levels are usually available for those approaching management level, for those already holding a management appointment, and for those with management experience. These courses deal with the skills of branch management and seek to develop lending skills. In some cases practice using close-circuit television is provided to develop interviewing techniques, and sometimes the art of public speaking is considered. Senior bank staff, in particular those at general management level, attend management courses outside the bank and sometimes at specialist institutions overseas.

Banking in the Future

As earlier pages have made clear, there have been considerable changes in banking in the post-war years. The pace of change is likely to continue and although to some extent it is possible to imagine banking in the future, the speed at which change will occur is difficult to predict. One certainty is that younger bankers will need a flexibility of approach enabling them to deal with change and an ability to take advantage of new challenges as they appear.

One attribute required from bank staff has been a capacity to cope effectively with routine and somewhat tedious work. In 1977 the clearing banks pointed out that about sixty per cent of their U.K. staff were involved in money transmission services. The development of information technology and the use of the computer have already changed the nature of clerical operations – ledger accounts and customers' statements posted by hand are now forgotten by most bank staff.

The growing use of automated teller machines, point-of-sale terminals, and no doubt the future spread of home banking can be expected to play a large part in changing the daily life of bank staff. Increased competition between banks and with other financial institutions has already led to greater emphasis being given to the marketing of bank services and increasingly staff will need to have a sound knowledge of the many services a large banking group can offer and to develop skills in marketing them.

Changes in the organisation and operations of The Stock Exchange in the mid–1980s and the links made by banks with stockbrokers and jobbers can be expected to increase bank involvement in security dealing with the possibility that stocks and shares will be available for purchase and sale at bank branches and offices in much the same way as foreign currency can be bought and sold today.

Banking as a Career

Despite the many changes affecting banking, it is likely that many routine tasks will remain and staff will need to accept this situation in the knowledge that their working conditions and terms of employment are generally very good, a fact supported by the relative lack of labour disputes in the industry.

Career bankers, those seeking promotion and more demanding jobs, will need to recognise that hard work performed with care and accuracy must be matched by improved understanding of a banker's technical skills. Becoming an Associate of The Institute of Bankers should be an early career aim, an ongoing interest in all financial matters should be cultivated, and management skills should be developed.

Banking is a worthwhile occupation. Those working in the industry provide a valuable community service. There is great satisfaction in knowing that financial help has assisted a local business, has resulted perhaps in the construction of an oil-rig, or has helped the progress of a developing country. There is satisfaction too in knowing that international banking activities are making a significant contribution to the health of the U.K.'s balance of payments.

Banking is big business, an international business, whose success demands the application of sound management and technical skills. These are the skills required of a career banker whose success depends on an ability to acquire and to apply them. But something else is needed, a thing which cannot be learned – Good Luck.

PERSONAL ASSIGNMENTS

1 Write a short essay entitled 'My work in a bank'.

2 List the personal qualities you feel are most important for a successful bank officer to possess.

3 Your bank tells you that in a month's time you are to go overseas to work in a branch of the bank for two years. What information would you seek to help you with your new job?

4 Write a brief account of how the structure and nature of banking is likely to change in the next twenty years.

5 What factors are likely to determine the speed at which banking innovations can be introduced?

6 What factors have to be considered by a bank's personnel manager when establishing plans for future staff recruitment and development?

7 Outline the structure of examinations offered by The Institute of Bankers.

APPENDIX

Increased competition, new technology, and legal and other developments led to frequent and important changes in the financial system during the 1980s. Banks have not been excluded from these frequent changes and the purpose of this Appendix is to provide the most up-to-date information available on some of the more interesting and important developments taking place towards the end of 1985.

London and Scottish Clearing Banks

In October 1985 the business of Williams and Glyn's bank was merged with that of the Royal Bank of Scotland. Williams and Glyn's was formed in 1970 from three existing banks: Glyn, Mills & Co.; the English branches of the National Bank; and Williams Deacon's bank. Although wholly owned by the Royal Bank of Scotland group, Williams and Glyn's operated under its own name until the merger and was one of the members of the Committee of London Clearing Bankers.

Prior to the merger the Committee of London Clearing Bankers (CLCB) invited the Royal Bank of Scotland and the Bank of Scotland to join them. The third Scottish clearing bank – Clydesdale – was not invited because it is represented by the Midland, its parent bank. The enlarged committee is now called the *Committee of London and Scottish Bankers* (CLSB) and now consists of the two Scottish banks, Barclays, Lloyds, Midland, and National Westminster as well as Standard Chartered Bank. The CLCB has ceased to exist but there still remains the *Committee of Scottish Clearing Bankers* (CSCB) to deal with Scottish affairs.

Clearing systems

Proposals contained in the Child report at the end of 1984 were accepted by the clearing banks and became effective by the end of 1985. These banks passed responsibility for clearing systems and related activities to the *Association for Payment Clearing Services* (APACS), the body responsible for three companies each of which looks after different parts of the clearing system: for the general and credit clearings, for BACS, and for the town clearing and CHAPS.

The new arrangements enable direct participation in clearing operations to be available to more banks than in the past and in due course will probably allow some building societies to enjoy the same facilities.

By the end of 1985 the payment systems were currently handling about 10 million transactions every working day worth £40 billion.

Building societies

Legally building societies have been allowed to raise funds only for the purpose of lending on mortgage, such lending being confined to first mortgages. Increasingly the societies have sought greater freedom to compete, notably with the banks, and in early 1983 they issued a report calling for legislation to enable them to play an extended role in the provision of financial services.

Such legislation will probably be introduced in 1986 but judging by the Government's proposals published in July 1984 it seems unlikely that building societies will win all the freedoms they originally asked for. It is expected that they will be required to continue to devote a large part of their resources in the provision of finance by means of first mortgages on owner-occupied residential property. However it is expected that they will have authority to lend limited sums in other ways, for example by second mortgages. Major building societies will probably also be allowed to devote part of their resources to unsecured consumer lending, to the ownership of land, and possibly to investment in company shares. Power to act as estate agents and to develop property is also expected whilst the provision of investment advice and insurance services may be permitted.

The new legislation is expected to result in the establishment of a *Building Societies Commission* which will take over the existing function of the Registrar of Friendly Societies as the authority responsible for the prudential control of the societies, including the monitoring of their capital adequacy. It is expected that a procedure will be established enabling societies to appeal against decisions of the Commission and that an *Investors Protection Board* will be set up to guarantee deposits in a way similar to that provided for bank depositors.

Securities markets

Many changes of considerable importance were in progress during 1985 in the U.K. securities markets. Traditional methods of operating were about to cease after many years and the financial world was preparing for the 'big bang' due towards the end of 1986.

The abandonment of traditional procedures largely concerned The Stock Exchange whose members in practice had been the only people able to deal in U.K. securities, either as jobbers or brokers. A clear distinction existed between banking and the securities business. A bank's customer wishing to purchase or to sell government securities ('gilts') or shares issued by a company had to deal through a broker, either direct or through a bank.

Restrictive arrangements existed which ensured that Stock Exchange members operated in a *single or separated capacity*. Brokers were allowed to undertake business only as agents, buying securities from or selling them to jobbers on behalf of clients. Jobbers on the other hand dealt on their own behalf using their own capital or borrowed funds to hold securities which could be sold to investors only through the agency of a broker.

A challenge to The Stock Exchange over its right to impose minimum rates of dealing commissions together with increasing competitive pressure from non-members – particularly from those dealing in the international securities markets – led to important changes and as these changes had not been introduced gradually over a period of time, the term 'big bang' was coined for the timing of the occasion when the changes became effective.

In preparation, banking and other financial groups both from home and overseas commenced to acquire stakes in Stock Exchange member firms. In a number of cases banks have acquired interests in both jobbing and broking firms thus enabling them in due course to buy and to sell securities on behalf of their customers and other investors as well as on their own behalf. Thus in the new situation banks as well as other organisations will be able to act in a *dual capacity*, offering both a jobbing and broking service.

These changes have meant that a number of difficulties have had to be faced, among them:

1. The need to ensure that the Bank of England has an active and well-organised market in government securities in which it can conduct its operations.

2. Safeguarding the interests of investors.

3. The requirement that the safety of the banking system be ensured.

The Bank of England has recognised twenty-nine market makers whom it feels have the necessary resources to make a market in gilt-edged securities and to whom the Bank will provide the necessary facilities for their successful operations. As well as providing a satisfactory market for the purchase and sale of government securities the arrangements are designed to achieve a high level of investor protection.

Further protection from the beginning of 1987 for investors in a number of markets will be the responsibility of a new statutory body, the *Securities and Investments Board* (SIB), and possibly also the *Marketing of Investments Board* (MIB). Day to day responsibility for regulating different markets will be in the hands of a number of *Self-Regulatory Organisations* (SROs) operating directly under the authority of the SIB. The Stock Exchange will be an important SRO whilst the responsibility of other SROs will include that for investment management, dealing in international securities, and the selling of life assurance and unit trusts.

Bank supervision

The entry of banks into new activities has emphasised the need for a strengthening of the supervisory procedures of the Bank of England which already had been subject to criticism. In 1985 steps were taken to increase the number of Bank supervisory staff as well as to improve the level of staff expertise. A high-level committee was also formed under the chairmanship of the Deputy-Governor to supervise this part of the Bank's work.

Ahead of the changes affecting the securities markets consideration had been given to the activities of the Bank in implementing the Banking Act of 1979. New legislation amending this act was expected to remove the distinction between a Recognised Bank and a Licensed Deposit-Taker, to set limits on a bank's lending to a single borrower, and to strengthen a bank's internal controls of its own affairs. It was also expected that steps would be taken to make it possible for a regular dialogue to take place between a bank's auditors and the Bank's supervisory staff.

Consumer Credit Act

The final stages of the Consumer Credit Act of 1974 became effective in May 1985. A *regulated agreement* under the Act is one for the advance of credit to an individual customer of up to £15,000. The Act does not apply to corporate borrowers.

From May 1985 a regulated agreement must be refinanced if its terms are altered. Thus if an increase in a loan is needed or there are to be changes in the security or repayment arrangements, the existing loan account has to be closed and a new one opened. Personal borrowers are entitled to a written quotation from a bank and this must show the *Annual Percentage Rate* (APR) and the *Total Cost of Credit* (TCC) a figure which takes account of any fees payable for arranging the advance and of any legal costs that have to be paid.

The Act establishes rules concerning the action needed when a customer dies or defaults and the information that must be given to a borrower or to someone acting as a surety. There are rules concerning the issue of credit cards and cash dispenser cards as well as about the times when bank statements must be sent to customers. All joint account holders must receive a separate copy of the bank statement unless they agree otherwise.

National savings

In November 1985 a new savings product became available to the public, an *Indexed-Income Bond*. Interest on the bond is paid monthly without prior deduction of any tax that is payable. Over a ten-year period the rate of interest changes in line with the general level of retail prices but this protection against inflation applies only to interest payments and not to the capital sum invested. When the bonds were first issued a minimum subscription of £5,000 was required.

Ombudsman

Towards the end of 1985 steps were taken by eighteen banks to establish a council with responsibility for selecting an Ombudsman to investigate complaints by personal customers about the banks' services. The banking Ombudsman – a lawyer – commenced his duties at the beginning of 1986 and is responsible to the council that appointed him. This consists of an independent chairman, three banking members, and three other members. The role of the Ombudsman is to resolve disputes between customers and their banks after all existing procedures for dealing with complaints have been exhausted. He has authority to make awards of up to £50,000 but a customer is not precluded from pursuing a claim through a court of law if that seems desirable.

Self-Examination Questions

These questions are designed to help you discover how well you understand the nature of banking after reading this book.

1 Explain the role of central banks with particular reference to the work of the Bank of England.

2 Explain briefly the functions of *two* markets in which U.K. banks operate.

3 Discuss the statement: 'Banks are just like any other firm'.

4 'Banks are merely moneylenders in grandiose premises.' To what extent do you feel this is true?

5 Consider the effects of a fall in interest rates in the U.S. on the interest rates charged by banks in your country. How is this likely to affect your currency's rate of exchange with the U.S. dollar and your country's balance of payments position with other countries?

6 'The trouble with banks is that they are only interested in making profits. They no longer care about the service they give to private customers.' Discuss.

7 How true is it to say that banks have now become financial supermarkets?

8 'The trouble with banks is that they will only lend you money if you have something to give them as security.' Is this true?

9 Should competition between banks be encouraged?

10 'Bank staff are just pen-pushers.' True?

--- **CASE STUDY I** ---

You have just received the following letter from the Secretary of a club you joined a little over a year ago:

Dear Porgy,

Sorry to bother you but I'm wondering whether you can help me and the Club. Rather stupidly I agreed at the last committee meeting to organise a debate about banking and it was suggested that the motion for consideration should be: 'The large British banks should be nationalised'.

Pat and Don have agreed to speak in support of the motion. I think this is very decent of them since they both work in banks and I thought they might be in trouble if their banks found out. However, they don't seem to be worried as this will be a local affair and the newspaper reporters won't be there.

I know you have been studying banking and I wonder whether you could speak *against* the motion. We start at 7.30 in the usual place on the 26th of next month so you have plenty of time to prepare for the big occasion. The idea is that you should speak for only five minutes so it shouldn't be too difficult.

I do hope you will agree to help. We shall need someone else to speak against the motion and when I've found a volunteer I'll let you know so that you can get together and work out what you are going to say.

I hope to hear from you soon. Meanwhile here's to the 26th.

Regards,
Bess

Required:

Notes for a five-minute talk *opposing* the motion: 'The large British banks should be nationalised'.

CASE STUDY II

George Smith has just become engaged to be married. The wedding is planned to take place in a year's time and the newly-weds will need to find somewhere to live. George at present lives with his parents near the Sussex coast. He travels about 50 miles each day to London where he works for a large supermarket, buying supplies of tinned foods for all their branches.

He is aged 25 and has a salary of £8,500 a year. He reckons that he spends about £1,000 a year on fares for travelling to work and he gives his mother £15 a week to pay for his food and accommodation.

The supermarket operates a pension scheme to which George contributes six per cent of his salary. He saves £20 a month in national savings and has built up a balance of just over £5,000 on a share account with his building society. He has a current account with a major bank and has no difficulty in maintaining a minimum balance of £100. He is paid monthly and always tries to increase his building society balance on payday.

As soon as they have married and settled down, George and his fiancée plan to start a family. Meanwhile, his fiancée wants to continue her job as a staff nurse.

Required:
Advise George on the steps he should take to obtain accommodation for when he marries. Bear in mind that he might continue to live at home, but also that various types of property can be bought or rented.

Include in your advice an indication of where George should live, what sources of finance are available to him, and what limit should he set to his accommodation costs.

CASE STUDY III

A branch manager of one of the large U.K. banks has recently received an application from Mr X for an advance of £5,000, details of which are as follows:

The application is for a firm that was incorporated as a limited liability company two years ago. Mr X and a friend are directors. Mr X is unemployed but his friend is working part-time as a secretary.

Finance is required to enable the company to purchase pigs' trotters at about £0.04 each to preserve them in salt, and then to export them to African countries where they currently sell for about £0.50 each. The company has not previously traded in pigs' trotters.

At present the company is operating from a council flat in London where a room has been set aside as an office with a telephone and office furniture. Mr X would like to have an office with a London business address with space for himself, a secretary and an accounts clerk. He plans to purchase pigs' trotters from an abattoir on the east coast and to employ five people there for weighing, washing and cleaning, salting, and packing the pigs' trotters in barrels. The barrels will be sealed and transported in containers to London where they will be stored preparatory to shipment. The abattoir has agreed to allow its premises to be used by the five employees and has also agreed to provide some supervision of the processing.

The figures overleaf have been produced to support the application based on a throughput of 100 trotters a barrel, 280 barrels a container, and 5 container shipments a year.

		£
Estimated Income	Sales	140,000
	Bank loan	5,000
	Private input	1,000
		146,000

Estimated Outgoings	Purchases	6,000
	Warehousing	2,200
	Wages and salaries	31,500
	Packaging	8,000
	Rent and rates	2,400
	Telephone etc.	2,000
	Leasing	2,200
	Transport	3,000
	Insurance	2,000
	Loan repayment	5,400
	Professional fees	600
	Advertising	7,800
	Sundries	1,700
	Contingencies	10,000
		84,800

The loan application was refused. Mr X has written to the bank's chief executive complaining of racial discrimination and the branch manager has been required to report on why the advance was refused.

Required:
The branch manager's report to his chief executive.

CASE STUDY IV

Louise, an old schoolfriend of yours, recently opened a small boutique in a small parade of shops close to a large high-class estate of new houses built recently on the outskirts of your town. After school she attended college and obtained very good examination results following her studies in dress design, clothing materials, and fashion. You understand from other friends that the business is doing well and you are therefore surprised when Louise calls to see you for urgent advice.

It appears that she is very worried because her bank account is overdrawn and the local branch manager has asked her to call to discuss the state of her account with him. She has never met this man before and has come to see you for advice before she visits the bank.

She tells you that the new business is doing very well. The shop is in a good position, the local people seem to have a lot of money, and she is very busy, particularly on Saturdays when the shop is always crowded with young people anxious to buy the latest fashions. She finds that business is very good – she has even had to employ another girl to help her on Saturdays – and her profits are so high that she has considered opening another shop in a different part of the town. She thinks that one of the things that has helped is the fact that she allows customers to pay for their purchases weekly over a period of four to six weeks. People are very honest and everybody has paid for their goods by the end of the period allowed.

Louise cannot understand why she is overdrawn when the business has been doing so well.

Required:
What information should you seek from Louise and what advice would you give her?

Among the customers that visited your branch of the bank today was a Mr Jones who works for a large company whose products are mainly exported to the Middle East. He explained that his firm has arranged for him to spend twelve months abroad touring a number of countries in an effort to expand overseas sales.

Mr Jones is very concerned about this. His wife is expecting a baby when he is away and there are already two young children to look after. He has a flat in a large house which he owns, the two remaining flats being let by him on a monthly basis. One of the tenants has been slow in paying his rent and the other may be leaving soon as she has been offered a job in a town some miles away.

This will be Mr Jones' first visit abroad and he has been told to make his own travel arrangements, to decide which countries to visit, and whom to meet. He is worried about this and also about the problems his wife will face in looking after the house and children and in dealing with tenants whilst he is away. He has always paid the bills, provided the housekeeping, and dealt with his own tax and investment affairs.

His employers are determined that he should make the trip and are prepared to meet all the expenses needed to make this possible. They have told him to arrange for the well-being of his family should he become ill or have an accident.

Required:
A brief note of the services the bank can offer to help to solve Mr Jones' problems.

FURTHER READING

BOND, P. *Monetary Economics*, Northwick Publishers: 1984.

COMMITTEE OF LONDON CLEARING BANKS. *Evidence to the Committee to Review the Functioning of Financial Institutions*, Committee of London Clearing Bankers: 1978.

COWAN, L. D. *Personnel Management and Banking*, The Institute of Bankers: Gilbart Lectures: 1983.

CRICK, W. F. and WADSWORTH, J. E. *A Hundred Years of Joint Stock Banking,* Hodder and Stoughton 3rd edn: 1958.

DYER, L. S. *A Practical Approach to Bank Lending*, The Institute of Bankers: 1983.

EDWARDS, J. R. and MELLETT, H. *Accountancy for Banking Students,* The Institute of Bankers: 1985.

GOFF, T. G. *Theory and Practice of Investment,* Heinemann: 1983.

HANSON, D. G. *Service Banking: the arrival of the all-purpose bank, The Institute of Bankers: 1982.*

THE INSTITUTE OF BANKERS The Banks and Technology in the 1980s: 1982.

The Banks and their Competitors: 1980.

KELLY, J. E. *Practice of Banking 1*, Macdonald and Evans: 1984.

LIVY, B. L. (ed.) *Management and People in Banking*, The Institute of Bankers: 1985.

MACKENZIE, C. *Realms of Silver*, Routledge: 1954.

MCIVER, C. and NAYLOR, G. *Marketing Financial Services*, The Institute of Bankers: 1985.

REEDAY, T. G. *Law Relating to Banking*, Butterworths: 1985.

REID, M. *The Secondary Bank Crisis, 1973–75*, Macmillan: 1982.

SHAW, E. R. *The London Money Market*, Heinemann: 1984.

TOFT, K. S. *Practical Bank Management*, Macdonald and Evans: 1977.

WATSON, A. J. W. *Finance of International Trade*, The Institute of Bankers: 1985.

INDEX

Acceptance, 38, 40
Acceptance credits, 42, 143
Accepting Houses, *see* Banks, merchant
Acceptors, 38
Accounting ratios, 109–10
Account payee, 178
Acid test, 110
Administrators, 136
Advertising strategy, 154
All-moneys debentures, 192
Annual Percentage Rate (APR), 107, 163, 208
APACS, *see* Association for Payments Clearing Services
Appropriation accounts, 50, 109
APR, *see* Annual Percentage Rate
Articles of association, 23, 169
Assignment, 185–7
Association for Payment Clearing Services (APACS), 205
ATMs, *see* Automated Teller Machines
Attitude surveys, 150
Authorised capital, 23
Automated Teller Machines (ATMs), 129–30

BACS, *see* Bankers' Automated Clearing Services Ltd
Bailees, 170, 194–5
Balance of payments, 68–70, 115
Balance of trade, 68
Balance sheets, 47–8, 53–4
Bank Charter Act, 1844, 34–5
Bankers' Automated Clearing Services Ltd (BACS), 127, 205
Bankers' Clearing House, 122–4
Bankers draft, 180–1
Banker's lien, 184
Bank Giro credits, 125
Banking:
   contract, 163–4

   controls, 12–13
   correspondent banks, 131–2
   inputs, 6–7, 9
   international, 1
   mandates, 165–6
   ombudsman, 208
   outputs, 2–3
   retail, 44, 55
   secrecy, 164–5
   services, 3, 134 *et seq.*
   wholesale, 44, 55
Banking Act 1979, 35, 101, 125, 159–62, 207
Bank notes, 34–6, 82–3, 120–1
Bank of England, 32–6, 40–1, 43, 99–100, 159–62, 206
Bank of England Act, 1946, 35
Banks:
   balance sheets of, 53–7
   colonial, 37
   joint stock, 33–4
   lending by, 3, 5–6, 29–30, 32, 103 *et seq.*
   liquidity of, 12, 40–1, 57–8, 161–2
   management of, 6–8
   marketing by, 149–50
   merchant, 42, 143
   overseas, 37
   recognised, 2, 160, 207
   staffing of, 2, 198–9
   supervision of, 159–62, 207
Barter, 76–8
Base rates, 112
Bid bonds, 145
Bid price, 25
Bill brokers, *see* Brokers
Bills of exchange, 38–41, 144, 181–2
Bills of Exchange Act, 1882, 39, 172 *et seq.*
Bills of lading, 182
Blank transfer, 188

Blue chip company, 113
Breach of duty, 170
Brokers:
  bill brokers, 40
  Lloyd's brokers, 140
  money brokers, 44
  stock brokers, 24, 147, 206
Budget accounts, 107
Building societies, 3, 10, 20–2, 27–8, 41,
  84, 130, 205
Building Societies Commission, 205
Buyers credit, 145

Capital, 23–4
Capital gains tax, 139
Capital gearing, 111
Capital transfer tax, 139
Cash flow forecasts and statements, 50,
  110–11
CDs, see Certificates of Deposit
Central banking, see Bank of England
Certificate of incorporation, 23, 169
Certificates of Deposit (CDs), 22, 41–2,
  55
Chain of title, 189
CHAPS, see Clearing House Automated
  Payments System
Charge cards, 129
Cheque cards, 128–9, 131, 180
Cheques:
  clearing, 121–4
  crossings, 176
  definition, 39, 172–3
  dishonoured, 174
  endorsements, 175–6
  overdue, postdated and stale, 175
  stopped, 174
Cheques Act, 1957, 175–8
Child report, 204
Choses in action and in possession, 185
CLCB, see Committee of London
  Clearing Bankers
Clean credits, 182
Clearing House Automated Payments
  System (CHAPS), 127, 206
CLSB, see Committee of London and
  Scottish Bankers
Coin, 82, 120–1
Collateral security, 192
Committee of London Clearing Bankers
  (CLCB), 204
Committee of London and Scottish
  Bankers (CLSB), 205

Committee of Scottish Clearing Bankers
  (CSCB), 204
Companies acts, 23, 159, 169
Company registrars, 147
Computer bureau, 146
Consortium banks, 115
Consumer Credit Act, 1974, 162–4, 207
Consumer durables, 28–9
Contractual capacity, 104
Contract uberrimae fidei, 187, 193
Conversion, 170, 178, 194
Conveyances, 189
Corporate planning, 8–10, 149–50
Corporate trustees, 135
Corporation of Lloyd's, 140
Corset, 100
Country risk, 116
Court of Protection, 168
Credit cards, 128–9, 131
Credit clearing, 124–5
Credit, definition, 4–5
Credit intelligence, 142, 146
Credit reference agency, 146
Credit sale, 28, 141
Credit scoring, 107–8
Cross-selling, 153
CSCB, see Committee of Scottish
  Clearing Banks
Current accounts, 53, 55
Current assets and liabilities, 53
Current ratio, 109–10

Debentures, 138, 191–2
Debt, government, 15–16
Deeds, 189–90
Defamation, 170
Delivery orders, 188
Demand curves and schedules, 63–6
Deposit bonds, 17–18
Deposit insurance, 161, 207
Deposits, 53–5
Direct costs, 49
Direct debits, 126–7
Direct exchange, 76
Discount houses, see Discount market
Discounting, 38
Discount market, 40–2
Documentary credits, 144, 182
Double entry bookkeeping, 46, 51–2
Drawers and drawees, 38

ECGD, see Export Credits Guarantee
  Department

Economic objectives, 91–2
Economic weapons, 92–3
EFTPOS, *see* Electronic Funds Transfer at Point of Sale
Elasticity of demand, 66
Electronic Funds Transfer at Point of Sale (EFTPOS), 130
Electronic Random Number Indicator Equipment (ERNIE), 19
Endorsements, 39, 175–6
Endowment policies, 26–7, 186
Equilibrium price, 63–5
ERNIE, *see* Electronic Random Number Indicator Equipment
Estate agents, 147, 205
Estoppel, doctrine of, 166, 177
Eurobonds, 146
Eurodollar and eurocurrency markets, 70–1, 113–14, 145–6
Exchange control, 100
Executors, 135–6, 167
Export Credits Guarantees Department (ECGD), 145

Factors and factoring, 141–2
Fair Trading Act 1973, 163
Finance Corporation for Industry (FCI), 116
Finance houses, 28–9, 141
Financial intermediation, 10–12
Fiscal policy, 93
Fixed and floating charges, 191
Fixed assets, 53
Foley v Hill, 1848, 164
Foreign exchange market, 67–8, 132
Forfaiting, 143
Forward rates of exchange, 67–8
Freehold land, 189

Garnishee orders, 165
Gearing, 111
General clearing, 123–5
General lien, 184
Going concern, 108–9, 112
Goldsmiths, 32
Gone concern, 109, 112
Goodwill, 112
Government debt, 15–16
Gratuitous bailees, 194
Gross profit, 49
Guarantees, 192–4

Hedging, 67, 206

Hire purchase, 28, 141
Holder for value and holder in due course, 179–80
Housing finance, 27–8, 205
Hypothecation, 185

IBELS, *see* Interest-bearing Eligible Liabilities
ICFC, *see* Industrial and Commercial Finance Corporation
Income bonds, 17, 208
Indemnity, 192–3
Index linking, 16–19, 72, 86, 208
Index numbers, 84–7
Indigenisation, 37
Indirect costs, 49
Indirect exchange, 78
Industrial and Commercial Finance Corporation (ICFC), 116
Institute of Bankers, The, 135, 143, 201
Insurable interest, 187
Insurance, 205
Inter-bank market, 44, 112–13
Interest-Bearing Eligible Liabilities (IBELS), 100
Interest rates, 63, 68, 71–3, 99, 112–13
Investment services, 136–8, 205
Investment trusts, 25–6
Investors in Industry (3i), 116
Investors Protection Board, 205
Invisible trade, 68–9
Invoice discounting, 142
Issuing houses, 24

Joachimson v Swiss Bank, 1921, 164
Jobbers, 24, 147, 206
Joint and several liability, 166, 193
Joint stock companies, 22

Land Charges Register and Land Registry, 189–90
LDT, *see* Licensed Deposit-Taker
Lead manager, 115
Leasehold land, 189
Leasing, 141
Legal tender, 82–3
Lender of last resort, 36, 41
Lessee and lessor, 141
Letter of hypothecation, 185
Letter of introduction, 144
Letter of pledge, 188
Letters of administration, 167
Letters of credit, 131, 144

Libel, 170
LIBOR, *see* London Inter-Bank Offered Rate
Licensed Deposit-Taker (LDT), 2, 160–1, 207
Lien, 184
Life assurance, 26–7, 207
LIFFE, *see* London International Financial Futures Exchange
Limited liability, 22
Liquidity, *see* Banks, liquidity of
Liquidity ratio, 110
Lloyd's see Corporation of Lloyd's
Loan syndication, 143
Local authority bills, 44
Local authority market, 44
Logo, 155
London Inter-Bank Offered Rate (LIBOR), 44, 112, 145
London International Financial Futures Exchange (LIFFE), 73–4

Magnetic Ink Character Recognition (MICR), 124
Manager's Discretionary Limit (MDL), 117
Manufacturing accounts, 109
Marketing of Investments Board (MIB), 207
Marketing strategy, 150–1
Market research, 150
Market segmentation, 151–2
Maturity transformation, 12
MDL, *see* Manager's Discretionary Limit
Memorandum of association, 23, 169
Memorandum of deposit, 187
MIB, *see* Marketing of Investments Board
MICR, *see* Magnetic Ink Character Recognition
Minors, 167, 192
Mint, 82, 121
Misrepresentation, 170
Monetarism, 95
Monetary controls, 13, 96–101
Monetary policy, 93, 98–100
Money:
  aggregates, 95–8
  creation, 87–9
  forms of, 80–2
  functions, 78–80
  near money, 83–4

quantity theory of, 94
supply, 95–8
value, 84–7
Money brokers, *see* Brokers
Money illusion, 63
Money markets, 44
Monopolies and mergers commission, 163
Mortgage, 21–2, 185
Mortgage debentures, 191–2

Naked debentures, 191
National Girobank, 122, 125–6
National savings, 16–20, 208
National Savings Bank, 17–18
National savings certificates, 16–18
National savings stock register, 19
Near money, 83–4
Negligence, 170
Negotiability, 172
Negotiable instruments, 172 *et seq.*
Net profit, 50
Net worth, 48
Night safes, 120
Nominal accounts, 51
Nominal capital, 23
Northern Ireland banks, 121–3
Nostro accounts, 132
Notes, *see* Bank notes

Offer price, 25
Office of Fair Trading, 163
Ombudsman, 208
Ordinary shares, 23
Overdrafts, 103
Over-funding, 98
Overseas banks, 37
Overtrading, 110

Packaging, 155
Paid bailees, 194
Paid-up policy, 186
Particular lien, 184
Partnership Act, 1890, 168
Patents, 112
Payee, 38
Paying banker, 174–7
Payroll service, 146
Pension schemes, 26–7, 138
Performance bonds, 145
Personal Identification Number (PIN), 129
Personal loans, 106–7

Personal representatives, 135
PIN, *see* Personal Identification Number
Pledge, 184
Power of attorney, 190
Preference shares, 23
Premium bonds, 18–19
Price elasticity, 66
Pricing strategy, 154
Private Sector Liquidity (PSL), 96
Probate, 137, 167, 195
Profit and loss accounts, 48–51
Promissory notes, 172, 180
Prudential controls, 13
PSBR, *see* Public Sector Borrowing
    Requirement
PSL, *see* Private Sector Liquidity
Public relations, 155–6
Public Sector Borrowing Requirement
    (PSBR), 93, 97–9
Puisne mortgages, 190

Quick ratio, 110

Rates of exchange, 67–8
Real accounts, 51
Real interest rates, 63
Receivables, 142
Receivers, 168
Recognised banks, 2, 160, 207
Registered land, 189
Registrar of Companies, 23, 159, 169
Registrar of Friendly Societies, 21, 205
Regulated agreements, 207
Rescheduling, 115–16
Reserve assets, 100
Restrictive covenants, 190
Retail Prices Index (RPI), 17, 19, 86
Return on capital, 109
Revolving credit, 107
Risk capital, 116
Risk transformation, 12
Roll-over, 145
Round tripping, 113
Royal Mint, *see* Mint
RPI, *see* Retail Prices Index
Rule in Clayton's Case, 166, 193

Safe custody, 137, 170, 194–5
Sales promotion, 154–5
Save As You Earn (SAYE), 18–19
Saving, personal, 19
SAYE, *see* Save As You Earn
Scottish banking, 121–2, 204

Searches, 190
Securities and Investments Board (SIB),
    207
Self-liquidating advances, 105, 134
Self-Regulatory Organisations (SROs),
    207
Set-off, right of, 165
Shares, 23
SIB, *see* Securities and Investments
    Board
Slander, 170
Society for World-Wide Interbank
    Financial Telecommunications
    (S.W.I.F.T.), 131–2
Special deposits, 36, 100
Spot rates of exchange, 67–8
SROs, *see* Self-Regulatory Organisations
Stagflation, 92
Standing orders, 126
Sterling M3 counterparts, 97–8
Stock brokers and jobbers, 24, 147, 206
Stock Exchange, The, 16, 24–5, 63,
    191, 201, 206
Stocking facility, 29
Supplementary special deposits, 100
Supplier credit, 145
Supply curves and schedules, 64–6
Surrender value, 186
S.W.I.F.T., *see* Society for World-Wide
    Interbank Financial
    Telecommunications

TCC, *see* Total Cost of Credit
Tender bonds, 145
Testator, 135
Test marketing, 155
Three i (3i), *see* Investors in Industry
Total Cost of Credit (TCC), 208
Town clearing, 123, 125, 127, 205
Tournier v National Provincial and
    Union Bank of England, 1924, 164
Trade marks, 112
Trading accounts, 49, 51
Transferability, 172
Travel agency, 147
Travellers cheques, 131
Treasury bills, 35, 42, 56
Trial balance, 52
Trustees, 25, 136, 138, 167
Trustee Savings Bank, 122–3, 130
Trusts, 167

Ultra vires, 169

Underwriters, 140
Undue influence, 193
Unit costs, 66
Unit trusts, 25–6, 138
Unregistered land, 189–90

Variable direct debits, 126–7
Venture capital, 116
Visible trade, 68–9
Vostro accounts, 132

Whole life policies, 26, 186
With profit policies, 27, 186
Working capital, 110
Work-in-progress, 112

Yearling bonds, 44
Yearly plan, 18, 126
Yield curve, 71–2
Yields, 16